THE BEST
AUSTRALIAN
ESSAYS
2 0 1 1

THE BEST
AUSTRALIAN
ESSAYS
2011

Edited by
RAMONA KOVAL

Published by Black Inc.,
an imprint of Schwartz Media Pty Ltd

37–39 Langridge Street
Collingwood Vic 3066 Australia
email: enquiries@blackincbooks.com
http://www.blackincbooks.com

Introduction & this collection © Ramona Koval
& Black Inc., 2011.
Individual essays © retained by the authors.
Typeset by J&M Typesetting

Every effort has been made to contact the copyright holders
of material in this book. However, where an omission has
occurred, the publisher will gladly include acknowledgement in any future edition.

ISBN 9781863955478

Printed in Australia by Griffin Press. The paper this book is printed on
is certified against the Forest Stewardship Council® Standards.
Griffin Press holds FSC chain of custody certification SGS-COC-005088.
FSC promotes environmentally responsible, socially beneficial
and economically viable management of the world's forests.

Contents

Introduction

The essay can be short or long, serious or trifling, about God and Spinoza, or about turtles and Cheapside ... It should lay us under a spell with its first word, and we should only wake, refreshed, with its last ... The essay must lap us about and draw its curtain across the world.

—Virginia Woolf

In the first volume of the excellent *Lapham's Quarterly*, the American editor and essayist Lewis Lapham describes his years editing *Harper's Magazine*, trawling through newspapers, periodicals, books and unsolicited manuscripts for the best things to read and the best writers to publish.

During his search, Lapham came up with a test based on the sound of the human voice.

'If the voice is there, I'll read anything,' he says. 'I'll read, for example, about giant ants in Peru. Or schemes in the White House basement. The subject is less important than what I can sense as the integrity of the voice.'

I followed his model when reading essays for this volume. I imagined a journey on the arm of the writer, who calls for me with the suggestion that we take a stroll. We start with an intriguing destination in mind, but on the way we get thrillingly lost. We take the road less travelled, we pause and set ourselves down, I'm shown something I've never seen, or shown it in a different light. We emerge at the end of our time together having learned something, been moved, even changed.

It begins with the voice. And the voice beckons.

It was a year of great, world-changing events, and they were brought to our attention on air, in print and online. There was the massive wave that inundated northern Japan, a global digital tidal wave called WikiLeaks, a scandal at the heart of the world's most influential media company, a movement for change called the Arab Spring and, at the end of the post 9/11 decade, the death of bin Laden.

The world got hotter and drier.

These were shared events, but some of the essays I've chosen concern private moments, written from a need to explain, to understand or to celebrate. As Michel de Montaigne said, 'You can tie up all moral philosophy with a common and private life just as well as with a life of richer stuff. Each man bears the entire form of man's estate.' In his essay 'Of Vanity' he is thinking about running his household while planning his escape from domesticity, musing on the pleasures and difficulties of travel while contemplating death, politics and astrology, and dismissing the use of umbrellas.

I hope this collection tells a story of the past year, as told by Australian writers looking inwards and outwards, or by others looking at Australia or at Australian people.

In his 1936 book of essays *Lucid Intervals*, Walter Murdoch joked that 'An essay is a newspaper article, exhumed, reprinted in larger type on thicker paper, and placed, along with other articles, between cloth covers.' Yet only a few essays here are from newspapers, and they are rare exceptions to what is often found in the inky dailies. The treasures that are to be found in our serious periodicals and literary journals, by contrast, underscore the vitality of this oft-overlooked sector of our literary culture.

For many years my day job has made me attuned to books, writers and writing of all kinds, and so a few of these pieces chime with a fascination with what to write and how to write, and whether to write, and about being distracted, and on not writing at all.

For me it has been a year of encountering birth and death, and looking at this selection I see my natural impulse has been towards writing that makes sense of these first and last breaths. But there are also pieces on all that happens in between: on eating and music and sport and passion and bravery and heroes – some falling, some fallen.

We start with the journey through pleasure to death and end with 'the endless cycle of return, in the stillness, between two waves of the sea.'

Now turn the page and hear the voices within.

Ramona Koval

Fairy Death

Gillian Mears

Before sitting at my desk I walk outside. Almost full moon and the wild early spring winds of the last few days have gone. I look up at the clouds this evening and long for my writing about love and desire to be like them; so effortlessly powerful, with perfect swerves and sweeps.

To have lost the ability to orgasm before it is time for such a disappearance seems inconceivable. Although in desperate prayers I have begged for this very outcome, for the price of an orgasm had become seven days of losing the ability to walk, the eerie absence now makes me cry. On the old Richter scale of pleasure would any charge register? Nothing, so far as I can tell. No neurologist has ever fully warned me that this was on the cards. At forty-six years old I've now had multiple sclerosis, this slow road to death, one third of my life.

The artist's wife died much more swiftly. She was only twenty-four I think and even over a decade on, though we never met, I find myself thinking of her. The manner of her passing has haunted me ever since I was told the story by someone who also loved her. I imagine that she was as lovely as the Little Prince's rose and as beloved.

I come from a family addicted to assessing its appearance. If no mirror is readily to hand we are all adept at making do. A pane of glass in a door is good for a full-length impression but smaller windows work well too, to check hair or the appearance of your nose in profile before that meeting with someone you haven't seen for a long time. In the presence of a camera we pretend not to prance or preen but when it's time for the shot to be shown, glance anxiously to see if we've come out well.

Once in Langley's Cafe I saw my father find his face in my cup of tea and well pleased, smiling. For me this was as wonderful as a moment in the 1956 Albert Lamorisse classic *Le Ballon Rouge*. In the film the balloon seeks out its reflection in a large mirror for sale at some pavement markets of Paris. The small boy hero examines a life-size portrait of a girl with a hoop but his red balloon friend is dancing up and down a little in delight at its own reflection.

*

The invitation from photographer Vincent Long arrived early in 2009. Would I be interested in taking part in his portrait series of Australian writers? Each participant would appear with a helium-filled red balloon, a kind of homage to the Lamorisse film, as well as symbolising in some sense the writer's muse.

On Vincent's website I saw what seemed to be a strange young 21st-century Madonna. The way he'd taken this photo was such that the surveillance mirror against shoplifters in a 7/11 served as her halo. If there was sadness in her expression, that she was seemingly without child, at least there were lots of chips and confectionery within easy arm's reach as compensation.

For the red balloon writer series, any location could be chosen. Think about a favourite childhood place, Vincent suggested to me, or possibly a spot that had been significant in a previous book.

Although I tinkered with the thought of the Grafton footbridge, or my balloon in the presence of a horse or cat, straight away I knew that I wanted to be unclad in *Decateur South*, the sea cubby built by sculptor Marr Grounds some twenty years before on the south coast, just two hours from the Victorian border. Where else had I ever been more beautiful? Where ever again could I appear so poised for pleasure?

There was no doubt in my mind. For me it had to be nude at Marr's for my portrait or not at all.

When I'd first lain on the old orange futon in the cubby I felt the astonishment every visitor must. The mystical minimalism of the tiny room came flowing through into my own body. Beneath the simple pane of mirror glass, bolted over the cubby's futon, it was possible to be more beautiful than you really were.

I'd reached an age where even without a chronic illness it could be a shock to accidentally catch sight of my chin's appearance in say a CD or saucepan lid. A slightly older friend laughed consolingly as she confessed it was around this year in her own life that she'd stopped riding her lover's rantipole. Or would do so only if the lighting was soft. 'Lest he take fright. Lest he think "My God, there's a skeleton on board!"'

Marr's mirror had the exact opposite effect. My skin tautened. MS and all, I looked ready for anything. The mirror made me remember outlandish dreams – to lead the Mardi Gras parade of 1994 with my girlfriend, riding our black mares topless except for gold skin-paint. Or to return to a Paris orgy I'd left early in '92, as if the huge mirror at the back of a stranger's living room even now holds the bodies of a naked and relentless crowd.

Growing up in the 1970s I used to babysit for a couple with a very large ceiling mirror framed by aluminium love cherubs. Once I'd got their children to sleep I'd lie on the grown-ups' bed, full of a Goldilocks-like disdain that lumpy old Mr and Mrs D did things under the mirror apparently without their clothes on. Yet when Mr D would walk me safely home all I'd long for was for him to do unsafe things to me in the dark shadows cast by the oldest shade trees of McHugh Street.

The mirror in Marr's cubby was as pure in contrast as a mountain pool to a swingers' club jacuzzi. Straightaway I named it The Mirror of Beauty, for even lying beneath it alone, it emphasised all that was lovely about being naked. Not long afterwards Marr started calling me *Modigliani*, as much for his love of the five-syllable sound as for any resemblance I bore to one of that artist's models. *Modigliani*, so that in his mouth I sounded like creek water over little stones.

From the outside the cubby resembled a shrine to Nereus as imagined by Ovid. 'Not bright with gold and marble but a timber frame of beams and shaded by an ancient grove.' Inside, there were not even any lining boards. Instead, silver insulation foil held in place by wire gave such an impression of scales, it was easy to believe in mermaids and nereides.

Under that mirror you could be Procris waiting for her father or a merciful sea nymph allowing a sailor she has saved from drowning to kiss his thanks.

The cubby perched on a headland so close to the sea that in a storm the Pacific Ocean sounded as though it was going to explode through the row of windows on the eastern side; as if the sea king himself had come to rape me. I drew a heart in the mist on the window. In recognition that I've always loved much older men, condensation immediately formed a stem; a romantic outline of a flower that persisted for many days.

A photo of the building taken from the air even captured the shape of a huge woman, her body formed by the southern beach at low tide; her truly magnificent breast jutting into the inlet directly opposite Manning Clark's old property 'Ness.'

In 2006 when I first took off my clothes underneath the mirror and was not alone, the tintinnabula of the bellbirds went wild. Through the little western-facing window and beyond the coastal mahoganies, the birds had the sound of triumphant madness.

Marr was thirty-five years older and I was semi-crippled but from the first I only saw our beauty. Although ungainly I was without pain and rated MS as one of the better diseases. On one walking stick it was easy to be jaunty. Years of yoga had given me a flexibility I rashly took for granted. I could lie down without thought in matsyasana, pose of the fish, and say to Marr, see how even my legs form the letter M? Our hands were exactly the same size and my initials were his in reverse.

One day, early summer, a miniature pipe made of tiny circles appeared on the gauze of the cubby's screen door. Had Marr somehow rolled fifty or more tiny spheres? No, they were genuine insect eggs, laid in the shape of a firm little pipe. Then came the feeling that the whole cubby was either part of a smoke ring blown by a blue caterpillar or else a vision in a dream by some Antipodean Coleridge; a fragment I basked in for some months to come.

Beneath the mirror it was impossible not to have the erotic ghosts of others who had lain together there cavorting into mind. It made me think of beautiful men and beautiful women known and unknown. It made me perch Marr's antique SLR Nikon on my breastbone to take photos of myself. The sandiness in the mechanism also recalled a memory of childhood from when I wanted my history teacher to touch me with far more than the piece of grass he was using to keep mozzies off my neck on an extracurricular excursion to the midden near Angourie.

In those first photos I gleamed with sexual lustre. I looked agile, strong, semi-wild. With the rule-breaking and passionate Marr, what hadn't been possible? I wanted to send copies to all who had ever loved me, for the photos also hold the blaze of something sad, as if deep in my legs lay the knowledge that my days as a sexual being were numbered.

However, I can't ever recall Marr's tiny, almost black nipples without also thinking of a favourite line from John Berger: 'The past grows gradually around one, like a placenta for dying.'

*

Perhaps this explains the inexplicable ardour of my hope that Vincent agree we meet in the cubby? I was going to cheat MS, I thought. I'd get to see Marr whom I hadn't seen for almost three years. In his beloved presence surely once again I'd be able to skylark up and down hills with his dog. I would re-find the strength in my legs and there'd be photos to prove it so.

'By all means,' wrote back Vincent. 'No clothes if that's what you want. It's your shot,' and arranged to meet at Marr's a few months later. However, over a year was to go by as one obstacle after another delayed our meeting.

*

Are you born with a certain quota of pleasure? Did mine come to such an abrupt end because I was awakened so young? I was the kind of shy girl who knew a lot about sexual magic beneath her own fingers before she was even eleven years old; not knowing what the waves of pleasure were. Only that they must be hidden and not abandoned.

I remember being no more than thirteen years old in a sitting room full of people, one of my mother's parties, and with the eyes of the insurance agent watching, unpeeling into ecstasy at the touch of one of my bare feet against the other. So that thirty-five years later when by chance I met that man again, he with his hang gut, me barely able to walk, something in both our bodies remembered and was glad, I think, in the way staggering along on a walking stick can make you recollect to a total stranger how once your legs could fly down the grass lane of the school oval for the 100 metres sprint on Sports Day in less than thirteen seconds.

As a seventeen-year-old I was quietly triumphant watching *Annie Hall*. Woody Allen wouldn't have had to almost dislocate his jaw if I was under his tongue. Later, my schoolteacher who'd taken me to the film would put his mouth on me as I sat in the passenger seat of his Corolla. Without thinking anything of it, I came three times before heading back for Sydney on the Mail train with windows that still opened.

The orgasms of childhood are like very ripe raspberries bursting open under your finger, exquisite enough but swiftly past. Those under Marr's mirror were of a different order. A molten cord flung itself up and out from my middle, lasting almost forever and apparently altering the shape of every other part of me.

Because the man who had been my schoolteacher had first fallen in love with my writing, he was always wanting to buy me fountain pens from a shop near Martin Place. For quite a few years I would wonder, with a jab of hope, was he right? Had my essays really been of the calibre of A.J.P. Taylor's or Manning Clark's prose? Or was he just overcome by the slit on the left-hand side of my uniform that showed a thigh burnished brown in the summer holidays?

Who initiated rating pleasure on the Richter scale? Who first began to call what hung between his legs Faber Castell? Who first spread a tissue on his tummy, like a doll's picnic rug, to catch what he didn't yet dare allow to leave inside me because for months there was no penetration? I can't remember. Goldfaber pencils carry the image of a set of scales in perfect balance. I still use them to this day, sometimes with a tender memory of being that full of sexual enchantment.

In the early 1980s, when an Italian girl at uni confessed that she'd never so far had an orgasm, I filled with disbelief. How could that be possible given the outrageous perfection of her breasts, always available to the gaze from either side view of her lace singlets? Her breasts were as perfect as Man Ray's girlfriend Ady's on a picnic at Picasso's house, Mougins, 1937, as photographed by Lee Miller, and only a fool would look up and away to the sky.

Another decade later my girlfriend with the breasts of a fourteen-year-old schoolgirl slipped a sugar-coated almond into me direct from her mouth. I watched the sea, hoping no one would walk around the cove as she gave me the easy sweet flowering I thought would always be mine.

*

By the time I finally meet Vincent at Marr's place much else besides sexual pleasure has vanished. In anticipation of the handover of the coastal property to NPWS the cubby has board by board been dismantled and rebuilt in spotted gum bushland.

Without the ocean rolling in from the eastern windows I feel a powerful disorientation. It is winter and the orchard, netted in a way that so resembles the shadow of the dome of pleasure, floats with a few remnant leaves of autumn. All the sculptures have also been relocated, including the only one ever made by Marr's famous father. It now stands sentinel-like on the southern side of the cubby, its forehead bowed.

Marr's works are elsewhere, in a cool grove of she-oaks where already two stones that look like breasts are in position for his dog's ashes and also his own. If you possess enough courage and agility, many of Marr's larger sculptures can be climbed. Climb at your own risk though, for to fall off the tree trunk hewn in half to give access to that biblical houseboat high up in the spotted gum canopy could mean death or severe disablement; yet Marr still walks up there as nonchalant as if he were strolling in a park, Umar his dog padding behind. Of my declaration from 2006, that when next I returned I'd walk up wearing only a pair of red high heels, we say nothing.

The longest night of the year will soon be here.

So what will Vincent be like, I wonder? Will it come easily to be naked in front of a stranger's camera? I've never earned an easy $50 as an artist's model for any life drawing class and as a rule feel shy even wearing a pair of swimmers in public.

My first tentative look in the cubby mirror in 2010 is all it takes to make me realise the stupidity of my suggestion. That longings have ever coursed through these stick-like limbs seems outlandish. There's nothing lush left of this body. I'm as light as the schoolgirl I used to be but my belly is drawn and old. Even under The Mirror of Beauty, my breasts stay like little flat animals, meekly waiting; their faces down. It is clear what has taken place. Absence has re-shaped my body. Pain has replaced pleasure and I draw my dressing-gown shut, full of shame.

I resemble nothing so much as the small dead rock wallaby of Chambers Gorge west of Tibooburra. I took its photo because the blazing summer had given its hide the appearance of 'gold to aery thinness beat.' Also, it had died with its arms in such a position of contrition I couldn't help but think of crusaders or even Christ.

But it was my younger sister, visiting me in Adelaide earlier in the year, who first saw something really magical in the wallaby photo that hangs on my wall in a second-hand gilt frame.

'Is that a picture of a fairy?'

'What?'

'Did someone sketch you a fairy?'

'No, that's a picture I took in 1999. Up north. It's a dead wallaby.'

But even as I was speaking, my sister was drawing a small winged girl in a riding habit.

'Oh yes. I see!' For within the placement of thin bones there was indeed, unmistakeably, the figure of a fairy. My sister also sketched in the presence of a large hare just behind, with giant spangled ears, as if this fairy's steed too might be capable of flight.

*

On the morning of my red balloon photo I'm up early enough to see the old crescent moon hanging as if positioned, exact centre over the upside-down lifeboat lychgate. Over to the north-west, like pieces of a giant puzzle in the sky, are other older Marr sculptures.

The cubby has been rebuilt beside a pavilion made of black towering poles and upside-down trees. The roots resemble the heads of gnarled black-headed gods hammered out of some colossal forge and flattened on that black stump anvil over there; yet the colour of the spotted gum country is almost overwhelmingly lyrical, all smoky pink with dapples. Down beneath the northern hill the water of Marr's lake is pitch black. Was I really able to swim up and down its inky curves four years ago? There is a quality of brooding to the scene, a waiting feeling, and the sea is nowhere in sight.

I hear the crunch of the photographer's boots on the river-pebble path outside. The sculpture above the door, made so many years ago by Marr using tiny bird bones, prayer paper and feathers, seems best to hold the fragility of this attempt.

'Vincent!' I greet him with a fake eagerness. After so much organisation, impossible to pull back now. He has an interesting face with the kind of wrinkles carved into certain planes that I usually associate with hard living. He has just come from photographing Bryce Courtenay with the balloon. Then his car broke down, hence the bits of grass and little leaves decorating his dark hair. A bit of a Heathcliff, I think, and that once we might've enjoyed getting drunk together.

Being naked in front of a stranger is easier than anticipated. I tilt this way and that, in time to each suggestion, feeling half pleased after all. We are the same age and ideas, memories and confessions unfurl between us as he lies on the floor a good hour or so taking photos. If he lived in Adelaide I feel we'd be friends.

I tell him about the Board Game of Life and of how it's time for me to throw the double six that lands you on The Black Square. *Congratulations. No More Turns. You are Dead.*

As I take Victor's photo afterwards at a café in Tanja I can still see myself in the mirror of his sunglasses. *Ha, ha, ha* laughs an advertising kookaburra on the wall immediately behind his head. My legs are heating up to that point where soon they won't be able to move. When I get hot MS makes my legs feel on fire even as my waist fills with the sensation that someone's pouring in cold cement. Panic begins. Vincent is ready to get going. He has many more Red Balloon portraits; a tight schedule set.

'This is embarrassing,' I say, staggering between two walking sticks before finally reaching the passenger seat. 'But I'm afraid you'll have to bend my legs for me.'

'Are you sure?' He grabs my ankles. 'Like this?'

'Harder. You'll have to be harder. If you ever want to reach Melbourne by tomorrow.'

*

That night under The Mirror of Beauty the MS spasms go wild. 'Legs, wait! Stop!' But they are less obedient than the red balloon of the film and do not feel playful. Once upon a time the paroxysms would've been all about pleasure.

In the middle of the night, an acrid quality enters my gaze. If I were a Pu-erh tea it's as if I've been brewed by someone overly patient, I've grown so dark and bitter. The right foot crosses sharply over the left, both feet coming to rest so exactly in the shape of a tail that it's impossible not to think of *The Little Mermaid*. Do I really want to be her story in reverse? There is no choice. I am losing my legs. That which used to lie within, that Marr might sometimes call his Little Pink Rice Flower, is closing. As if in readiness for a return to childhood, my triangle of womanly hair grows softer and softer.

High in the pantheon of special books of childhood was my sister Karin's copy of *The Little Mermaid*. The hardcover special edition held a beautiful illustration of the mermaid floating amongst her coral garden. If the picture was tilted her eyes appeared to open wider as if in readiness for the pain she was about to choose.

In special honour of Karin's love of this story, in 1973 Dad drove the hired campervan to Denmark specifically so that his second-born daughter could see the famous statue sitting on her rock in Copenhagen harbour. When not a week or two later the statue was decapitated a feeling of luck swept through my family.

Imagine if instead of her wistful gaze we'd found that kind of violence? Head missing? An arm half sawn off or worse?

*

Marr will turn eighty in October. To escape any surprise celebrations, he's going to Shanghai. Yes, he says, he will look out for *The Little Mermaid*, uprooted from her harbour for the World Trade Fair.

I'm as awed as ever by how many generations he has lived. Tell me again about having a date with Elizabeth Taylor with her chauffeur as chaperone in The Brown Derby Cafe, when you were just eleven. What about sailing your snipe *Beloved* up San Francisco Bay to the brothel when you were fourteen, before beating a terrified retreat at the sight of aged women carrying douche pots past where you and your best friend Wing sat waiting? Did you really hear Cannonball Adderley in the Black Hawk Cafe? I could listen forever to these incredible tales from the past.

On the last morning of my visit I hold Marr's hand beneath the mirror, certain that I will never visit again. The bush is not easy when there's almost no working leg muscle left. The bush is no place for the wheelchair I've been warned time and again is waiting for me. I'm as wistful as that strand of flowering grass curving out of the tiny vase Marr has shaped using a Nicorette as clay.

Beneath my other hand parts of Marr are still capable of thinking themselves far younger. We smile at this. In the safety of the mirror. I say it is the most royal plinth of all and beneath my mouth feel the dark helmet grow huge with yearning. At my request, as part of our farewell, he's going to read aloud some of Antoine de Saint-Exupéry's *The Little Prince*.

He has never read this before and his gravelly laugh sounds like a thousand bells in the stars. I try to halt my rising sadness but as only the beautiful Katherine Woods translation makes clear, 'It is such a secret place, the land of tears.'

*

Fairy Death, who will you come riding for first? Who will be at whose funeral? In the manner of a school debate of old, far easier not to go last. If I could kiss Hans Christian Andersen I would find lips as bisexual and lonely as my own. Had he lived in this century would he ever have clicked open a few porn sites as recommended by my new neurologist as a way of sparking up lost libido? Do lovers I once knew? Do I? At the neurologist's behest, I give it a try.

Who on earth are all these girls and women opening their shaved selves, legs all akimbo, to dicks of this or that size and capacity? They make me remember a careless time in my life when if my breasts had been more perfect I would've been applying for topless waitressing jobs. I imagine us as babies, all sparkly with new life, for as the Taoist saints said, 'When we are born we are all good, with no evil.'

If I was still of the age where blunt graffiti on the desks of the Fisher Library stack once saw me heading to the disabled toilet to give myself a quick jasm, this internet pornography might've helped. Later there was one swift tryst in the same toilet with an older student with an interest in Japan. In Kyoto, he said, lifting my skirt, were vending machines selling the underwear of schoolgirls and I never knew if this was for real or just another fantasy.

Now I prefer to imagine holding the fairytale writer's face in my hands; looking into his fatherly eyes. If I could kiss the edge of his bony brow and other more delicate perimeters, with Marr, old swinger that he was, close by watching, Hans Christian Andersen would grant me one wish.

Then *Fairy Death* shall arrive tonight. I will unpeel her glove and hold the dainty bones of her hand, relief sweeping through in the way of the afternoon southerlies reaching the now land-locked cubby.

The mouths of men stay beautiful because their skin is stronger. Their eyes, especially at dusk, become very kind. Older men have always rejoiced in my presence. I think this is because I in turn have always rejoiced in the still gallant scope of their flirt; the sheer audacity of their hopes. Even on one walking stick I've been amazed by the frequency of rash propositions.

An old Greek man at dusk on a street in Prospect mimes that he can still get an erection. 'I can still be hard! I will feed you fruit,' he calls as I make haste to hobble away. 'In the bedroom of my second house. I will take you there.'

For a time, on buses, trains and planes, I find myself studying the lips of strangers. Has that bald businessman's face ever arisen from between his wife's legs as wet as if from a swim in a sea of crushed mangoes? Has his tongue ever been taught to bring her to ecstasy?

Marr's mouth is not that of an old man. Though the moon of his life is a waning, westward-facing one, his lips are ageless. His lips are shapely, the top one with a bow-like crest I've never tired of studying. Whenever his warm mouth has brushed my neck there always comes a feeling of the kind of light-filled, deep love written about by the poets.

When we kiss goodbye, in the way of the Little Mermaid seeing her beloved prince with his new wife, my heart feels a fleck of sea foam at its edges.

*

Back in Adelaide, one glimpse in a shopfront window as I stomp along behind a walking frame on wheels is all it takes to end a lifetime of hunting out accidental mirrors. The frame makes me move forward in a way that most resembles a famous homeless man of the Devonshire tunnel of two decades ago. *Slab* would lurch along as if pinioned beneath his baggy trousers by a pair of callipers. With newspapers tucked under both arms it seemed he had some secret contract to move only millimetres away from the tunnel wall. Or my appearance calls to mind that tiny bird of a woman always at the Country Trains section of Central Railway Station. After my romantic assignations with my old schoolteacher, she'd be in the vicinity of the clock, her head almost at a right angle, taking a rest. She pulled her life possessions along in a vinyl shopping trolley as cracked by wrinkles as her face and seemed always to harken my way with some kind of crooked warning imminent.

On a walking frame you become instantly vulnerable to the sympathy of strangers. Kisses of pity not passion suddenly start landing on the top of your head.

These enrage me but what can I say? The strangers think that Jesus-like they are the milk of human kindness and, suddenly embarrassed, wipe their lips and rush away.

Not so long after the appearance of the walking frame follows the invasion of the wheelchairs. The ratchet of pain set up by MS spasms gives me little choice. A standard MS society wheelchair would make anyone weep. Somehow, three have been delivered.

They are each bigger, blacker, than any old fashioned perambulator. They droop in doorways in the way of Mirkwood forest spider webs.

The vase of flowers in front of my writing light is throwing huge shadows onto the opposite wall. The flowers, delivered from a florist and meant to assuage my sadness, have absolutely no fragrance. How is this so? Does this Velcro twenty-first century also have glass houses full of rose scientists intent on breeding blooms from which no perfume can ever float? What would the Little Prince's friend the fox or his own precious and precocious Rose have to say about this?

Marr sends a note with some frigate bird feathers from a bird that didn't make it through the winter storms. After swifts, these sea birds are the most aerial of all, graceful and soaring and perhaps, it is thought, even sleeping on the wing after bad weather. The down is the colour of sea mist. Fixed to prayer paper, the feathers are a little parted, as if to permanently recall for me the delicacy of desire.

The bad weather of my own life deepens.

I realise that if I'm serious about driving out into the mallee in search of, if not the elusive fairy, then the Little Prince's yellow snake, then I'd better not leave it too much longer. I'm disappointed in myself that I keep finding reason to delay such a deliberate and dramatic end. I revoke my licence and awake in an ordinary, mirrorless bed.

Fairy Death, when are you coming? I listen to Arvo Pärt's *Spiegel im Spiegel*, Mirror in the Mirror, and find some relief. The cello reflects the piano endlessly and, in like fashion, back and forth I flick resignation and sadness. Is that piano speaking Latin, as in *Vehimur in altum*, the sun rising in golden glory over the horizon where the cubby used to face, *we are carried out into the deep*?

I think again of the artist's young and beautiful new wife; how swiftly exquisite her passing: an aneurism at the moment of orgasm. Only twenty-four years old and gone. A gift from her lover's mouth like no other.

If I could pick such an end it would be in the *Decateur South* cubby before it was moved. Pleasure splintering me. The Little Pink Rice Flower opening one last time in rapture with Marr, 'God stepping through our loins,' D.H. Lawrence style, 'in one bright stride.' A huge sea crashing against the shores of a land far away.

But when Vincent Long sends the photo, I see the unexpected. I see myself motionless on the futon, as if thrown from a horse. It is as if I am lying there winded, wondering if I'll be able to move. I see that my longing has become manifest so truly that I resemble no one so much as *Fairy Death* herself.

Humour cuts through such observations better than anything.

'Do you think Marr really *did* get Nembutal last time he went to the States?' I remembered to ask Marr's gardener before leaving.

The gardener, his wit as black as Marr's lake, replied in a flash. 'Oh yes, actually. He did. Took it. Didn't work.'

HEAT

Photography by Vincent L. Long, from *The Red Balloon Project.*

Happiness in the Flesh

David Malouf

One of the most striking features of 21st-century living, in what we think of as our part of the world, is the return of the body as our most immediate, and in some cases our only, assurance of presence, of the rich and crowded and actively happening world-we-are-in.

The body has become natural again, and essentially good. It is subject to decay, of course, and eventually to death, but for most of us it is a source of innocent pleasure and happiness, of joy in the flesh, and increasingly for some of a kind of worship in which, as I shall want to suggest later, it has largely replaced what in earlier times would have been called the Self. This is only to say that for a large number of people these days the material or physical world is more important than the inner life. The body is what most completely represents them, even to themselves. If we no longer see it as fallen or corrupt, it is because we no longer see nature that way, and it is to nature that it belongs.

This is both a new and a very old view of the body. It has its roots in that part of our culture that derives from the classical world, and is one of the things that were revived and returned to us with what we call the Renaissance.

For the Greeks and Romans, the human body was an animal body. Clearly, humanity, endowed as it is with reason, speech, a capacity for inventing and making, and for social organisation of a most complex kind, stands at the top of the animal ladder; but as in other world views – Hinduism, Buddhism, for example – the separation between the species was not absolute. In classical mythology, girls could be turned, on the whim of the gods, into birds, like Philomela the nightingale, or trees or plants, like Daphne the laurel, the reed Syrinx, Clytie the sunflower, or even into a bear, like Callisto. Zeus, in his role as lover, could take the form of an eagle, a bull, a swan; young men, after death, return as flowers (Hyacinthus, Narcissus) or become constellations like the twins (Gemini) Castor and Pollux.

This fluidity of forms is what animates Ovid's book of 'changes,' the *Metamorphoses*. In the medium of words, as virtuosic syntactical act and visual event, he made the emergence of one life out of another, the melting before our eyes of girlish sinuosity into the flow of water, the breaking of limbs into branches and leaves, so convincing in their actuality as to be 'real,' and if ordinary men and women did not believe in them as *fact* – belief in our sense of the word was not required – they did recognise that what these 'fables' pointed to was a larger and more general truth. That all of creation was connected, and shared the same life-energy; was part of a continuity. That the world, *this* world, was whole and 'good.' Animals, including humans, were innocent. The pleasures of the body were also innocent, a source of happiness and ease. Sensual delight was a gift of the gods that was meant to be celebrated, and whose celebration, in games, in dance, in eating and drinking, in lovemaking, was its own way of showing gratitude for the gift.

What the classical moralists recommended was moderation – as a guarantee of psychological balance as well as good health – *nec nimis* (nothing in excess) is the phrase that Horace, who has a supreme gift for such concise and memorable formulations, has passed down to us; but they did not think of carnal pleasure as sinful or as a reason for shame.

The body was not holy – a temple as the Church would later call it – to be preserved from unhallowed use; it was meant to be used – that is, enjoyed. If the sexual life involved distress or evil, this had nothing to do with the sinfulness of the flesh, but with such psychological factors as jealousy, loss of self-containment and control, the pain of rejection or betrayal and the shaming anger and self-disgust that may follow upon them – all these the human consequences of the war between the sexes as Catullus and others report upon it, writing in, from its battle-zones and skirmishes, with personal accounts of triumph or of humiliation and defeat.

Carnal pleasure, which involves and interests us all, is one of the major subjects of classical writing from Sappho and the poets of the Greek Anthology to a long line of Latin poets: Catullus, Horace, Propertius, Ovid. Ovid especially has a sensibility so 'modern,' so contemporary to all times, that he has been a living voice in every period from Ronsard and Donne to Frank O'Hara in our own.

His *Ars Amatoria*, a cheeky exercise in youthful exhibitionism and the pursuit of sexual adventure in the big city, is the work of a young man-about-town (a *persona*, in fact: Ovid when he wrote it was nearly fifty) who delights in every form of doubtful behaviour, rejects every respectable career that might be available to a Roman of his class, and, as opportunistic seducer, sometime lover, hero not of the battlefield or the law courts but of the bedchamber and bed, devotes the whole range of his energy and interest to the pleasures of the flesh.

This is the classical work that poets and writers throughout Europe in the sixteenth century turn back to as their textbook and guide to a freer form of living, and the rediscovery of the body as a new world of pleasure and happiness.

Pietro Aretino in Italy produces a suite of sonnets, the *Sonetti Lussuriosi* (Lascivious Sonnets), that break with the Petrarchan tradition of idealised love in poems that are frankly and provocatively carnal – and which he takes to a point that even now seems close to the limits of the permissible.

In France, Rabelais sets up, in his Abbey of Thélème, a parody religious order whose only rule is *Fay çe que vouldras* (Do what thou wilt), an institution devoted to the breaking of all taboos and the restoration of the flesh as a source of riotous but harmless and joyful misrule.

Half a century later, Ovid provides the model again for the stance that John Donne adopts, and the voice he uses, to challenge convention, defy authority and claim his own place in the world as nothing less, or more, than poet and lover. The scramble for office – in law, in the army, at court – he leaves to what he scornfully calls 'country ants.' An early member of his own Me Generation, he makes a grand rejection of all social ties, all ties to nation or polity, in favour of a community that consists solely of his mistress and himself: 'She is all States, and all Princes I, Nothing else is.' He even challenges the centrality of the sun (that newish scientific concept), which he now harnesses to their private universe and use:

> *Thou, Sun, art half as happy as we,*
> *In that the world's contracted thus ...*
> *Shine here to us, and thou art everywhere;*
> *This bed thy centre is, these walls, thy sphere.*

His celebration of his mistress's body is free, happy, entirely without shame or guilt, and expresses itself in language so active and sensual that it not only reproduces, as far as language can, his own energy and excitement, but attempts to transfer that energy, with its kinetic rhythms, to us as we read:

> *Licence my roving hands, and let them go*
> *Behind, before, above, between, below ...*
> *Oh my America, my new found land.*

*

The body has always been a source of joy of the kind Donne is expressing, and if there were those, during the long period when Christianity and its teachings held sway in Europe, for whom it was guilty joy, shameful, even degrading, there must have been many who felt nothing of this: felt, that is, as Donne did and held their tongue about it. Sexual joy is too overwhelmingly physical to be ignored. Such sceptics, or secret heretics, must have decided that the Church Fathers were somehow wrong about the body, and that their parish priests were either equally wrong or liars; or that they themselves were somehow lost but happy about it, or lost and not.

Certainly there were times and places, among the Cathars, for example, in south-western France in the thirteenth century, where sexual energy and the open expression of it could not be contained and broke out as revolt. And of course there were other parts of the world, equally religious, where sexual energy and its joyful expression were not incompatible with a sense of the sacred or the practice of faith. The temples of India, with their exuberant facades where sculptured figures rejoice in voluptuous poses and engagements of every kind, are monuments to the sacredness of the flesh, and to moments of carnal and spiritual union.

*

The frank expression of sexual happiness in a poem, in words, is one thing. Painting and the depiction of sensual joy in paint – despite Horace's famous phrase that links poetry and painting as sister arts – is something quite other.

Though flat and two-dimensional, painting tricks the eye into perceiving a third, creating depth and distance where there is none, giving a bare arm or leg a roundness it does not have, but also a softness, since the visual is not the only sense that painting appeals to and plays with. Objects it picks out on the flat surface of a canvas or a plaster wall have textures we feel we could reach out and test between our fingers. Flesh, and the blood that gives it colour, has a palpable warmth, but the shadow it throws is cool. No painter better controls these effects, or deploys them more richly, than the Flemish artist Peter Paul Rubens.

Almost exactly Donne's contemporary, Rubens – already, at sixty, by the standards of his time an old man (Shakespeare was dead at fifty-two) – sets out to paint his second wife, Helena Fourment. The painting still has the power, even in our own century, to shock.

Caught bare-footed and naked in a room with a crimson carpet and a crimson cushion at her feet, she has snatched up a black fur cape with a gold border to cover herself, but this spur-of-the-moment act only serves to emphasise her nudity: bare feet and legs, bare shoulders, the cape caught up below her belly so that she has to use her arms in an inadequate, endearingly awkward way to cover her breasts. She seems younger than her twenty-four years. Perhaps Rubens was thinking of her as she was when he married her, his sixteen-year-old bride.

It is a 'corridor' moment, an after-dark household moment to which only her husband might be privy, or should be.

Peter Paul Rubens, *Het Pelsken* (*Hélène Fourment in a Fur Wrap*), c. 1630s, Kunsthistorisches Museum, Vienna.

Instead he paints it to express and share – but with whom, we wonder – the immense joy he finds in her presence: her being, her youth, her glowing beauty, her flesh; and to confess – again, to whom? – how happy they are in their togetherness in the flesh. The gratitude he feels is part of the offering. He is showing, in the surest way that is possible to him, in paint, the privilege he feels in her having given herself to him.

All this is so intensely private, sacred perhaps, that we are astonished that the painting is there to be seen. We know that Rubens regarded it as a personal possession, a precious record of their intimate life together; he names it, *Het Pelsken*, in his will, and leaves it to her.

But paintings are *made* to be seen. There is something here that Rubens wanted revealed, and in such a way that it would be powerfully clear. It is something not only about the woman, the girl, his wife Helena Fourment, about the way he sees her and the sensual response she wakes in him, which is everywhere in the painting. It is his own brimming happiness that he wants to show.

*

Three years earlier, Rubens's younger contemporary Rembrandt had produced a famous double portrait, if that is what it is, of himself and his young wife, Saskia. The painting, where it hangs now in the Gemäldegalerie in Dresden, is called *The Prodigal Son with a Whore*.

Rubens and Rembrandt both work as Northern painters often do, close to home. Household and studio are sometimes one. We know the interior of these Flemish and Dutch houses from the paintings: closed, half-dark, stocked with heavy furniture, crowded with objects of every sort – oriental carpets, furs, brocaded silks, satins, leather, old pieces of armour, glazed pitchers, metal ewers – that can be glimpsed, from one painting to the next, as background decoration in domestic portraits and genre pictures, or as 'props' in a mythological set-piece.

We also recognise the painters' wives, as a young woman is called upon to set her child aside for a moment, strip and, as directed, raising an arm here, inclining her neck there, shifting her weight from the left foot to the right, strike a pose as Callisto or Andromeda or Flora, or as a close convenient servant-girl and bed companion (only much later a wife) take on the role of Bathsheba or A Woman Bathing.

The world these Northern painters work in is grounded in the domestic but moves easily from the homely to the theatrical, and from contemporary moments to the remote mythological past. In a way that seems essentially Baroque, the cluttered rooms of these interiors, with so many props close at hand, suggest the back-stage 'tyring rooms' of a private theatre where someone is always undressing or dressing up.

So it happens that in the Rembrandt double portrait we cannot be quite sure what it is we have got. It may be the illustration of a parable, the exposure – with, in that case, a deal of good-natured sympathy – of youthful debauchery, though that is not the message we take from its cheerful exuberance.

What it clearly is, whatever the 'subject,' is the picture of a couple, caught here in a private moment but not at all disconcerted by our intrusion.

He, elaborately decked out as a cavalier, with a sword at his waist and a glowing feather in his hat, looks back over his shoulder, sees us and bursts out laughing. (How often in these Northern pictures people laugh outright – an expression of excessive emotion too undignified and naturalistic, too distorting of the ideal, for Italian painting.)

Rembrandt Van Rijn, *The Prodigal Son with a Whore* (self-portrait with Saskia), c. 1635, Gemäldegalerie, Dresden.

She too, made aware perhaps by his burst of laughter that we have come upon them, turns and meets our gaze; we have caught her seated on his knee. She is demure but dignified. Confident. Preparing to smile. They are on their way to bed, but show no sign of embarrassment; he raises his long glass and toasts us. Held high, it resembles a lamp that floods with light her face, her neck, the gold chain she is wearing, the shallow scoop of white lawn below the collar of her gown, his snowy feather, his left hand on the gleaming folds of her skirt.

What the man, who is clearly the painter, seems to be celebrating and to be inviting us, since we have so unexpectedly appeared, to witness, is a moment of domestic bliss, of conjugal felicity. Perhaps the dressing-up part of it is a piece of private theatre, the acting out of a sexual fantasy, titillating foreplay. If it is, that too he is willing to show without embarrassment and to share.

What he is also sharing with us is the ordinary richness of the world, its press of objects, some of them useful in an ordinary way, some of them both that and props to be taken up and given a new use and significance in the theatre of happy play: all of them – fringed cushion, oriental rug, gold chain, silk skirt, glass, brocaded curtain, feather, sword-hilt, glowing flesh – brush-stroked in, since he is after all Rembrandt the painter, with the greatest possible appeal to the senses in their varied textures and the play of light upon them, in the utter joy, one would want to say, that he finds in all this as artist and technician. Not simply in the moment, and in the two human participants and what they are making for, but in his being-in-the-world, and in all these objects that he has so lovingly rendered.

Amsterdam and Antwerp at this moment, like Venice just decades before, are great trading centres. Objects – commodities – matter. Making them visually actual, in brushstrokes on canvas, is the artist's way of dealing with what merchants handle in the world of affairs: a feeling for materiality – the texture, weight, colour, of cloth or fur or metal, but also of such exotic blooms as peonies and tulips, the iridescent plumage of partridge and peacock, the rind of melons and pomegranates. The bringing alive of all this in paint is another form of the same energy that goes, elsewhere, into adventuring and trading out there in the Caribbean or the Indies, and can be made visible in the domestic world of a couple, the painter *en zijn huysvroouw*, on their way to bed. Part of that energy is sexual. It is a close step, as Donne shows, from the adventuring of 'Behind, before, above, between, below' to 'Oh my America, my new found land.'

Perhaps the closest we get in painting to the bold and joyful sensuality of Donne's poem is in Rubens's extraordinary image

of Helena Fourment. What it reaches for is a moment of spontaneous appearance that seems too fleeting for paint – for the
painstaking business of preparing the canvas, making a sketch,
mixing the paints, getting the model to hold her pose. Rubens
here is reproducing what struck his senses in the instant when
the image of this woman flashed on his eye. What the picture
anticipates is the candid camera-flash, a figure caught in bright
light as she steps out of the dark.

Rubens, of course, is the master in his period, the Baroque,
of the large-scale historical painting that is all drama, spectacle,
dynamic action and energy. These vast works came in dozens
from the Rubens workshop, Biblical or mythological scenes, alle-
gorical set-pieces, contemporary events – the cycle he painted,
for example, for Marie de Medici in France – in which, given all
the paraphernalia, and bravura and dash of Rubens's 'theatre,'
the political is raised to the status of myth and endowed with
'divine' authority. He produced these compositions to order,
employing an astonishing flair for dramatic gesture, and drawing on his memory, which was vast and encyclopedic, for poses
from the classical repertoire or the modern Italian masters that
he could, in each case, shape to his own occasion and play with
in such a way that they both recalled the past, and his creative
continuity with it, and at the same time displayed his individual
boldness and originality; and when it came to convincing background detail for this period or that, the Biblical, or the classical world of Greece or Rome, there was again his encyclopedic
memory to call upon for antiquarian accuracy.

Skilled workmen executed what Rubens had designed and he
added the finishing touches: the adjustment of a pose, a dash of
colour no assistant would dare aspire to, individual brushstrokes. His genius was essential to these works, but the question
remains of how 'authentic' they are, how much they are his. The
eye and the mind are his but not the hand. Which is why we put
such a high value on the bravura sketches, which are so full of
the immediate energy of conception and so characteristic in the
boldness of their lines and washes (as executed they are small,
but already gigantic in their dynamic power, in the scope of what
they have imagined) but also on the late landscapes, which we
know were so personally dear to him, and the domestic images

of Helena and her children (the last of whom, a girl, was born eight months after Rubens's death).

What makes a 'private' work like *Het Pelsken* so precious, and rare at this late point in Rubens's career, is that we know that it is his hand, and the energy of his mind and body, that produced every brushstroke. The painting is the product not just of his vision, his powers of composition, but of his *presence*, as we know him – the man himself – from other more public occasions.

Wordsworth defined the making of poetry as 'emotion recollected in tranquility.' The poet makes the emotion he creates real to us *now*, but to him it belongs to experience that has to be called up out of the past and re-collected. What he needs for the making of it now is a quiet moment when he can be still, and, by thinking, relive what he felt as words.

Het Pelsken is nothing like that. Painting is a physical act in which the painter's energy is dynamically of the moment, in the quickness of his eye, the sureness of his hand, as brushstrokes and paint reproduce what he feels in the moment itself. That energy is a form of joy. What he is setting down, direct onto the canvas, is his happiness, and this, perhaps, is as close as we will ever get to it, to another man's being; the closest we will get – and we take the phrase in both senses – to happiness in the flesh.

The Happy Life

Living Hard, Dying Young in the Kimberley

Nicolas Rothwell

The funeral, brief and heart-rending, was held in the shade of a half-wrecked basketball court. The music was gospel-country, the service Catholic, modified a touch to suit East Kimberley traditional beliefs. At the grave site were plastic flowers: birthday flowers. It would have been the twenty-third birthday of the young woman who was being laid in the ground: at the front of the crowd of wailing mourners, her little daughter, in a bright dress, looked on.

Another dreadful death in the Kimberley Aboriginal world, another with alcohol involved. Another piece in the interlocking jigsaw of grief, reaction and self-destructive behaviour that has shadowed the entire Kimberley throughout the past wet season's most oppressive months. The recent suicide statistics for the region are terrifying: they gravely understate the social disaster's true scale. Violence, alcoholic drinking, drug-taking and self-harm all form part of a pattern of behaviour entrenched among the young Indigenous population in the wide belt of country that runs from Broome along the highway to Wyndham in the north. When fragments of this picture are reported, it can seem that a whole society is going under. What exactly is happening, and what can be done?

*

Each unhappy region of remote Aboriginal Australia is unhappy in its own way, but the most striking aspect of the tragedy that has been unfolding in the red range country of the far north-west is how well documented and closely tracked it has been. The Kimberley is an expanse, its dispersed people bound by family ties: just over 40,000 people live there, half that total Indigenous, their median age twenty-one: many of that number are without work and unable to read or write to any degree of competence. This vast area, twice the size of Victoria, enfolds both cosmopolitan Broome and a set of extremely remote communities and outstations, where 40 per cent of the population is under fifteen years of age. In such places, young people lack authority figures: the steadying balance of experiences and influences in society has been broken. Five years ago, a spate of suicides in the region triggered an inquiry by West Australian coroner Alastair Hope, and profound reforms. Policing was stepped up, alcohol controls were brought in. Large-scale investments aimed at reshaping Indigenous Kimberley life began. But the signs of social breakdown and despair have spiked again. Since late December last year eleven suicides have been recorded, almost all in remote Aboriginal areas, together with many failed attempts and self-harm episodes. WA Mental Health Minister Helen Morton is blunt in speaking of a 'crisis.' Federal and state funds have been urgently channelled to the region's special mental health and suicide prevention programs. The StandBy Response Service, an interagency panel, is strikingly well informed and sober in the private assessments it compiles of the social landscape. North-West Mental Health recently tallied the figures: it had 300 people on its books and 330 new referrals. It sees the present stage of the crisis as 'acute' and calls for the presence of specialists, more workers on the ground, massive investment to address the grave shortfall in Indigenous housing.

'This is larger scale than a cluster – bigger than anyone can respond to at the moment,' said one NWMH figure recently behind closed doors. Police intelligence has probed the circumstances behind the recent suicides as much as possible. Only two of the cases were directly related to each other: nine involved hanging, one cutting. One was an identified past victim of sex abuse, one had a few domestic violence reports. In the little

East Kimberley metropolis of Kununurra, police have listed twenty-five 'at risk' individuals who have threatened or attempted suicide in the recent past. But they know, as the social workers know, and as Aboriginal leaders very well know, that there are overarching factors, and the picture is much more complicated. Alcohol is almost always part of the story. 'People become highly impulsive,' says a veteran health worker. 'They drink, argue and kill themselves – it's always the way, and each suicide spreads out like a ripple, people are so devastated they want to follow.' Death feeds on death. Cycles of mourning can't unfurl properly, there's not the time between funerals for sadness and anger to be dissipated, the grief and loss counsellors who might serve as calming voices simply aren't present on the ground. The suicides are only the peaks in a complicated range: a massif of violence, numbness, drink and dark atmospherics.

How to respond? 'We can see where we are, and what's failing,' says long-time West Australian state parliamentarian Tom Stephens, a former Minister for the Kimberley. 'But we only respond with more departments, with bureaucracies of families and community services, organisations that actually have nothing to do with their names. There's a disconnect from people on the ground.'

The statistics and trend figures somehow disguise the effects of grief in small societies of the scale found in the remote Kimberley. Consider the funeral described above. It was held in Turkey Creek, the 'dry' community where the death took place. The young woman died in a house just up the road from a new police station. She and her friends had visited Wyndham, where a baby from a family they knew had died in a distressing accident. They were grieving. They came back to Turkey Creek: they were in a house close by a large tree from which a young friend of theirs had hanged himself. He tried three times. The first time, his family lopped off the low branch he used for the rope; the second time, the second lowest branch; the third time, he crept out at night; they were too late. In the shadow of that tree, the drinking, and mourning, began: the young woman was not a habitual drinker: she vomited, inhaled her vomit, and died. Technically, her death was not a suicide: in truth, it was part of a tangled chain of grief and loss. That chain stretches far and wide: the mourners at her funeral last month came from as far afield as Wyndham, Kununurra and Wave Hill. A few days after her death, a flood of Biblical proportions swept through Turkey Creek, devastating the community, wrecking almost all its houses, and forcing an evacuation of the entire population: they are being housed in a workers' camp 200 kilometres away while the place is rebuilt and emergency quarters set up in its shell. A disaster, says the state government. A cleansing flood, say the old Gija men and women who saw the waters rise: the action of the 'Ngarringgarni' – what we translate as the Dreamtime, but should describe as the inscrutable, fate-dealing cosmic power of the Kimberley Aboriginal world.

*

Given the central role of alcohol and binge-drinking as the release trigger for this tide of death and violence, it was only natural, once the emergence and the scale of the linked plagues of domestic aggression, sexual abuse and fetal alcohol syndrome (FAS) sweeping across the Kimberley were fully recognised, that restrictions on the unchecked supply of drink would be imposed; and after concerted lobbying by women's groups in the Fitzroy Valley, limits on the sale of full-strength grog were introduced at Fitzroy Crossing late in 2007. Similar restrictions followed in Halls Creek, another notorious Central Kimberley alcohol black spot, and in due course in the east Kimberley as well. Just last month, two more large communities requested blanket grog bans: in theory, much of the remote Kimberley is now 'dry.' Drinking unfolds for the most part in the towns, though grog-running into the outlying areas is also rife. Medical research into the extent of the damage is ongoing: social programs enfold the region in a tightening, compassionate net. The results of the changes in drink supply have been closely monitored: at first, there were spectacular reductions in violence and alcohol-caused emergencies, but after two years of restrictions in Fitzroy Crossing it is apparent that the beneficial effects of the controls erode over time, with drinkers finding ways to bring in outside supplies, or moving to areas where the flow of alcohol is less constrained: hundreds of Halls Creek people have moved to semi-permanent drinking camps in Broome and Kununurra. Hence the appeal by some local Indigenous leaders to treat the whole area as a single province of control, and give restrictions universal scope. But control of the region's supply of drink is just one component in the management of the Kimberley crisis: controlling the conditions that produce the demand for the intoxicating drug is the second key, and policy designers have been less able to influence this element. After deep re-assessments at federal and state level, large-scale employment and development projects have been unveiled for the both the far west and east Kimberley: in Broome, where a strong investment is being made in a new Aboriginal development corporation, and in Kununurra, where the second stage of the Ord Valley irrigation project is now being built by a workforce with an Indigenous component. Such schemes are the late-dawning hope. But they can capture only a small proportion of the ill-educated, welfare-dependent youth of the region, those who feed the domestic violence statistics and coronial reports.

*

Most coverage of the Aboriginal Kimberley treats these individuals from an outside perspective, through police bulletins and the words of social workers. But what is the life they experience? Can we describe it? What follows is based on long acquaintance with a set of families from the East Kimberley, the epicentre of the latest troubles. They inhabit a distressing world.

Let's stroll through the well-kept centre of Kununurra, the little regional hub, as darkness falls, and the temperature drops: the mainstream families retreat to their elegant, tropically accented suburbs, and the Aboriginal drinkers and their families and children take to the streets. Here come two little groups of young adults, the men pushing prams, toddlers walking and tumbling alongside: in each pram is a child-sized thirty-pack of mid-strength being wheeled tenderly out to the drinking camps. Along the verges of the roadways, and in the parklands, figures lie prone on the grass, passed out. Shouts and cries of anger and anguish fill the air. The nightly bacchanal is underway. Rival gangs congregate, for the town is a crossroads of different peoples, from different cultural regions, as far afield as Ringers Soak and Mount Barnett. Most of the locals, the Miriuwung people, live, often twenty to a house, in the crowded reserves just outside the town centre; many occupy the tattered Aboriginal dwellings strewn through the inner streets. Look inside: no furniture: only mattresses and TV and stereo, an empty fridge, decaying food in the sink: why do the dish-washing, when someone else will leave more mess to clean up? Tension is in the night. The 300 Gija refugees from Turkey Creek are stabled for now down the road in the Ord Valley development scheme's plush 150-bed workers' camp, with nothing much to do: it is run at a cost to the government of $50,000 a week, free food and lodging provided, so the residents have much more welfare money in their pocket than usual, and little to occupy them, except downtown Kununurra, with its bright lights. Hence the uptick in the 'night-walking' that sees the town come alive by dark: hundreds of young men and women swarm about. Hence, too, the night-fighting: 'Big fight,' says senior artist Peggy Patrick after a long battle just outside her house at Lakeside, while the detectives in their unmarked 4WDs cruise the scene. 'Too many – you just couldn't see!'

Darkness is drinking time: the restrictions on full-strength alcohol sale keep takeaways to the window from 5 to 8 p.m., so consumption starts late and runs through to dawn. In theory, the limit is one thirty-pack a day (forty-five standard drinks), or a one-litre bottle of rum: but there's no identification requirement or information sharing between outlets. A breathalyser checks for intoxication if the vendor has suspicions, and that's it: a committed drinker can buy his daily ration at Gulliver's in town, drop the plunder at the reserve nearby, come back, repeat the purchase at the Kununurra Hotel, loop round again and buy more at the well-appointed bottle-shop at Coles. Experts monitor the pattern, and almost despair: almost – because there are intriguing pointers from this real-life behavioural lab. On Sundays across the East Kimberley, no take-away is allowed, but drinkers can have their full-strength alcohol at the bar: alcohol-related hospital emergencies and crimes almost vanish on that day, lending at least a modicum of support to those advocates who suggest the promotion of convivial drinking environments as well as control regimes.

But there are other channels to keep up some of the flow: four sly-grog operators thrive in Kununurra, two white, two Aboriginal. Fifty dollars buys a six-pack of green cans. The patterns of the trade fluctuate; they can be baroque. One local reseller liked to line up his customers in a row at 6 a.m., and dispense rum by the glass in return for sex. Alcohol is not the only substance in the bloodstreams of the young night-walkers on the streets. Ganja is everywhere in town: strong marijuana, heads of weed, brought up from South Australia by a white dealer, then split up for distribution by local couriers. Fifty dollars for a half-gram, six times higher than the capital-city price. Strong dependency and tolerance of THC develops fast: many smokers consume ten to twenty cones a day. The money to fund this heavy intake of intoxicants comes from welfare and artwork payments, constantly distributed through family networks, and from burglaries as well. Not all the property crime in Kununurra, though, is purely the expression of economic need. The other night the local resource centre was vandalised: eleven cars and several laptops were damaged; the fire extinguishers were let off.

This was anger: Miriuwung children feel displaced by the incomers to their town. On an average evening, four or five groups of young men and women, maybe a dozen in each, are marauding about, coalescing and then separating, talking, sparring, heading from here to there. Many check in at the sobering up shelter to see who's in. Many others stop in at the Chilling Out Space at the Mirima Reserve. There are good reasons for keeping on the move by night, if you're young, and live in a crowded house. Children often bunk down at home on their shared floor-mattresses wearing five or six layers of clothing, well aware men from their extended families – 'men behaving like bloody goannas' – may pounce. Some try to spend their nights in the designated grog-free houses, with those optimistic 'No grog, no ganja, Police will be called' notices on the front doors. Some form their own little groups and take shelter at the high red-rock peak of Kelly's Knob just outside town. If you climb up there, you can see their campsites, and the cans of butane-rich

Lynx deodorant spray scattered round, those tell-tale badges of youth; the night-walkers inhale them in their bid for entry to a gentler psychic space.

And here we have come close to the hidden heart of East Kimberley life-paths today. Sex is a theatre of troubles for the young of the far north-west: it expresses their world's tone, and it causes it: sex as violence; sex as power. The pattern is linked to life in crowded, chaotic circumstances. Almost two-thirds of young women have been interfered with in some profound way before they begin having sex with partners of their own age cohort, around the age of twelve – the age when Kimberley doctors routinely administer the long-acting contraceptive Implanon to Miriuwung and Gija girls. The abuse rate is probably about the same for boys – though such things are not easily mentioned. This is consistent with the picture compiled over recent years by investigators in ultra-troubled remote North Kimberley communities, like Kalumburu, and Oombulgurri, a place so hellish it has now been effectively closed down by the West Australian government. Pack rape is the most frequent mode of initiation into young sex for pretty girls: these episodes are so distressing they rarely come out: but they show, of course, for years afterwards, in the strange, troubled behaviours of teenagers. How to bear such things? How to live with such constants in the world surrounding you? Toughness, gang formation, hard drinking and readiness for fighting take on a logic of their own. Having children, oddly, can be a kind of defence, as well as a welfare income source: most women are mothers by the age of twenty; there are four girls aged fifteen or younger with new babies in little Kununurra today. This is the landscape, with death, pressure, grief and violence forming a perfect trap – and round that trap, as further barriers to escape, lie the burdens of illiteracy, overcrowding and poor health.

'It's getting worse,' says Kimberley health worker Giancarlo Mazzella, speaking from his seventeen years experience. 'There's been a huge under-investment in mental health. What we see is clear: the young don't have any hope, they don't have goals. They're losing their language and their culture. Violence is all around them. There's no safe, basic shelter for people, no shelter from the storm.'

What underpins this pattern? Intense research is underway, aimed at providing some understanding of the ground causes, and some exit from the trap. Psychiatrists, medical specialists and anthropologists throng the region: Fitzroy Crossing is a centre for world-class fetal alcohol syndrome research, in much the way the Warsaw ghetto was home to the doctors who first studied starvation's effects on human subjects. It is increasingly accepted that 'structural violence' is one key to the terrifying syndromes observed in much of the region. When your society has been oppressed, you tend to oppress. The Kimberley's colonisation pattern was hard; even today, race relations are pretty tough. Hence suicide and self-harm are a return of the submerged past: those marginalised through poverty, gender inequality and frontier violence hit out at victims they can target – their own peers, and themselves.

This process spreads in myriad ways. Consider 'growth faltering,' a special focus of eminent paediatrician John Boulton, who now works in the North. Kimberley children today often fail to find the food they need when young because social patterns are disrupted: the age pyramid has inverted completely: young teenagers are having children of their own, but the elder women who helped feed them in traditional Aboriginal family life are missing from the picture: co-operative parenting has collapsed. Parents today can actually be harm-bringers: mothers who drink in pregnancy may leave even children who seem untouched by FAS with threshold neurological problems that resist easy detection, yet explain a widespread failure to learn. As for the younger men, they have no obvious role in the welfare space: their old place was as hunters, providers, cattlemen: what now, sidelined? Mourning and depression do their work as well: but there are other optics through which to see the personal histories traced out in the modern Kimberley. Bravado is to the fore. The prevailing lifestyle has a strong touch of 'Live Fast, Die Young' about it: early child-bearing, dramatic adventures, flame-out, death. And why not, when all your friends burst into sexual maturity in their early teens, and fight constantly, and lead lives of drink and violence, and slow asset accumulation and economic progress are simply off the map? Better to leave a good-looking corpse, and many plastic flowers, and make the funeral parade the pulse of life.

Another feature of this strangely adapted world strikes some of the researchers who surround it, and ponder ways of modifying its plight. Kimberley Aboriginal languages are dying out: fast. Bunuba, Miriuwung, Gija and many others are going: the young understand them at a surface level, but do not speak them. Nor, though, do they speak standard English with great confidence, though, strangely, they may think they do. They tend to speak a reduced form of the language, along with the high-paced Kimberley Kriol. Kriol has its keen defenders – by some definitions it is the largest Aboriginal language. But it is not an organically formed vehicle for the expression of mental depth or examined feelings, in the way the old tongues were; it is a vernacular, at a time when emotions are flowing, and demand expression. There is a strange sense of near horizon about the language world of the Kimberley today: and when words fail, gestures, and strong frustrations, come into play.

Even those members of the small Indigenous leadership cadre in the north-west who move fluently between the mainstream and the remote Aboriginal worlds tend to find the going hard. The system administers, from the top down, rather than including local perspectives. State MP Tom Stephens, like other long-view politicians, regards remote Aboriginal Australia today as a 'failed state.'

'The record of recent times is a complete indictment of official structures and their interaction with this part of the country, so as to grind people into the dust. The despair that's there is in part because of the failure of a system designed to reward bureaucrats, not help their subjects.' Many observers think the evident crisis in remote area governance is structural, linked to the presence of three ill-coordinated tiers of administration, and insoluble without radical redesign.

*

Such factors as these help compose the overall region's human landscape. But what is the Kimberley difference? Why the pattern we now dimly see? Alcohol is just the touch-paper. By the logic of history, the Kimberley's Aboriginal culture-world should be relatively intact. It was settled late; indeed, it was almost the last place where the frontier closed. But settlement's speed was faster here than anywhere: cattle station regimes came swiftly, then vanished, to be replaced by remote community ghettoes: whole tribal groups were displaced, there was sexual exploitation, land was appropriated, used, then handed back. The new Kimberley generations have been thrust into modernity without education, and without much in the way of blueprint. Of course there is a Kimberley plan: resource development – but rent is the best the newly enfranchised first occupants can dream of in that scenario. Mining jobs are all around, but they require some basic literacy and numeracy: they also require a will to escape the gentle bonds of welfare. By the standards of Australian governments, the much-criticised authorities in Perth have performed moderately well in their tasks of stewardship in recent years: one only needs to cross the border into the Northern Territory to see the contrasting pattern of underfunding and neglect. Plainly the unmet need is vast: West Australian departments could spend much more, build more houses, fund more schools and medical intervention programs.

But there is a shadow here. It is the help, the assistance, that defines, and condemns. Young Aboriginal people in the East Kimberley know their position: they see it every day. Their contact with other Australians is close, and constant, yet it is contact with another world: a world of houses, jobs and opportunities they find themselves ill-suited for. Many of the mainstream people they encounter are there to look after and manage and tend them: the Kimberley is increasingly like a large open-air emergency ward, constantly watched. The presence of the healers and the therapists may even help perpetuate the sickness of dependency among the subjects. So much, by way of speculation: that, though, is one aspect of the mood in the air among the young people who subsist from night to night on the streets of Kununurra and the surrounding towns. It is breakdown time. Everyone can see, and no one says. A crisis of grief is unfolding: a spiritual collapse so deep it cannot be held back or gainsaid. The acts of self-harm are not inadvertent, they are not mistakes, not just the ill-judged results of too much drink and too much drugs, not something to be solved by simply lowering the levels of intoxication. Those watching, on both sides of the divide between peoples, struggle for words, and fear they may be watching as an entire culture, acting collectively, destroys itself.

The Australian

The Cypherpunk Revolutionary:
Julian Assange

Robert Manne

Less than twenty years ago, Julian Assange was sleeping rough.
Even a year ago hardly anyone knew his name. Today he is one
of the best-known and most-respected human beings on earth.
Assange was the overwhelming winner of the popular vote for
Time magazine's 'Person of the Year' and *Le Monde*'s less politically correct 'Man of the Year.' If Rupert Murdoch, who recently
turned eighty, is the most influential Australian of the post-war
era, Julian Assange, who will soon turn forty, is undoubtedly the
most consequential Australian of the present time. Murdoch's
importance rests in his responsibility for injecting, through Fox
News, the poison of rabid populist conservatism into the political culture of the United States; Assange's in the revolutionary
threat that his idea of publishing damaging documentary information sent by anonymous insiders to WikiLeaks poses to governments and corporations across the globe.

Julian Assange has told the story of his childhood and adolescence twice, most recently to a journalist from the *New Yorker*,
Raffi Khatchadourian, and some fifteen years ago, secretly but
in greater detail, to Suelette Dreyfus, the author of a fascinating
book on the first generation of computer hacking, *Underground*,
for which Assange was the primary researcher. In what is called
the 'Researcher's Introduction,' Assange begins with a cryptic

quote from Oscar Wilde: 'Man is least himself when he talks in his own person. Give him a mask, and he will tell you the truth.' Nothing about Assange has ever been straightforward. One of the main characters in *Underground* is the Melbourne hacker Mendax. Although there is no way readers at that time could have known it, Mendax is Julian Assange. Putting Khatchadourian and Dreyfus together, and adding a little detail from a blog that Assange published on the internet in 2006–07 and checking it against commonsense and some material that has emerged since his rise to fame, the story of Assange's childhood and adolescence can be told in some detail. There is, however, a problem. Journalists as senior as David Leigh of the *Guardian* or John F. Burns of the *New York Times* in general accept on trust many of Assange's stories about himself. They do not understand that, like many natural writers, he has fashioned his life into a fable.

According to Assange, his mother, Christine Hawkins, left her Queensland home for Sydney at the age of seventeen, around 1970, at the time of the anti–Vietnam War movement when the settled culture of the Western world was breaking up. Christine's father, Dr Warren Hawkins, was the principal of the Northern Rivers College of Advanced Education; her mother was a specialist in medieval literature. Christine fell in love with a man called John Shipton in Sydney. A year or so after Julian was born, in Townsville, they parted. Assange did not meet Shipton again till he was twenty-five.

When Julian was about one, Christine met and married a roving theatrical producer and member of what was by now called the counter-culture, Brett Assange. According to what Julian told Khatchadourian, Brett was the descendant of a Chinese immigrant who had settled on Thursday Island, Ah Sang or Mr Sang. Together Brett and Christine travelled around the country, performing. He painted a vivid portrait for Khatchadourian of an idyllic life after the family settled for a time on Magnetic Island. 'Most of this time was pretty Tom Sawyer. I had my own horse. I built my own raft. I went fishing. I was going down mine shafts and tunnels.' To Dreyfus, Julian claimed his stepfather was a decent man but also an alcoholic. By the time he was addressing audiences worldwide, his 'father' – which Assange informed me is an amalgam of Brett Assange and John Shipton, created to protect their identities – had become idealised as a 'good and generous man' who had taught him the most fundamental lesson in life: to nurture victims rather than to create them. Assange also told Dreyfus about a foundational political memory, an incident that had occurred while he was about four but was much spoken of later. His mother and a male friend had discovered evidence concerning the British atomic bomb tests that had taken place in Maralinga in greatest secrecy, which they intended to give to an Adelaide journalist. The male friend had been beaten by police to silence him. Christine had been warned that she was in danger of being charged with being 'an unfit mother.' She was advised to stay out of politics.

When Julian was eight or nine years old, Christine and Brett Assange separated and then divorced. His mother now formed a 'tempestuous' relationship with an amateur musician, Keith Hamilton, with whom she had another child, a boy. To Dreyfus, Julian described Hamilton as a 'manipulative and violent psychopath.' A brief bitter battle over access to Julian's half-brother was fought. Christine's family was now once more on the move – this time not as before on a 'happy-go-lucky odyssey,' but hiding on both sides of the continent in permanent terror. In his final years of education Julian was home-schooled or independently educated either by professors encountered on their travels or by following his curiosity in public libraries. He did, however, attend very many schools. According to Dreyfus, by the time Mendax was fifteen he 'had lived in a dozen different places' and had 'enrolled in at least as many different schools.' His lawyer in his trial of 1996, Paul Galbally, also told the court Assange had been enrolled in about twelve schools. By 2006, Assange claimed he had attended thirty-seven different schools. To answer my doubt, Assange explained: 'Since my mother was going to be a witness and could only reliably remember the schools I had spent a long time at ... we claimed merely twelve to be safe. The figure of thirty-seven includes schools I spent a single day attending.'

One of the schools Julian attended was in rural Victoria. In the blog he posted on 18 July 2006, there is an account of his and another outsider's experience at this school.

We were bright sensitive kids who didn't fit into the dominant sub-culture and fiercely castigated those who did as irredeemable boneheads.

This unwillingness to accept the authority of a peer group considered risible was not appreciated. I was quick to anger and brutal statements such as 'You're a bunch of mindless apes out of Lord of the Flies' when faced with standover tactics were enough to ensure I got into a series of extreme fights and I wasn't sorry to leave when presented with the dental bills of my tormentors.

Eventually Julian's family settled on the outskirts of Melbourne in Emerald and then Tecoma, according to Dreyfus. Christine bought Julian a $700 computer and a modem. Assange fell in love with a sixteen-year-old girl, Teresa, whom he claims to have met through a program for gifted children. He left home and then married his girlfriend. They had a son. This was the period when the underground subculture of hacking was forming in Melbourne. Around 1988 Assange joined it under the handle Mendax. By October 1989 an attack was mounted from Australia on the NASA computer system via the introduction of what was called the WANK worm in an attempt to sabotage the Jupiter launch of the Galileo rocket as part of an action of anti-nuclear activists. No one claimed responsibility for this attack, which is outlined in the first chapter of *Underground*. In a Swedish television documentary, *WikiRebels*, made with Assange's co-operation, there are hints he was responsible.

Mendax formed a closed group with two other hackers – Trax and Prime Suspect. They called themselves the International Subversives. According to Dreyfus, their politics were fiercely anti-establishment; their motives adventure and intellectual curiosity; their strict ethic not to profit by their hacking or to harm the computers they entered. Mendax wrote a program called Sycophant. It allowed the International Subversives to conduct 'massive attacks on the US military.' The list of the computers they could recall finding their way into 'read like a Who's Who of the American military-industrial complex.' Eventually Mendax penetrated the computer system of the Canadian telecommunications corporation Nortel. It was here that his hacking was first discovered. The Australian Federal Police conducted a long investigation into the International Subversives, Operation Weather. Eventually Trax lost his nerve and began to talk. He told the police that the International Subversives had been hacking on a scale never achieved before. In October 1991 the Australian Federal Police raided Prime Suspect's and Mendax's homes. They found Assange in a state of near mental collapse. His young wife had recently left him, taking their son Daniel. Assange told Dreyfus that he had been dreaming incessantly of 'police raids ... of shadows in the pre-dawn darkness, of a gun-toting police squad bursting through his backdoor at 5 a.m.' When the police arrived, the incriminating disks, which he had been in the habit of hiding inside a beehive, were scattered by his computer. The evidence was removed.

Assange descended into a personal hell. He was admitted briefly to hospital, suffering from what Suelette Dreyfus describes as 'a deep depression and consuming rage.' He tried and failed to return home to live with his mother. He frequently slept along Merri Creek in Melbourne or in Sherbrooke Forest. He told Dreyfus that 1992 was 'the worst year in his life.' The formal charges against Assange were not laid until July 1994. His case was not finally settled until December 1996. Although Assange had been speaking in secretive tones about the technical possibility of a massive prison sentence, in the end he received a $5000 good behaviour bond and a $2100 reparations fine. The experience of arrest and trial nonetheless scarred his soul and helped shape his politics. In his blog of 17 July 2006, Assange wrote:

> If there is a book whose feeling captures me it is *First Circle* by Solzhenitsyn.
>
> To feel that home is the comraderie [sic] of persecuted, and in fact, prosecuted, polymaths in a Stalinist labor camp! How close the parallels to my own adventures! ... Such prosecution in youth is a defining peak experience. To know the state for what it really is! To see through that veneer the educated swear to disbelieve in but still slavishly follow with their hearts! ... True belief only begins with a jackboot at the door.

True belief forms when lead [sic] into the dock and referred
to in the third person. True belief is when a distant voice
booms 'the prisoner shall now rise' and no one else in the
room stands.

No doubt the experience of investigation and prolonged trial
was harrowing. Nonetheless, this is a rather self-dramatising
passage. Solzhenitsyn was incarcerated in the Gulag Archipelago,
harassed for years by the KGB and eventually expelled from the
Soviet Union. Assange was investigated by the AFP and received
a good behaviour bond and a fine.

*

Julian Assange was extremely sensitive about any public discussion of his impending trial. In 1994 he offered to assist the director of *Dogs in Space*, Richard Lowenstein, with a film about
hackers. Assange spoke about the 290 years he might theoretically spend in prison. He learned that Lowenstein had not
kept this information confidential. He was furious. He sent
Lowenstein a series of threatening emails in which he outlined
details of Lowenstein's sexual life. Assange explained to me he
did so to make Lowenstein aware of 'the significance of his con-
fidentiality breach by way of analogy.' Lowenstein protested.
Had Assange no understanding of the concept of privacy?
Privacy, Assange replied, is 'relative.' 'I could monitor your
keystrokes, intercept your phone and bug your residence. If I
could be bothered ... As one who's has [sic] one's life monitored
pretty closely, you quickly come to the realisation that trying to
achieve complete privacy is impossible.' If Lowenstein wanted
to keep details of his life confidential he should use encrypted
email. Lowenstein told Assange he had not realised that the
information was confidential. 'I do not doubt your reasons
were not malicious. Stupidity, ignorance and lack of respect
come to mind. You seem to think I have only one life. I have
many.'

While awaiting trial, Julian Assange began to try to recon-
struct his life. One overwhelming preoccupation was the bitter
struggle waged for the custody of his son, Daniel. In their

struggle, Julian and Christine Assange formed a small activist group – Parent Inquiry into Child Protection. They found sources of support inside the Victorian Department of Health and Community Services. An insider provided them with a document of great value to their cause – an internal departmental manual outlining the current rules determining custody disputes. He told Dreyfus that in his fight against government corruption in Victoria he had 'acted as a conduit for leaked documents.' On several occasions recently, in answering questions about the origin of WikiLeaks, Assange has spoken of a domain site registered in 1999, but with which he did nothing, known as 'leaks. org.' His interest in leaks must have preceded that. In November 1996 he sent the following enigmatic message to those on certain email lists he had created.

> A few pointy heads in Canberra have been considering your moderator's continued existence. Consequentially I've been called on to justify labour and resources spent on all projects under my control, particularly those that can't easily be quantified such as IQ, BOS, LACC, IS, LEAKS ...

All these lists were connected to an internet service provider, Suburbia Public Access Network, for which Assange was, as he puts it, 'the chief technical brains' and which he had taken over when its original owner, Mark Dorset, went to live in Sydney. He likened it to a 'low cost power-to-the-people enabling technology.' Suburbia was the vehicle for several email lists – Interesting Questions (IQ), Best of Security (BOS), Legal Aspects of Computer Crime (LACC), Inside-Source (IS) and, presumably, LEAKS – that Assange created. It was also the free site for several groups of Melbourne activists, artists and others – the Powerline Action Group; the Alternative Technology Association; the Centre for Contemporary Photography; the Australian Public Access Network Association and, strangely enough, the Private Inquiry Agents Association. It is because of the continued existence on the internet of some of the commentary he wrote for these lists in his mid-twenties that we can begin to hear, for the first time, the distinctive political voice of Julian Assange. In general, it is intelligent and assured. One of

Suburbia's clients had published some of the Church of Scientology's holy scriptures. The church threatened legal action against Suburbia. The client, Dave Gerard, fought back. In March 1996, Assange issued an appeal to join an anti-Scientology protest.

> What you have then is a Church based on brainwashing yuppies and other people with more money than sense ... If Nicole Kiddman [sic], Kate Cerbrano [sic], John Travolta, Burce [sic] Willis, Demi Moore and Tom Cruise want to spend their fortunes on learning that the earth is in reality the destroyed prison colony of aliens from outer space then so be it. However, money brings power and attracts the corrupt ... Their worst critic at the moment is not a person, or an organisation but a medium – the Internet. The Internet is by its very nature a censorship free zone ... The fight against the Church is far more than the Net versus a bunch of wackos. It is about corporate suppression of the Internet and free speech. It is about intellectual property and the big and rich versus the small and smart.

At this time, to judge by the pieces he wrote that have survived, Assange's main political preoccupation seems to have been the extraordinary democratic possibilities of the information-sharing virtual communities across the globe created by the internet, and the threat to its freedom and flourishing posed by censorious states, greedy corporations and repressive laws.

Not everything Assange wrote at this time was serious. He was interested in a computer security software program developed by Dan Farmer of Silicon Graphics known as SATAN. One evening in April 1995 he composed 'The Dan Farmer Rap' for 'firewalls,' a list to which he subscribed.

> I'm Dan Farmer you can't fool me –
> The only security consultant to be on MTV,
>
> I've got red hair – hey hands off man!
> don't touch the locks of the mighty Dan.

AC/DC – from the front or from behind,
you can fuck my arse but you can't touch my mind.

philosophy's the trip – evil 'n' stuff,
god, we know a lot, Mike me and Muff.

A real ardent feminist – just like she tells me to be,
See me out there rooting for sexual e-qual-ity ...

I coded it all – yes the mighty Dan did it alone,
if you can't believe it, you and your note pad can fuck off
    home.

I'm Dan Farmer – now take that down – it's not every
day you get to interview the world's biggest security clown.

Several subscribers to 'firewalls' were appalled. One wrote: 'Just reading this made me feel dirty. In 20+ years associated with this business, I don't think I've ever seen debate among professionals degraded to quite this slime-ball level. Mr Assange is an unprincipled ass ...' Assange wrote a sort-of apology. 'It was perhaps an error of judgment on my behalf to equate the people on this list with those who knew myself and Dan more fully. Such mistakes are ripe to happen when one is merry and full of wine in the wee hours of the morning.' Nonetheless, he expressed high amusement regarding all those who had publicly condemned him while privately sending their congratulations. 'You know who you are.' Assange's Dan Farmer 'peccadillo' was still remembered six years later by a British computer geek, Danny O'Brien.

By 1997 Julian Assange, with his friends Suelette Dreyfus and Ralf Weinmann, had written Rubberhose, a piece of 'deniable cryptography' for human rights activists and troublemakers, the purpose of which was to make it impossible for torturers or their victims to know whether all the encrypted data on a computer hard drive had been revealed. It was designed to make torture to extract passwords pointless, and defection and betrayal in the face of such torture impossible. The concept was Assange's. Assange argued a convoluted and rather improbable psychological case about why Rubberhose would cause rational torturers to put away their weapons. Danny O'Brien captured the obvious objection rather well. Despite Rubberhose's deniable cryptography, 'won't rational torturers just beat you up "forever"?' Assange disagrees. 'Rational torturers have opportunity costs and understand them.'

I am in no position to judge the sophistication of the Rubberhose software or the level of creativity it required. I can however assess the quality of the posting announcing its creation, which Assange sent to the firewalls list in June 1997. Assange called it 'One Man's Search for a Cryptographic Mythology.' His search to find a suitable name for Rubberhose takes him, in a zany and hilarious stream of consciousness, on a journey through Greek and Roman mythology, the incestuous Cerberus and the clichéd Janus; to the moral pessimism of David Hume, who argued the inescapable connection between joy and despondency; to an unexplained rejection of his request for mythological advice by the Princeton History Department; to Sigmund Freud, the Medusa's Head and the castration complex; to a spoof on Zen Buddhism; to a memory of a visit to a mercenary hypnotherapist in Melbourne's Swanston Street – until, through the suggestion of a Swedish friend with an interest in ancient Sumerian mythology – 'who calls himself Elk on odd days and Godflesh on even days. Don't ask why' – he finally arrives with a joyous heart at the Mesopotamian god MARUTUKKU, 'Master of the Arts of Protection.'

> If MARUTUKKU was my exquisite cryptographic good, of wit, effusive joy, ravishing pleasure and flattering hope; then where was the counter point? The figure to its ground – the sharper evil, the madness, the melancholy, the most cruel lassitudes and disgusts and the severest disappointments. Was Hume right?

Alas, he was. Assange, 'on a cold and wintry night here in Melbourne,' discovers in the 4000-year-old Babylonian tablets a reference to the supposedly secret eavesdropping intelligence agency in Maryland, the National Security Agency! It is a magnificently exuberant, bravura literary performance. Assange was not merely a talented code writer and computer geek. There was in him daring, wildness and a touch of genius. For a while he signed his emails not with his customary 'Proff.' but 'Prof. Julian Assange.'

Assange was by now a committed member of the free software movement, pioneered by Richard Stallman, whose aim was to regulate communication in cyberspace by software not by law. As members of the movement put it, freedom here meant free speech rather than free beer. The movement stressed democratic, collective contribution. Assange tended to be somewhat sceptical about the movement, on one occasion arguing that in reality usually one or two people did 80 per cent of the work. Assange was nonetheless involved in the development of NetBSD, an open source computer operating system derived from the original Berkeley Software Distribution source code. Some of the slogans he invented to spruik its virtues can still be found on the internet. Here are three. 'We put the OS in OrgaSm'; 'Bits for Tits'; 'More ports than a Norwegian crack whore' – all examples, as Assange now sees it, of his youthful 'ribald humour.'

By the time Assange was working on NetBSD he had been involved for several years with a movement known as the cypherpunks. It was the cypherpunks more than the free software movement who provided him with his political education. Although there are tens of thousands of articles on Julian Assange in the world's newspapers and magazines, no mainstream journalist so far has grasped the critical significance of the cypherpunks movement to Assange's intellectual development and the origin of WikiLeaks.

*

The cypherpunks emerged from a meeting of minds in late 1992 in the Bay Area of San Francisco. Its founders were Eric Hughes, a brilliant Berkeley mathematician; Timothy C. May, an already wealthy, former chief scientist at Intel who had retired at the age of thirty-four; and John Gilmore, another already retired and wealthy computer scientist – once number five at Sun Microsystems – who had co-founded an organisation to advance the cause of cyberspace freedom, the Electronic Frontier Foundation. They created a small group, which met monthly in

Gilmore's office at a business he had created, Cygnus. At one of the early meetings of the group, an editor at *Mondo 2000*, Jude Milhon, jokingly called them cypherpunks, a play on cyberpunk, the 'hi-tech, low-life' science-fiction genre. The name stuck. It soon referred to a vibrant email list, created shortly after the first meeting, which had grown to 700 by 1994 and perhaps 2000 by 1997 with by then up to a hundred postings per day. It also referred to a distinctive sub-culture – eventually there were cypherpunk novels, *Snowcrash, Cryptonomicon, Indecent Communications*; a cypherpunk porno film, *Cryptic Seduction*; and even a distinctive cypherpunk dress: broad-brimmed black hats. Most importantly, however, it referred to a political–ideological crusade.

At the core of the cypherpunk philosophy was the belief that the great question of politics in the age of the internet was whether the state would strangle individual freedom and privacy through its capacity for electronic surveillance or whether autonomous individuals would eventually undermine and even destroy the state through their deployment of electronic weapons newly at hand. Many cypherpunks were optimistic that in the battle for the future of humankind – between the State and the Individual – the individual would ultimately triumph. Their optimism was based on developments in intellectual history and computer software: the invention in the mid-1970s of public-key cryptography by Whitfield Diffie and Martin Hellman, and the creation by Phil Zimmerman in the early 1990s of a program known as PGP, 'Pretty Good Privacy.' The seminal historian of codes, David Kahn, argued that the Diffie–Hellman invention represented the most important development in cryptography since the Renaissance. Zimmerman's PGP program democratised their invention and provided individuals, free of cost, with access to public-key cryptography and thus the capacity to communicate with others in near-perfect privacy. Although George Orwell's *Nineteen Eighty-Four* was one of the cypherpunks' foundational texts, because of the combination of public-key cryptography and PGP software, they tended to believe that in the coming battle between Big Brother and Winston Smith, the victor might be Winston Smith.

At the time the cypherpunks formed, the American government strongly opposed the free circulation of public-key cryptography. It feared that making it available would strengthen the hands of the espionage agencies of America's enemies abroad and of terrorists, organised criminals, drug dealers and pornographers at home. For the cypherpunks, the question of whether cryptography would be freely available would determine the outcome of the great battle of the age. Their most important practical task was to write software that would expand the opportunities for anonymous communication made possible by public-key cryptography. One of the key projects of the cypherpunks was 'remailers,' software systems that made it impossible for governments to trace the passage from sender to receiver of encrypted email traffic. Another key project was 'digital cash,' a means of disguising financial transactions from the state.

Almost all cypherpunks were anarchists who regarded the state as the enemy. Most but not all were anarchists of the Right, or in American parlance, libertarians, who supported laissez-faire capitalism. The most authoritative political voice among the majority libertarian cypherpunks was Tim May, who, in 1994, composed a vast, truly remarkable document, 'Cyphernomicon.' May called his system crypto-anarchy. He regarded crypto-anarchy as the most original contribution to political ideology of contemporary times. May thought the state to be the source of evil in history. He envisaged the future as an Ayn Rand utopia of autonomous individuals dealing with each other as they pleased. Before this future arrived, he advocated tax avoidance, insider trading, money laundering, markets for information of all kinds, including military secrets, and what he called assassination markets not only for those who broke contracts or committed serious crime but also for state officials and the politicians he called 'Congressrodents.' He recognised that in his future world only elites with control over technology would prosper. No doubt 'the clueless 95%' – whom he described as 'inner city breeders' and as 'the unproductive, the halt and the lame' – 'would suffer, but that is only just.' May acknowledged that many cypherpunks would regard these ideas as extreme. He also acknowledged that, while the overwhelming majority of cypherpunks were, like him, anarcho-capitalist libertarians, some were strait-laced Republicans, left-leaning liberals, Wobblies or even Maoists. Neither fact concerned him. The cypherpunks formed a house of many rooms. The only thing they all shared was an understanding of the political significance of cryptography and the willingness to fight for privacy and unfettered freedom in cyberspace.

Like an inverse Marxist, Tim May tended to believe that the inexorable expansion of private cryptography made the victory of crypto-anarchism inevitable. A new 'balance of power between individuals and larger entities' was already emerging. He predicted with some confidence 'the end of governments as we know them.' Another even more extreme cypherpunk of the libertarian Right, Jim Bell, like an inverse Leninist, thought that history might need a push. In mid-1995, drawing upon May's recommendation of assassination markets, he began a series explaining his 'revolutionary idea,' which he called 'Assassination Politics.' These were perhaps the most notorious and controversial postings in the history of the cypherpunks list. Bell devised a system in which citizens could contribute towards a lottery fund for the assassination of particular government officials. The prize would go to the person who correctly predicted the date of the death. The winner would obviously be the official's murderer. However, through the use of public-key cryptography, remailers and digital cash, from the time they entered the competition to the collection of the prize no one except the murderer would be aware of their identity. Under the rubric 'tax is theft' all government officials and politicians were legitimate targets of assassination. Journalists would begin to ask of politicians, 'Why should you not be killed?' As prudence would eventually dictate that no one take the job, the state would simply wither away. Moreover, as assassination lotteries could be extended across borders, no leader would again risk taking their people to war. Eventually, through the idea of the assassination lottery, then, not only would the era of anarchy arise across the globe, the condition of permanent peace humankind had long dreamt of would finally come to pass. Bell ended his 20,000-word series of postings with these words. 'Is all this wishful thinking? I really don't know!' A year or so later he was arrested on tax avoidance charges.

Julian Assange informed me he joined the cypherpunks email list in late 1993 or early 1994. There were many reasons Assange was likely to be attracted to it. As his encounter with Richard Lowenstein had revealed, he was interested in the connection between privacy and encrypted communication. Even before his arrest he had feared the intrusion into his life of the totalitarian surveillance state. An atmosphere of paranoia pervaded the cypherpunks list. Assange believed that he had been wrongly convicted of what he called a 'victimless crime.' The struggle against victimless crimes – the right to consume pornography, to communicate in cyberspace anonymously, to distribute crypto-graphic software freely – was at the centre of the cypherpunks' political agenda. Moreover the atmosphere of the list was free-wheeling – racism, sexism, homophobia were common. Not only Tim May believed that political correctness had turned Americans into 'a nation of sheep.' On the cypherpunks list no one would disapprove of 'The Dan Farmer Rap.' Yet there was probably more to it than all this. Cypherpunks saw themselves as Silicon Valley Masters of the Universe. It must have been more than a lit-tle gratifying for a self-educated antipodean computer hacker, who had not even completed high school, to converse on equal terms with professors of mathematics, whiz-kid businessmen and some of the leading computer code-writers in the world.

Julian Assange contributed to the cypherpunks list until June 2002. As it happens, almost all his interventions have been placed on the internet. On the basis of what historians call pri-mary evidence, the mind and character of Julian Assange can be seen at the time of his obscurity.

The first thing that becomes clear is the brashness. Over a technical dispute, he writes: '[B]oy are you a dummy.' When someone asks for assistance in compiling a public list of hackers with handles, names, email addresses, Assange responds: 'Are you on this list of morons?' In a dispute over religion and intol-erance one cypherpunk had written: 'Because those being hate-fully intolerant have the 'right' beliefs as to what the Bible says. Am I a racist if I don't also include an example from the Koran?' 'No, just an illiterate,' Assange replied. Following a savaging from Assange for total computer incompetence, a hapless cypherpunk pointed out that he has been writing code since the age of fourteen. If one thing is clear from the cypherpunks list, it is that the young Julian Assange did not suffer those he regarded as fools gladly.

In his posts there is humour, although often it is sarcastic. In one of his earliest interventions Assange has read about the arrest of someone caught with diesel fuel and fertiliser. 'Looks like I've just been placed into the ranks of the pyro-terrorist. Golly, Deisel [sic] fuel. Gosh, Fertilizer. Ma, other items.' Some posts reflect his faith in the theory of evolution. Assange forwarded an article about the role played by the CIA in supplying crack gangs in Los Angeles. A cypherpunk responded: 'I wish they'd get back to the business, but add an overt poison to the product. Clean out the shit from the cities. Long live Darwinism.' 'Darwinism is working as well as it ever was. You may not like it but shit is being selected for,' Assange shot back. Other posts reflect his recent life experiences. Assange had helped Victoria Police break a paedophile ring in 1993. On the cypherpunks list he defended the circulation of child pornography on the internet on the grounds that it would cut the need for new production and make it easier for police to capture paedophiles. In another post he expressed deep anger at perceived injustice regarding those with whom he identifies – convicted hackers. One, Tsutomu Shimamura, had not only played a role in the hunting down of a notorious American fellow hacker, Kevin Mitnick (known personally to Assange through his research for *Underground*), but had even co-authored a book about it, *Takedown*. 'This makes me ill. Tsutomu, when Mitnick cracks will you dig up his grave and rent his hands out as ash trays?' Assange also posted on the reports of violence against another hacker, Ed Cummings aka Bernie S, imprisoned in the US. 'I was shocked. I've had some dealings with the SS ... Those that abuse their power and inflict grave violence on others must be held accountable and their crimes deplored and punished in the strongest manner. Failure to do so merely creates an environment where such behaviour becomes predominant.'

Already there are qualities in Assange's postings that are unusual in the standard cypherpunk. One is a fascination with language. Assange invented with Richard Jones a software program that created anagrams. The deepest institutional enemy of the cypherpunks was the National Security Agency. Assange put the name into his computer. Among the anagrams that emerged were: 'National Anti-Secrecy Guy'; 'Secret Analytic Guy Union'; 'Caution Laying Any Secret'; 'Insane, ugly, acne atrocity'; and, Assange's apparent favourite: 'National Gay Secrecy Unit.' He was also interested in what he described as 'tracking language drift; i.e. the relative change in word frequency on the internet as time goes by.' He informed the cypherpunks that he had just discovered that in a '10 billion word corpus' the following frequency occurred:

God – 2,177,242
America – 2,178,046
Designed – 2,181,106
Five – 2,189,194
December – 2,190,028

His eccentricity would also have been obvious after a member of the 'firewalls' list forwarded his MARUTUKKU fantasia to cypherpunks.

Where did Assange stand with regard to the radical cypherpunks agenda of Tim May? This question is best answered in two parts. On the question of cryptographic freedom and hostility towards the surveillance state and its chief embodiment – the National Security Agency – Assange was, if anything, even more absolute and extreme than May. In September 1996, Esther Dyson, the chair of the lobby group for freedom in cyberspace, the Electronic Frontier Foundation, was quoted in the *Los Angeles Times* as being in favour of certain extremely limited restrictions on internet anonymity. On the cypherpunks list a furious controversy, called 'The Esther Dyson Fuss,' broke out. Some cypherpunks defended Dyson on the ground that she had every right to argue a more nuanced position and that it was anyhow healthy for individuals to speak their mind. May vehemently disagreed. The issue was not her freedom of speech. A critical moment in the battle between freedom and surveillance had arrived. Dyson had defected to the enemy camp. Assange went further. He launched a stinging ad hominem attack.

Examining in detail Dyson's interests it appears she maintains a sizeable and longstanding interest in Eastern European technology companies. She is also very far to the right of the political spectrum (rampant capitalist would be putting it mildly). She also speaks Russian. I'm not saying she's been working for the CIA for the past decade, but I would be very surprised if the CIA has not exerted quite significant pressure … in order to bring her into their folds during that time period.

'At least you don't accuse me of being a Communist,' Dyson responded. 'For the record, I am not a tool of the CIA nor have they pressured me, but there's no reason for you to believe me.' Later, Assange informed me, they became friends. However, when Assange was in trouble last year Dyson wrote a piece on the Salon website arguing that even unpleasant characters need to be defended.

A month or so after September 11 a controversy broke out on the cypherpunks list over the report of a civilised discussion about increased FBI surveillance over internet communications between Mitch Kapor, a co-founder and former board member of the Electronic Frontier Foundation, and Stu Baker, an attorney who had once been employed by the National Security Agency. Some cypherpunks had some sympathy for Kapor's moderation. Even they recognised that with September 11 something major had occurred. One pointed out, in addition, that Stu Baker was 'a gun-for-hire, not a doctrinaire blinders-on true believer for either the surveillance enthusiasts or privacy freaks.' This was too much for Assange:

Stu is a well known NSA zealot. The only reason there's a bridge between Kapor and Baker is due to the cavernous ravine that lays [sic] between them. Kapor is now apparently half-way across, following Stu's silently beckoning finger, fearfully running from the sounds of angels [sic] wings; fooled into believing that they lie behind and not ahead of him.

From beginning to end Assange was, in short, a hardline member of the tendency among the cypherpunks that Tim May called the 'rejectionists,' an enemy of those who displayed even the slightest tendency to compromise on the question of Big Brother and the surveillance state.

On another question, however, Assange was at the opposite end of the cypherpunks spectrum from Tim May. At no stage did Assange show sympathy for the anarcho-capitalism of the cypherpunks mainstream which, as he explained to me, he regarded as 'naive' about 'the state tendencies of corporatism.' In October 1996, a prominent cypherpunk, Duncan Frissell, claimed that in the previous fiscal year the American government had seized more tax than any government in history. Assange pointed out that, as the US was the world's largest economy and its GDP had grown in the previous year, this was a ridiculous statement designed to be deceptive. In October 2001, Declan McCullagh expressed 'surprise' when a 'critique of laissez-faire capitalism' appeared on the cypherpunks list 'of all places.' Assange replied:

Declan, Declan.

Put away your straw man ... Nobel economic laureates have been telling us for years to be careful about idealised market models ... This years [sic] Nobel for Economics won by George A. Akerlof, A. Michael Spence and Joseph E. Stiglitz 'for their analysis of markets with assymmetric [sic] information' is typical. You don't need a Nobel to realize that the relationship between a large employer and employee is brutally assymmetric [sic] ... To counter this sort of assymetery. [sic] Employees naturally start trying to collectivise to increase their information processing and bargaining power. That's right. UNIONS Declan. Those devious entities that first world companies and governments have had a hand in suppressing all over the third world by curtailing freedom of association, speech and other basic political rights we take for granted.

Assange was, then, an absolutist crypto-anarchist but one who leant decidedly to the Left. Mainstream cypherpunks did not defend trade unions or speak negatively of 'rampant capitalists' and positively of 'human rights activists.' He was an electronic but not an economic libertarian.

There is also evidence that Assange was increasingly repelled by the corrosive cynicism common in cypherpunks ranks. Something in his spirit seems to have changed after his trial and the writing of his MARUTUKKU mythology. From 1997 to 2002 Julian Assange accompanied all his cypherpunks postings with this beautiful passage from Antoine de Saint-Exupéry: 'If you want to build a ship, don't drum up people together to collect wood and don't assign them tasks and work, but rather teach them to long for the endless immensity of the sea.' On one occasion in July 1999 William H. Geiger III presented standard Ayn Rand Objectivist praise of human selfishness. 'Everyone is a predator out to advance their own agenda at the expence [sic] of others. Tim is just more honest than most about it.' Assange replied with a defence of altruism, for Objectivists an evil.

> No … Everyone maybe self-interested, but some are self-interested in a way that is healthy (to you, or the people you care about), some in a way which is benign, and some in a manner that is pernicious. It is important to distinguish between these different behaviours and support or undermine them accordingly.

On another occasion, a cypherpunk suggested that in the great struggle for privacy and against censorship ordinary people could not give a damn. Perhaps with Tim May's contempt for 'the clueless 95%' in his mind, in March 2002, in what was one of his final cypherpunks postings, Assange responded: 'The 95% of the population which comprise the flock have never been my target and neither should they be yours; it's the 2.5% at either end of the normal that I find in my sights, one to be cherished and the other to be destroyed.' Already he seems to have imagined the future as a struggle to the death between autocratic elites and electronic freedom fighters. Increasingly, Assange began to mock Tim May. Many thought of May as an anti-Semite, with good reason. In November 2001, when May used a quote from a cypherpunk fellow traveller, David Friedman (Milton's son), Assange emailed: 'Quoting Jews again, Tim?'

Julian Assange was a regular contributor to the cypherpunks mailing list particularly before its decline in late 1997 following a meltdown over the question of the possible moderation of the list – censorship! – and the departure of John Gilmore. The cypherpunks list clearly mattered to him deeply. Shortly before his travels in 1998, Assange asked whether anyone could send him a complete archive of the list between 1992 and the present time. While commentators have comprehensively failed to see the significance of the cypherpunks in shaping the thought of Julian Assange, this is something insiders to the movement understand. When Jeanne Whalen from the *Wall Street Journal* approached John Young of Cryptome in August last year, he advised her to read the Assange cypherpunk postings he had just placed on the internet, and also Tim May's 'Cyphernomicon.' 'This background has not been explored in the WikiLeaks saga. And WikiLeaks cannot be understood without it.' Likewise, in his mordant online article on WikiLeaks and Assange, the influential cyberpunk novelist and author of *The Hacker Crackdown* Bruce Sterling wrote: 'At last – at long last – the homemade nitroglycerin in the old cypherpunks blast shack has gone off.'

*

In 2003 Julian Assange seems to have considered living a more conventional life. He went to the University of Melbourne to study mainly mathematics and physics. As a student of mathematics his results were mixed but generally mediocre. This can hardly be explained by lack of talent. No one worked more closely with Assange than Suelette Dreyfus. 'A geek friend of his once described Assange as having an IQ "in excess of 170,"' she wrote in the *Sydney Morning Herald* of 12 December 2010. 'I suspect this could be true.' Assange claimed that he became disillusioned with the applied maths department when he discovered its members were working with defence authorities in the US on a military bulldozer adapted to desert conditions known as 'The Grizzly Plough.' He also claimed that visits to the ANU were thoroughly dispiriting. On one occasion he represented University of Melbourne students at a competition. 'At the prize ceremony, the head of ANU physics motioned to us and said, "you are the cream of Australian physics." I looked around and thought, 'Christ Almighty I hope he's wrong."' On another occasion he saw 900 senior physicists in Canberra proudly carrying bags with the logo of the Defence Science and Technology Organisation. He described them as 'snivelling fearful conformists of woefully, woefully inferior character.'

Perhaps there were other reasons for dissatisfaction. By 2004 Assange had reached the elevated position of vice-president of the students' Mathematics and Statistics Society and chief organiser of their Puzzle Hunt – a quiz leading the winner to $200 of buried treasure. He described his role as 'plot/script, general nonsense, Abstract(ion), Caesar Cipher, Disc, Platonic, Score, Surstro:mming.' Assange explained that he 'invented/founded the competition to improve the intellectual climate in Australia.' Nonetheless, organising a puzzle hunt was a somewhat less engrossing ambition than planning world revolution. And towards the end of his studies this was exactly what he was doing. A female friend provided the journalist Nikki Barrowclough with a vivid portrait of the atmosphere of a share house close-by the University of Melbourne that Assange lived in at this time.

> There were beds everywhere, she says. There was even a bed in the kitchen. This woman slept on a mattress in Assange's room, and says she would sometimes wake up in the middle of the night to find him still glued to his computer. He frequently forgot to eat or sleep, wrote mathematical formulas all over the walls and the doors, and used only red light bulbs in his room – on the basis that early man, if waking suddenly, would see only the gentle light of the campfire, and fall asleep again.

Between July 2006 and August 2007 – the period when WikiLeaks was being planned and actualised – Julian Assange maintained a blog at IQ.ORG, some of which he collected under the title 'Selected Correspondence.' The correspondence can still be found on the internet. Because of its existence, a reasonably detailed map of his mind at the age of thirty-five and at the moment of WikiLeaks' creation is available. Strangely enough, even though there are now some 27 million Google entries on Assange, so far as I am aware no one has offered an analysis.

The blog reveals a young man of unusual intellectual range, ambition and curiosity. As expected, there are references to cypherpunks and his work as a code-writer in the free software movement. Assange writes of his loathing for the '"everything which is not explicitly permitted is denied" security types' who 'make concurrent salutes to the Fuhrer, Baal and Jack Straw.' He explains why as one of the committed developers of NetBSD he has refused to sign a proposed contract: 'The contract as well as being an instrument of the state is written in the demeaning language of the corporate state. It should have been written in the language of our programmer world.' Some entries, such as his defence of altruism, are familiar to those who have followed his postings on the cypherpunks list. Many others have the range and also eccentricity revealed in his MARUTUKKU performance. There are abstract speculations on philosophy, mathematics, neuroscience, human physiology, the law, history and sociology.

There are also very striking and revealing extracts. One is from a Buddhist text from 500 BC, *Ajita Kesakambali*, in defence of materialism. 'The words of those who speak of existence after death are false, empty chatter. With the break-up of the body, the wise and the foolish are alike annihilated, destroyed.' Another is a wonderful story from the Nazi concentration camp. A Jewish inmate can save his daughter if he chooses which eye of his guard is glass. He chooses the left eye, correctly. His guard asks how he knew. '"I'm sorry," trembled Moshe, "but the left eye looks at me with a kindly gleam."' Assange has great interest in the history of European totalitarianism. One extract is a poem – 'bad … but elevated by its monumental context' – about the atom bomb spies Ethel and Julius Rosenberg: 'Even so, we did what we believed in: / Treason, yes, perhaps, but with good cause.' There is also a long extract from an article about the problems besetting those possessing super-high IQs, such as the unfulfilled genius William James Sidis. It concludes with these words: 'And so we see that the explanation for the Sidis tragedy is simple. Sidis was a feral child; a true man born into a world filled with animals – a world filled with us.' It is not difficult to understand why this article interested him.

Many blog entries are personal. When Daniel Domscheit-Berg released his memoir, *Inside WikiLeaks*, there was excitement around the globe at his claim that Assange had boasted about fathering several children, something Assange fiercely denies. About one child at least there can be no doubt. On his blog, Assange includes a photo of a bonneted baby under the title 'Those Eyes' with the caption, 'All the pink ribbons in the world can't hide them.' She is his new daughter. Another entry referred obliquely to his mother's organisation of 'The Great Bikini March' against Sheikh Hilaly, who had recently compared women who dressed scantily to 'uncovered meat.' Some entries about women fleetingly encountered are awkward in a Mills & Boon kind of way. 'A lovely girl I knew … stood for a moment fully clothed in her shower before letting the wind and rain buffet her body as she made her tremulous approach to my door and of course I could not turn her away.' One – Assange's study of the etymology of the word 'cad' – seems to me rather sinister. 'Caddie or cadet used to denote the passenger of a horse-coach picked up for personal profit by the driver … So a "cad" is a man who picks up women, profits from them and leaves them by the road side … Such romantic etymology is enough to make a man want to don his oilskin and mount his horse with whip and smile at the ready.' The coldness of tone here, which Assange ascribes to his taste for 'black humour,' is striking precisely because other passages in the correspondence are so tender. Assange writes of meeting Antony, a country kid he had known since they were both fourteen, at a mental health centre in East Ringwood. 'His smile was shaky but characteristic. His physical edges rounded off by weight gain and his imagination dulled … His limbs and jaw gently shuddered with some frequency.' Assange visited him later still at a psychiatric hospital. 'When I asked about the cause of his shaking, suggesting a dopamine antagonist, he said, "No … If you look closely you'll notice a number of people around here acting the same way. Julian … we're all doing the Mont Park shuffle."'

What is most important about the correspondence, however, is that in it we can hear for the first time Julian Assange's distinctive political voice. As a former cypherpunk crypto-anarchist the enemy for him is, unsurprisingly, that abstraction he calls the State. 'Where words have power to change, the state tries hard to trap, burn or blank them, such is its fear of their power.' The state represents the principle of 'mendacity.' 'The state does what it can get away with.' True understanding requires the individual 'to know the state for what it really is.' Yet, unlike most of his fellow cypherpunks, by now Assange unambiguously extends his idea of the state to big business. In thinking about the US, in one blog entry, he asks: 'What kinds of states are giant corporations?' He answers in the following way. As executive power is wielded by a central committee; as there is unaccountable single-party rule; as there is no freedom of speech or association, and 'pervasive surveillance of movement and electronic communication,' what then do you have in that federation of giant corporations that control the US? What else but a 'United Soviet of America.' Assange is a profound anti-communist. But he regards power in Western society as belonging to political and economic elites offering ordinary people nothing more nourishing than a counterfeit conception of democracy and a soul-destroying consumption culture.

Assange's selected correspondence is addressed to a small coterie of followers. It involves a revolutionary call to arms. 'If we can only live once, then let it be a daring adventure that draws on all our powers ... Let our grandchildren delight to find the start of our stories in their ears but the endings all around in their wandering eyes.' Assange seems not particularly interested in future political institutions or in economic arrangements. The revolution he speaks about is moral. He believes that individual action can re-fashion the world. The state may do 'what it can get away with' but it does 'what we let it get away with' and even 'what we let ourselves get away with, for we, in our interactions with others, form the state.' Over the whole selected correspondence there is a quotation from the German–Jewish revolutionary anarchist Gustav Landauer, beaten to death by right-wing troops after the Munich soviet experiment of 1919. 'The state is a condition, a certain relationship between human beings, a mode of behaviour. We destroy it by contracting other relationships, by behaving differently toward one another ... We are the state and we shall continue to be the state until we have created the institutions that form a real community and society of men.' The question is how new institutions can be formed.

In the struggle to create a truly human society, Assange warns his interlocutors not to believe they can think globally but act locally. This is an illusion. Action must be taken on a truly global scale. He is also witheringly contemptuous of those he calls 'the typical shy intellectual.'

> This type is often of a noble heart, wilted by fear of conflict with authority. The power of their intellect and noble instincts may lead them to a courageous position, where they see the need to take up arms, but their instinctive fear of authority then motivates them to find rationalizations to avoid conflict.

For Assange the central political virtue is courage. One of his favourite sayings is: 'Courage is contagious.' He attributes it to the Pentagon Papers whistleblower Daniel Ellsberg. In fact it was coined by the evangelist Billy Graham. Assange's politics are also generational. 'Perhaps as an old man I will take great comfort in pottering around in a lab and gently talking to students in the summer evening and will accept suffering with insouciance. But not now; men in their prime, if they have convictions are tasked to act on them.'

For Assange the great moving forces in history are the need for Love and the thirst for Truth. In his final piece in the selected correspondence, Assange admits that often 'outcomes are treated with more reverence than Truth.'

> Yet just as we feel all hope is lost and we sink into the miasma, back to the shadow world of ghosts and gods, a miracle arises, everywhere before the direction of self interest is known, people yearn to see where its compass points and then they hunger for truth with passion and beauty and insight ... Here then is the truth to set them free. Free from the manipulations and constraints of the mendacious. Free to choose their path, free to remove the ring from their noses, free to look up into the infinite void and choose wonder over whatever gets them through. And before this feeling to cast blessings on the profits and prophets of truth ... on the Voltaires, the Galileos and Principias of truth, on the Gutenbergs, Marconis and Internets of truth, those serial killers of delusion, those

brutal, driven and obsessed miners of reality, smashing, smashing, smashing every rotten edifice until all is ruins and the seeds of the new.

But how will the rotten edifice be smashed? On 22 November 2006 Assange provides a link to a paper. He tells his coterie of readers: 'No. Don't skip to the good stuff. This is the good stuff.' He is pointing them to the central theoretical breakthrough that led to WikiLeaks.

Julian Assange published this paper twice, the first time on 10 November 2006 under the title 'State and Terrorist Conspiracies,' the second time, in more developed form, on 3 December under the title 'Conspiracy as Governance.' Stripped of its inessential mathematical gobbledegook, its argument goes like this. The world is at present dominated by the conspiratorial power of authoritarian governments and big business corporations. As President Theodore Roosevelt understood, behind 'ostensible governments,' there exists 'an invisible government owing no allegiance and acknowledging no responsibility to the people. To destroy this invisible government, to befoul this unholy alliance between corrupt business and corrupt politics is the first task of statesmanship.' Authoritarian governments and corporations maintain and entrench their power through a conspiracy. For Assange the conspiracy involves the maintenance of a network of links between the conspirators, some vital, some less so. Conspiracies naturally provoke resistance. Among revolutionaries of earlier generations resistance has involved the attempt to break the links between the leaders of the conspiracy by 'assassination ... killing, kidnapping, blackmailing, or otherwise marginalising or isolating some of the conspirators they were connected to.' Such methods are no longer appropriate. 'The act of assassination – the targeting of visible individuals, is the result of mental inclinations honed for the pre-literate societies in which our species evolved.' The new generation of revolutionaries 'must think beyond those who have gone before us, and discover technological changes that embolden us with ways to act in which our forebears could not.'

Contemporary conspiracies rely on unrestricted information flow to adapt to and control their environments. Conspirators need to be able to speak freely to each other and to disarm resistance by spreading disinformation among the people they control, something they presently very successfully achieve. Conspirators who have control over information flow are infinitely more powerful than those who do not. Drawing on a passage from Lord Halifax in which political parties are described as 'conspiracies against the rest of the nation,' Assange asks his readers to imagine what would happen in the struggle between the Republican and Democratic parties in the US 'if one of these parties gave up their mobile phones, fax and email correspondence – let alone the computer systems that manage their subscribes [sic], donors, budgets, polling, call centres and direct mail campaigns.' He asks them to think of the conspiracy as a living organism, 'a beast with arteries and veins whose blood may be thickened and slowed until it falls, stupefied; unable to sufficiently comprehend and control the forces in its environment.' Rather than attacking the conspiracy by assassinating its leading members, he believes it can be 'throttled' by cutting its information flows. 'Later,' he promises, 'we will see how new technology and insights into the psychological motivations of conspirators can give us practical methods for preventing or reducing important communication between authoritarian conspirators, foment strong resistance to authoritarian planning and create powerful incentives for more humane forms of governance.'

The promise is fulfilled in a blog entry of 31 December 2006. Here he outlines finally the idea at the core of the WikiLeaks strategy.

> The more secretive or unjust an organization is, the more leaks induce fear and paranoia in its leadership and planning coterie. This must result in minimization of efficient internal communications mechanisms (an increase in cognitive 'secrecy tax') and consequent system-wide cognitive decline resulting in decreased ability to hold onto power as the environment demands adaptation.
>
> Hence in a world where leaking is easy, secretive or unjust systems are nonlinearly hit relative to open, just systems. Since unjust systems, by their nature induce opponents, and in

many places barely have the upper hand, leaking leaves them exquisitely vulnerable to those who seek to replace them with more open forms of governance.

There is a link between Assange's cypherpunks period and the theory behind WikiLeaks. Assange was a contributor to the cypherpunks list at the time when Jim Bell's 'Assassination Politics' was being hotly discussed. There is evidence that Assange was intrigued by the idea. In January 1998 he had come upon an advertisement for a prize – 'Scoop the Grim Reaper. Who Will Live? Who Will Die?' – which was to be awarded to the person who guessed on what dates certain Hollywood celebrities would die. 'Anyone noticed this before?' Assange posted the advertisement on the cypherpunks list under the heading: 'Jim ... Bell ... lives ... on ... in ... Hollywood.' Although Assange assured me he was not thinking about 'Assassination Politics' at the time he was inventing WikiLeaks, there are similarities between Bell's thought and Assange's. Like Bell, Assange was possessed by a simple 'revolutionary idea' about how to create a better world. As with Bell, the idea emerged from reflection upon the political possibilities created by untraceable anony-mous communication, through the use of remailers and unbreakable public-key cryptography. The differences are also clear. Unlike with Bell, the revolution Assange imagined would be non-violent. The agent of change would not be the assassin but the whistleblower. The method would not be the bullet but the leak.

In arriving at this position, Assange had drawn together dif-ferent personal experiences. It was as a 'frontier hactivist' and as 'Australia's first electronic publisher' that he had become interested in the political potency of leaks. From his cypher-punk days he had become engaged in discussions about the political possibilities of untraceable encrypted communication. And from his involvement in the free software movement he had seen what collective democratic intellectual enterprise might achieve. In essence, his conclusion was that world politics could be transformed by staunching the flow of information among corrupt power elites by making them ever more fearful of insider leaks. He believed he could achieve this by establishing an organisation that would allow whistleblowers from all countries to pass on their information, confident that their identities would not be able to be discovered. He proposed that his organisation would then publish the information for the purpose of collective analysis so as to empower oppressed populations across the globe.

There are few original ideas in politics. In the creation of WikiLeaks, Julian Assange was responsible for one.

*

In late 2006 Assange sought a romantic partner through OKCupid using the name of Harry Harrison. Under the heading, 'What am I doing with my life?,' he answered: 'directing a consuming, dangerous human rights project which is, as you might expect, male-dominated.' Under the heading, 'I spend a lot of time thinking about,' he answered: 'Changing the world through passion, inspiration and trickery.' There was something distinctly Walter Mittyish about it all. Under the informal leadership of Julian Assange, a group of mainly young men, without resources and linked only by computers, now began to implement their plans for a peaceful global political revolution.

On 4 October 2006 Assange registered the domain name 'WikiLeaks.org' in the US. He called it WikiLeaks because he had been immensely impressed by the success of the Wikipedia experiment, where three million entries had been contributed through the input of a worldwide virtual community. As he put it, WikiLeaks would be to leaks what Wikipedia was to the encyclopedia. Strangely and perhaps revealingly, it was registered under the names of two fathers, his biological one, John Shipton, and his cypherpunk political one, John Young, a New York architect who ran the intelligence leak website Cryptome, which could be seen as WikiLeaks' predecessor. Assange explained his request for assistance to Young like this:

> You knew me under another name from cypherpunks days. I am involved in a project that you may have a feeling for ... The project is a mass document leaking project that requires someone with backbone to hold the .org domain registration ... We

expect the domain to come under the usual political and legal pressure. The policy for .org requires that registrants [sic] details not be false or misleading. It would be an easy play to cancel the domain unless someone were willing to stand up and claim to be the registrant.

The choice of Young reveals something about Assange. For Young was undoubtedly the most militant security cypherpunk of all, who had published on his website an aerial photo of Dick Cheney's hideout bunker, a photograph of the home of Fox News's Bill O'Reilly, and the names of 276 British and some 600 Japanese intelligence agents and 2619 CIA 'sources.' Young was also Jim Bell's greatest champion. After Bell's arrest and imprisonment, Young nominated him for the Chrysler Award for Innovation in Design. Bell had, he argued in his nomination, contributed 'an imaginative and sophisticated prospective for improving governmental accountability by way of a scheme for anonymous, untraceable political assassination.'

Serious work on the establishment of WikiLeaks began in December 2006. One of the first tasks was to decide upon a logo. Before opting for the hourglass, the WikiLeaks team thought seriously about a mole breaking through a wall above which stood three sinister authoritarian figures, arms folded. Another early task was to put together an advisory board. The first person he wanted was Daniel Ellsberg. Assange explained the purpose of WikiLeaks and why he had been approached:

> We'd like your advice and we'd like you to form part of our political armor. The more armor we have, particularly in the form of men and women sanctified by age, history and class, the more we can act like brazen young men and get away with it.

Here was one generation speaking to another. A month after being contacted Ellsberg replied. 'Your concept is terrific and I wish you the best of luck with it.' He did not agree to join the board. Two leading cypherpunks were approached – the British computer security specialist Ben Laurie and one of the cypherpunks' founders, John Gilmore. Laurie became actively involved.

Gilmore instead asked the Electronic Frontier Foundation he had also co-founded to help. Assange's old cypherpunk sparring partner, Danny O'Brien, now with the EFF, offered to assist. Also approached not long after were two Chinese Tiananmen Square dissidents, a member of the Tibetan Association in Washington and Australian journalist Phillip Adams. All agreed to join the board of advisers and, then, most seem never to have heard from WikiLeaks again.

What do the early internal documents reveal about the charge that WikiLeaks was an anti-American outfit posing as a freedom of information organisation? In his invitation to Gilmore, Assange had pledged that WikiLeaks 'will provide a catalyst that will bring down government through stealth everywhere, not least that of the Bushists.' In its first public statement, WikiLeaks argued that 'misleading leaks and misinformation are already well placed in the mainstream media … an obvious example being the lead-up to the Iraq war.' And in an email of 2 January 2007 Assange even argued that WikiLeaks could advance by several years 'the total annihilation of the current US regime and any other regime that holds its authority through mendacity alone.' And yet, despite these statements, the evidence surrounding WikiLeaks' foundation makes it abundantly clear that anti-Americanism was not the primary driving force. Time and again, in its internal documents, it argued that its 'roots are in dissident communities' and that its 'primary targets are those highly oppressive regimes in China, Russia and central Eurasia.' China is a special focus. One or more of WikiLeaks' inner coterie were Taiwanese hacking into Chinese government sources. At the time of its foundation, WikiLeaks claimed to have more than a million documents. Almost certainly almost all came from China. For this reason, WikiLeaks argued publicly that 'a politically motivated legal attack on us would be seen as a grave error in western administrations.' Concerning its targets, the formulation is precise. WikiLeaks has in its sights authoritarian governments, the increasingly authoritarian tendencies seen in the recent trajectory of the Western democracies, and the authoritarian nature of contemporary business corporations.

What then of the charge that WikiLeaks was a revolutionary organisation pretending to be concerned merely with reformist liberal issues such as exposure of corruption, open government and freedom of information and expression? The internal WikiLeaks documents show that the answer to this question is complex. At its foundation, Assange frequently argued that WikiLeaks' true nature did indeed need to be disguised. Because 'freedom of information is a respected liberal value,' Assange argued, 'we may get some sympathy' but it would not last. Inevitably governments would try to crush WikiLeaks. But if the mask of moderation was maintained, at least for some time, opposition would be 'limp wristed.' A quotation from the Book of Isaiah, he believed, might be suitable 'if we were to *front* as a Ploughshares [peace] organisation.' To John Young he wrote: 'We have the collective sources, personalities and learn-ing to be, *or rather appear to be*, the reclusive ubermensch of the 4th estate.' The emphases are mine. He also knew that if WikiLeaks was to prosper, and also to win support from philan-thropic bodies such as the Soros Foundation, the hacker–cypherpunk origin of the inner circle needed to be disguised. 'We expect difficult state lashback [sic] unless WikiLeaks can be given a sanctified frame ("center for human rights, democracy, good government and apple pie press freedom project" vs "hack-ers strike again").' The key to WikiLeaks was that its true revo-lutionary ambitions and its moderate liberal public face would be difficult for opponents to disentangle. Open government and freedom of information were standard liberal values. However, as explained in the theory outlined in 'Conspiracy as Governance,' they were the values in whose name authoritarian structures would be undermined worldwide, through the drying up of information flows and a paralysing fear of insider leaks.

It was not only opponents who found it difficult to keep the public and private faces of WikiLeaks distinct. Despite those involved understanding the need for disguise, at its foundation the excitement was so palpable and the ambition so boundless that, when it was called upon to explain itself, the mask of apple pie liberal reformist moderation instantly fell away. On 3 January 2007 a small crisis arose when WikiLeaks' existence was prematurely revealed. Assange immediately put together a brilliant description of WikiLeaks for public release.

> Principled leaking has changed the course of human history for the better; it can alter the course of history in the present; it can lead to a better future ... Public scrutiny of otherwise unaccountable and secretive institutions pressures them to act ethically. What official will chance a secret corrupt transaction when the public is likely to find out? ... When the risks of embarrassment through openness and honesty increase, the tables are turned against conspiracy, corruption, exploitation and oppression ...
>
> Instead of a couple of academic specialists, WL will provide a forum for the entire global community to examine any document relentlessly for credibility, plausibility, veracity and falsifiability ... WL may become the most powerful intelligence agency on earth, an intelligence agency of the people ... WL will be an anvil at which beats the hammer of the collective conscience of humanity ... WL, we hope, will be a new star in the political firmament of humanity.

Julian Assange recognised that the language of what amounted to the WikiLeaks Manifesto might appear a little 'overblown.' He recognised that it had about it too much the flavour of 'anarchy.' But in general when it was written he was pleased.

John Young was not. In early January 2007 he decided that WikiLeaks was a CIA-backed fraud. 'Fuck your cute hustle and disinformation campaign. Same old shit, working for the enemy ... Fuck 'em all.' 'We are going to fuck them all. Chinese mostly but not entirely a feint,' Assange cryptically replied. Young decided now to post all the WikiLeaks correspondence he had seen between early December 2006 and early January 2007 on his website. Later, in 2010, he published Assange's contributions to the cypherpunks list between 1995 and 2002. It is because of his baseless suspicion that the mind of Julian Assange and the intellectual origins of WikiLeaks are able to be understood.

*

In February 2007, Julian Assange travelled to Nairobi to attend the World Social Forum, a very large gathering of mainly left-wing human rights activists and NGOs. He stayed on in Kenya for several months, involved with anti-corruption forces but also fascinated and repelled by the world of superstition he encountered:

> Here, in Africa there was a two page fold out on the 'Night Runner' plague. Plague? Yes. Of people – typically old, who supposedly run around naked at night ... tapping on windows, throwing rocks on peoples [sic] roofs, snapping twigs, rustling grass, casting spells and getting lynched because it's the 'right thing to do.'
>
> Insofar as we can affect the world, let it be to utterly eliminate guilt and fear as a motivator of man and replace it cell for cell with love of one another and the passion of creation.

Assange was a true Enlightenment Man.

The next Social Forum was to be held between 27 June and 4 July in Atlanta. Assange wanted WikiLeaks volunteers to attend. Emails he sent in early June can be found on the internet. They provide the clearest evidence of his political viewpoint and strategic thinking at this time. In the first he assures his supporters that WikiLeaks' future is secure. '[T]he idea can't be stopped. It's everyone's now.' Some people have apparently argued that WikiLeaks' idealism or 'childlike naivety' is a weakness. He believes they are entirely wrong. 'Naivety is unfailingly attractive when it adorns strength. People rush forward to defend and fight for individuals and organizations imbued with this quality.' Confronted by it, 'virtuous sophisticates' are 'marooned.' Some people are clearly worried that WikiLeaks will be captured by 'the Left.' Assange assures his followers they need not be concerned. In the US the problem is rather that WikiLeaks is seen as too close to the CIA and American foreign policy. In fact, 'we'll take our torch to all.' Some people have clearly expressed doubts about Social Forum types. Assange more than shares them. They are by and large 'ineffectual pansies' who 'specialize in making movies about themselves and throwing 'dialogue' parties ... with foundation money,' while fantasising that 'the vast array of functional cogs in brute inhumanity ... would follow their lead, clapping, singing and videotaping their way up Mt. Mostly Harmless.' In Africa Assange has seen human rights fighters of real backbone. He warns his followers not to expect to find such people in the US. He quotes at length from Solzhenitsyn's 1979 Harvard address about the radical decline of 'civic courage' in the West especially among the 'ruling and intellectual elites.' Nonetheless, to advance WikiLeaks' cause, the Social Forum – the world's biggest NGO 'beach party' – matters. Assange anticipates that anti–Iraq War feeling will hold it together. Although WikiLeaks has so far concentrated on 'the most closed governments,' he explains that it is about to publish explosive material on American 'involvement in Iraq and Afghanistan.' He hopes that the anti-war movement will embrace these documents so that WikiLeaks can avoid the 'retributive' blast from pro-war forces. It is vital to position itself 'as everyone's friend.' If anyone still needs it, this despatch is proof that Assange has a biting tongue, a mordant wit and a brilliant political mind.

It is obvious that by June 2007 several members of the Left had indeed gravitated to WikiLeaks. In Assange's view, this group were thinking of publishing commentary on leaked documents in a way that allowed their political bias to show. He sent a different email to them:

> OK, you guys need to keep the Progressive/Commie/Socialist agendas and rhetoric to yourselves or you're going to go absolutely nowhere very, very fast. Now, now, don't get your dander up: if I can pass by gross mis-characterizations of the existing world order as 'capitalism' or 'white supremacy,' you can stay calm and listen a minute.

WikiLeaks was in danger, he argued, of being positioned either as a CIA front by John Young types or as a same-old left-wing outfit 'preaching to the choir.' All partisanship would be lethal. WikiLeaks needed to keep itself open to whistleblowers of all stripes – even 'conservative and religious types waking up to the fact that they've been taken for a ride.' 'What you need to strive for is the same level of objectivity and analytical disinterest as the League of Women Voters. No, even higher. Else I'll be so disheartened that I'll lower myself to government contracting work.' This email is not only illuminating from the point of view of WikiLeaks' grand strategy. It is also decisive as to his true political position. Assange might have been on the left of the spectrum by anarcho-capitalist cypherpunk standards but he was by no means a standard leftist. His politics were anti-establishment but genuinely beyond Left and Right.

Between 2007 and 2010 Assange's political thinking was shaped by two key ideas. The first, as we have seen, was that all authoritarian structures – both governments and corporations – were vulnerable to insider leaks. Fear would throttle information flows. Assange called this a 'secrecy tax.' Inevitably, he argued, because of this tax, governments and corporations with nothing to hide would triumph over their secretive, unjust conspiratorial competitors. This aspect of his politics amounted to a kind of political Darwinism, a belief not in the survival of the fittest but of the most transparent and most just. As an organisation that encouraged whistleblowers and published their documents, WikiLeaks was aiding and speeding up this process.

There was, however, another dimension of his politics that reflected his long association with the cypherpunks. Assange believed that, in the era of globalisation, laws determining communication were going to be harmonised. The world would either opt for a closed system akin to Chinese political secrecy and American intellectual property laws, or an open system found to some extent in Belgium and Sweden. Once more, Assange hoped that WikiLeaks was assisting a positive outcome to this struggle through its role as what he called a global publisher of last resort. If WikiLeaks could survive the attacks certain to be mounted by governments and corporations, the rights of human beings to communicate freely with each other without the intervention of governments would be entrenched. WikiLeaks was, according to this argument, the canary in the mine. Assange was taken with the famous Orwell quote. 'He who controls the present controls the past and he who controls the past controls the future.' The world was at a turning point. Either Big Brother would take control of the internet or an era of unprecedented freedom of communication would arrive.

Assange was by now in the habit of composing motivational emails for his volunteers. This is the message he sent them on 12 March 2008:

> Mankind has successfully adapted changes as monumental as electricity and the engine. It can also adapt to a world where state sponsored violence against the communications of consenting adults is not only unlawful, but physically impossible. As knowledge flows across nations it is time to sum the great freedoms of every nation and not subtract them. It is time for the world as an international collective of communicating peoples to arise and say 'here I am.'

This might have come straight out of a cypherpunks manifesto. In the first weeks of 2010 Assange was involved in an ultimately successful political manoeuvre to turn Iceland into the world's first 'data haven' with the most politically progressive anti-censorship laws on Earth.

There was an aspect of WikiLeaks' work that was, through 2008 and 2009, beginning to trouble Assange. Although it was a peripatetic organisation with a small permanent staff, WikiLeaks had proven to be an outstanding success in attracting leaks and then publishing them. By late 2009 it had published documents concerning an Islamist assassination order from Somalia; massive corruption in Daniel arap Moi's Kenya; tax avoidance by the largest Swiss bank, Julius Baer; an oil spill in Peru, a nuclear accident in Iran and toxic chemical dumping by the Trafigura corporation off the Ivory Coast. Further, it had released the Guantanamo Bay operational manuals; secret film of dissent in Tibet; the emails of Sarah Palin; a suppressed report into an assassination squad operating in Kenya; American intelligence reports on the battle of Fallujah, and reports into the conditions in its jails; the Climategate emails; the internet censorship lists from Australia; and, finally, the loans book of the Icelandic bank Kaupthing. WikiLeaks had never been successfully sued, although Julius Baer had tried. None of the identities of the whistleblowers who sought to conceal them had been uncovered. WikiLeaks had won awards from the *Economist*, in 2008, and from Amnesty International, in 2009. Assange believed that WikiLeaks' information had determined a Kenyan election. He knew that the publication of the loans book in Iceland had riveted the nation, especially after Kaupthing had brought down an injunction against the national broadcaster's evening television news. And yet, as his internal communications make clear, he was puzzled and appalled by the world's indifference to his leaks.

Assange had once regarded WikiLeaks as the people's intelligence agency. In January 2007 he sincerely believed that when WikiLeaks published commentary on the Somalia assassination order document it would be 'very closely collaboratively analysed by hundreds of Wikipedia editors' and by 'thousands of refugees from the Somali, Ethiopian and Chinese expat communities.' This simply had not happened. Commentary by the people on material produced by their intelligence agency never would. He had once hoped for engaged analysis from the blogosphere. What he now discovered were what he thought of as indifferent narcissists repeating the views of the mainstream media on 'the issues de jour' with an additional flourish along the lines of 'their pussy cat predicted it all along.' Even the smaller newspapers were hopeless. They relied on press releases, ignorant commentary and theft. They never reported the vitally significant leaks without WikiLeaks intervention. Counterintuitively, only the major newspapers in the world, such as the *New York Times* or the *Guardian*, undertook any serious analysis but even they were self-censoring and their reportage dominated by the interests of powerful lobby groups. No one seemed truly interested in the vital material WikiLeaks offered or willing to do their own work. He wrote to his volunteers:

> What does it mean when only those facts about the world with economic powers behind them can be heard, when the truth lays [sic] naked before the world and no one will be the first to speak without a bribe?
>
> WikiLeaks' unreported material is only the most visible wave on an ocean of truth rotting in draws [sic] of the fourth estate, waiting for a lobby to subsidize its revelation into a profitable endeavour.

In Iraq, a junior American intelligence analyst, Private Bradley
Manning – at least according to very convincing evidence yet to
be tested in court – had been following WikiLeaks' activities with
interest. On 25 November 2009 WikiLeaks released a document
comprising 573,000 messages from September 11. As this material could only come from a National Security Agency leak,
Manning was now convinced that WikiLeaks was genuine.
Eventually, after sending WikiLeaks some cables concerning the
American Ambassador in Iceland, he decided to download
93,000 logs from the Afghan War, 400,000 incident reports
from the war in Iraq and 250,000 State Department cables, to
which he and hundreds of thousands of American officials had
access, and to send them to WikiLeaks. As a cover, he brought
along Lady Gaga CDs and, while downloading these documents
onto disc, pretended to be mouthing the words to the music.
Some time after, he confessed to a convicted hacker, Adrian
Lamo, what he had done. The most secure encryption and
remailing systems were powerless against human, all-too-human
frailty. Lamo in turn informed the FBI and American military
authorities. Shortly after, Manning was arrested and taken to a
military prison in West Virginia. Lamo also went with his evidence to a longstanding acquaintance, another convicted hacker,
Kevin Poulsen, who worked at the magazine *Wired*. Poulsen published the log of some of the alleged conversation between
Manning and Lamo.

(12.15:11 PM) bradass87: hypothetical question: if you had
free reign [sic] over classified networks for long periods of
time ... say 8-9 months ... and you saw incredible things, awful
things ... things that belonged in the public domain, and not
on some server stored in a dark room in Washington DC ...
what would you do?

(12.26:09 PM) bradass87: lets just say 'someone' I know
intimately well, has been penetrating US classified networks,
mining data like the ones described ... and been transferring
that data from the classified networks over the 'air gap' onto
a commercial network computer ... sorting the data, com-
pressing it, encrypting it, and uploading it to a crazy white
haired aussie who can't seem to stay in one country very long.

One of the items sent to WikiLeaks was a video of a cold-blooded, American Apache helicopter attack on a group of Iraqis, in which up to fifteen men were gunned down. Assange made the decision to concentrate the resources and the energies of WikiLeaks on publishing it under the title: 'Collateral Murder.' In early April 2010 he flew to Washington to launch it, with his temporary chief-of-staff in Iceland (where the video had been edited), Rop Gonggrijp, the Dutch veteran of Berlin's Chaos Computer Club. On 5 April Assange addressed the National Press Club. His frustration with the indifference of the world was, to put it mildly, about to end.

*

For once, the cliché is true. What happened over the next ten months is stranger than fiction. With the release of the 'Collateral Murder' footage, WikiLeaks became instantly famous. Assange decided to publish the new material he had received from Manning anonymously in association with some of the world's best newspapers or magazines. Complex and heated negotiations between WikiLeaks and the *Guardian*, the *New York Times* and *Der Spiegel* were now conducted. Even though these negotiations are one of the less interesting aspects of this story, already three books from the news outlets involved offering their own perspectives have been published. Assange had long regarded the Western media as narcissistic. It is likely that his judgement was now confirmed.

In July the first of the Manning tranche, the 'Afghan War Diary,' was published. Assange held back only 15,000 of the 93,000 reports. Unforgivably, those released included the names of perhaps 300 Afghans who had assisted Western forces. A Taliban spokesperson, Zabiullah Mujahid, claimed that a nine-member commission had been created after the documents were released 'to find out about people who were spying.' Assange was unrepentant. In a speech in Sweden of 14 August, in talking about the practical impossibility of redacting names from the 93,000 reports, he distinguished between those who are 'innocent' and those who are not. Regarding the latter he asked: 'Are they entitled to retribution or not?' He did, however, learn from the experience. When the Iraq War logs were released in October most names had been redacted.

By now, fissures were emerging inside WikiLeaks. Relations between Assange and Domscheit-Berg became increasingly tense, especially after Assange warned him, in April 2010, regarding the exposure of sources: 'If you fuck up, I'll hunt you down and kill you.' Birgitta Jónsdóttir, the anarchist Icelandic parliamentarian, was concerned about what she saw as the cavalier way in which Assange had handled the moral issue of the Afghan War Diary. The young Icelandic anarchist historian, Herbert Snorrason, resented what he thought of as the increasingly dictatorial tendency inside the organisation. He claimed that Assange had warned: 'I don't like your tone. If it continues you're out. I am the heart and soul of this organization, its founder, philosopher, spokesperson, original coder, organizer, financier, and all of the rest. If you have a problem … piss off.'

On 21 August, Assange discovered that he was under investigation for sexual crimes after he slept with two Swedish supporters during a triumphal visit to Stockholm, one of whom, Anna Ardin, to complicate matters, had published advice on her blog concerning seven lawful kinds of revenge women might take after sexual mistreatment. Facing these charges, Assange expected total loyalty. Neither Domscheit-Berg nor Jónsdóttir were willing to give him what he wanted. Domscheit-Berg was suspended from WikiLeaks; Jónsdóttir quit. The man Domscheit-Berg called 'the architect' followed. He and Domscheit-Berg took the WikiLeaks' submissions with them, at least temporarily, on the grounds that its sources needed far more scrupulous protection. Assange regards this as a pure 'post facto fabrication.' Yet there was more to the troubles at WikiLeaks than supposed concerns about Assange's laxity over security or his cavalier and dictatorial behaviour. In December, Rop Gonggrijp confessed to the Chaos Computer Club: 'I guess I could make up all sorts of stories about how I disagreed with people or decisions, but the truth is that [during] the period that I helped out, the possible ramifications of WikiLeaks scared the bejezus out of me. Courage is contagious, my ass.' Assange had taken on the power of the American state without flinching. His identification with Solzhenitsyn was no longer empty.

Assange decided to release the 250,000 US Department of State cables WikiLeaks still had in its possession on drip-feed so their content could be absorbed. On 28 November the first batch was published. The American vice president, Joe Biden, called Assange a 'high-tech terrorist.' The rival vice-presidential candidate of 2008, Sarah Palin, thought he should be hunted down like Osama bin Laden, a suggestion that led Assange to quip to *Paris Match* that at least that option assured him of a further ten years of freedom. Visa, MasterCard and PayPal severed connections with WikiLeaks. A global guerrilla hacker army of WikiLeaks supporters, Anonymous, mounted an instant counter-attack.

Assange was by now facing two legal threats – extradition to Sweden to be interviewed about his relations with Anna Ardin and Sofia Wilén or extradition to the US where a secret grand jury had been established to look into whether he had committed crimes outlined in the 1917 *Espionage Act* or broken some other law. After a preliminary hearing in London on the Swedish extradition request, he was first imprisoned in Wandsworth gaol and then placed under a form of house arrest.

In early April 2010 hardly anyone had heard of Julian Assange. By December he was one of the most famous people on Earth, with very powerful enemies and very passionate friends. A future extradition to the US was almost certain to ignite a vast Left versus Right global cultural war, a kind of 21st-century equivalent of the Dreyfus Affair. Ironically, if that broke out, his staunchest and most eloquent defenders were likely to be people Assange assured me he now genuinely admires, such as John Pilger or Tariq Ali or Michael Moore. These are the kind of thinkers whom Assange privately had once derided as followers of the 'Progressive Commie Socialist' agenda. Domscheit-Berg tells us Assange considered Moore 'an idiot.' In an email Assange denied this with considerable eloquence: 'I would never call someone as successful and influential as Moore an "idiot" ... His precise position is, I suspect, more a function of his market than his limitations. Similarly when people have called George W.

Bush "an idiot," I think they are wrong, and that they are wishfully blind to other forms of intelligence.' In the coming cultural war, he would also be championed by millions of 'average shy intellectuals' across the Western world who had watched on passively as the political and business elites and their spin-masters in the US and beyond plunged Iraq into bloody turmoil, brought chaos to the global financial markets and resisted action over the civilisational crisis of climate change.

Assange had long grasped the political significance of his compatriot, Rupert Murdoch. In 'Conspiracy as Governance' he had called the disinformation the political and business elites fed the people to safeguard their power and their interests the 'Fox News Effect.' As the pressure on Assange mounted, Murdoch was clearly on his mind. In December, he spoke to Pilger in the *New Statesman* of an 'insurance file' on Murdoch and News Corp. his supporters would release if the future work of WikiLeaks was threatened by his arrest and to *Paris Match* about Murdoch's supposed 'tax havens.' If a culture war was engaged over Assange's extradition to the US it would involve, strangely enough, the clash of cultural armies mobilised by the creators of Fox News and WikiLeaks, the two most influential Australians of the era.

The Monthly

Hack Work: A Tabloid Culture Runs Amok

Anthony Lane

On 21 March 2002, a thirteen-year-old English schoolgirl took the train home. Usually, she took it all the way to Hersham, seventeen miles from London, where she lived, but on that day she got off one stop before, at Walton-on-Thames, to get something to eat. From that decision flowed two events, one terrible and final, the other more ambiguous and by no means complete. The first was the death of the girl, whose name was Milly Dowler. Walking home from Walton, she was abducted and murdered by a man named Levi Bellfield. Her body was found six months later, in a field twenty-five miles away, by mushroom pickers. The second consequence has been the fraying of an empire, and the sight of its emperor under siege. Many people have dreamed of such a day; far fewer would have predicted the swiftness with which it arrived; others view it as an overreaction tinged with hypocrisy and hysteria; and only the unworldly would claim that the end is nigh. Empires strike back.

The emperor is, of course, Rupert Murdoch, the chairman and CEO of News Corporation; the owner of Twentieth Century Fox, Fox News and the *Wall Street Journal;* the proprietor, in Britain, of the *Times*, the *Sunday Times* and the *Sun*, and the holder of a 39.1 per cent stake in BSkyB, the country's leading satellite-broadcasting company; an Australian by birth and an American by choice; the proud father of six children; the 38th-richest person in this country; and, in the words of his mother, the adamantine Dame Elisabeth Murdoch, now a hundred and two years old, 'that wretched boy of mine.' Never underestimate the wish, in the heart of a child, even a child aged eighty, to please the matriarch and prove himself less wretched in her eyes. It takes only three minutes, near the start of *Citizen Kane*, to shift from the stony stare of Mrs Kane, as she watches young Charles leave forever, to the bullish proposal of the grown lad: 'I think it would be fun to run a newspaper.'

In the past weeks, the fun has leached away. Readers and viewers who know Murdoch purely as a name – or as one of those figures so wealthy, and granted such frictionless mobility by their wealth, that they never seem to be in the part of the world that you expect them to be – were startled to see a senior gent, with sparse white hair and a clownish smile, descend upon London. He was seen jogging in one of the parks, in the thrall of a personal trainer. She was blonde and wholly fearsome, like someone whom Sylvester Stallone very nearly married before changing his mind and hiding under the bed. As for her trainee, he was photographed with milk-white shanks exposed unkindly to the elements. This was Rupert Murdoch? The man to whom prime ministers bend the knee? More unfamiliar still was the contrite figure who emerged from a meeting in a London hotel and pronounced himself 'appalled to find out what had happened.' He was also 'humbled to give a full and sincere apology to the Dowler family,' according to the Dowlers' solicitor. Of all the words one never thought to find in the vicinity of Murdoch, 'humbled,' especially in the passive voice, would top the list. But what was he apologising for?

Chronology matters here, if one is to chart the rising tide. Bellfield, who is serving life imprisonment for two other killings, committed in 2003 and 2004, was tried for Milly's murder and convicted on 23 June of this year. The following day, the Dowlers complained of their legal ordeal; Milly's father, Robert, who had been an early suspect, had endured fierce cross-questioning. So had Milly's mother, Sally, who was made to listen to Milly's private notes, and who collapsed after giving evidence. 'My family have had to pay too high a price for justice for Milly,' Robert Dowler said. On 25 June, the chief constable in charge of the investigation, Mark Rowley, said that the Dowlers' privacy had been 'destroyed.' He contrasted their position with that of celebrities who seek to guard their follies through legal injunctions – Ryan Giggs, for instance, a Manchester United soccer player whose sexual exploits had been concealed, protected by such an injunction, until unloosed on the internet.

What links all these disparate details is a confused and volatile concern about how, and even whether, our lives still belong to us. Who can possibly remain a closed book, when others try to open it and leaf through? Have the millions who volunteer their thoughts, on Facebook and in other social media, made it more treacherous for others – and for themselves – when a secret begs to be kept? The hungering quest to know, in short, and the debatable right to pry were already being stirred in the public mind. A sportsman with too many girlfriends could be jeered like a baited bear, but bereaved parents, who had sought no fame, were another matter. Something had to give, and it came on 4 July, with the allegation that the *News of the World*, the Sunday paper owned by Murdoch, had hacked into Milly Dowler's cell phone. In the days after she vanished, it was said, journalists had deleted messages on her phone, in order to clear space for more. This may have compromised the police inquiry and had also, more damnably, given her family false hope that she might be alive.

The story was broken by the *Guardian*, the upmarket daily paper that has been pursuing the matter of illegal conduct by the tabloids since 2002. The royal editor of the *News of the World* and a private investigator employed by the paper had already been jailed for hacking into phones used by members of the royal family, yet it would be fair to say that such occurrences had been met, by the wider public, with a shrug. So what was different now? The received wisdom – that the extreme sufferings of ordinary folk do not merit exploitation – is correct. There was, furthermore, a sense that the hacking of Milly Dowler's messages represented a desecration of the dead. The obloquy deepened in the ensuing days, during which it was reported that the cell phones of families of British soldiers killed in Iraq and Afghanistan may also have been hacked. These are, as yet, allegations: nothing has been proved, although little has been denied. What hackers could conceivably have gleaned from such activity, apart from listening to messages of condolence, is hard to imagine; maybe hacking, profitable or not, had stiffened into a reflex.

From here, the outcry gathered force and rolled over those who stood in its path. On 8 July, Andy Coulson, a former editor of the *News of the World* who later became the communications director in the office of David Cameron, the prime minister, was arrested in connection with the allegations. On 14 July, the same fate befell Neil Wallis, who had been the deputy editor first of the *Sun* and later of the *News of the World*, where he rose to become executive editor. The next day, Les Hinton, the CEO of Dow Jones, a subsidiary of News Corporation, and a colleague of Murdoch's for half a century, resigned his post, as did Rebekah Brooks, the chief executive of News International, which publishes all the Murdoch newspapers in Britain. She had edited the *Sun* from 2003 to 2009, and before that the *News of the World*, from 2000 to 2003 – the period that included the alleged hacking of Milly Dowler's phone. Brooks is evidently close to Murdoch, who, on 10 July, having arrived in London to limit the damage, was asked what his greatest priority was. 'This one,' he replied, indicating Brooks. A week later, she was arrested.

Later that day, Sir Paul Stephenson, the commissioner of the Metropolitan Police, and thus the senior law-enforcement official in the land, also quit his job. He had been hobbled by the revelation – and here we are treading close to farce – that Neil Wallis, after leaving the *News of the World* in 2009, had been hired by the Metropolitan Police (the Met, as it is known) as a public-relations consultant. Stephenson, in his resignation speech, pointed out that Wallis, unlike Andy Coulson, had not been forced to resign from the paper. The prime minister had nonetheless gone ahead and hired Coulson. Cameron was, and remains, under fire not just for his naïveté in that appointment but for the ease with which he had mingled with members of News International; lips were pursed at his personal amity with Brooks, who was a neighbour of Cameron's, in Oxfordshire. (Her husband, a racehorse trainer, was educated at Eton, as was the prime minister: nothing suspicious about that, but it does oil the wheels.) How high would this scandal rise? Could it not merely corrode but pull down a government?

Of all the charges being levelled, the social one – that the prime minister was fraternising with the wrong sort – is at once the most splenetic and the weakest, especially to anyone familiar with the dance that politicians and newspapers have led one another in the past hundred years. No waltz could have been merrier than the weekend gathering, in November 1923, at Cherkley Court, a resplendent country house in Surrey. The guests included David Lloyd George, Winston Churchill, Austen Chamberlain (a former chancellor of the exchequer) and Lord Birkenhead, until recently lord chancellor. Their plan was to discomfit the prime minister, Stanley Baldwin, and form a new coalition – a scheme abetted by their host, Lord Beaverbrook, the owner of the *Daily Express*, then a newspaper of great potency and reach. 'I think Baldwin will be defeated,' Beaverbrook wired to another press baron, Lord Rothermere, who owned not just the *Daily Mail* but also the *Daily Mirror*. Later, in the Second World War, Beaverbrook became, at Churchill's invitation, minister of aircraft production. His colleague Ernest Bevin, the wartime minister of labour, said that, when it came to Beaverbrook, Churchill 'was like a man who's married a whore; he knows she's a whore but he loves her just the same.' Churchill himself, incidentally, once wrote for the *News of the World*.

The joke is that the anti-Baldwin plotting petered out; when it comes to moguls and ministers, not all convenings are conspiracies, and few conspiracies succeed. It is natural, in the present frenzy, that Carl Bernstein, writing in *Newsweek*, should claim that comparisons with the Watergate affair are 'inevitable.' But is that so? On the presidential watch, men were hired to commit criminal acts; Cameron, by comparison, took on a man, Coulson, who had been tarnished by association with criminality and gave him a respectable (if serpentine) job, which by all accounts Coulson performed with aplomb. The prime minister erred, but was he guilty of anything darker than lousy judgement? Ian Katz, the deputy editor of the *Guardian*, may well be right when he says, 'The conspiracy reading is that Cameron wasn't prepared to risk the ire of News International by dumping Coulson overboard, because once he dumped Coulson, the whole thing would chase back up the ladder towards Murdoch. I don't really buy that. I think it was more a combination of arrogance and a reluctance to confront a really difficult situation.'

If the Nixonian shadow falls anywhere in this case, it is not on Cameron but on Murdoch, for it was doubtless under his aegis that cell phones were allegedly hacked, and the law transgressed. As he admitted, 'I don't know any better than anyone else where the electronic age is taking us, or how it will affect a large newspaper company.' Those words were quoted in *Fortune*, in February 1984. Whether he is wiser now, more than a quarter of a century later, God only knows. And, as yet, no one has hacked his phone.

*

For a small nation, Britain has an awful lot of national newspapers. Six days of the week, you can choose among five tabloids, some of them known, for reasons of design rather than of ideology, as 'red-tops' (the *Sun*, the *Daily Mirror*, the *Daily Express*, the *Daily Star* and the *Daily Mail*), and five broadsheets (the *Times*, the *Guardian*, the *Independent*, the *Financial Times* and the *Daily Telegraph*). Only the last two are still technically broadsheets, in terms of their page size, but the term has adhered to anything that lays claim to higher ground. (There is also a new kid, simply called *i*, which the *Independent* launched last year, and which fillets much of its content from its elder brother.) On Sunday, there is the *Sunday Times*, the *Sunday Telegraph*, the *Independent on Sunday* and the *Observer*, and, at the more perspiring end of the market, the *Sunday Mirror*, the *Mail on Sunday*, the *Daily Star Sunday*, the *People* and the *Sunday Express*. There was the *News of the World*, the heaviest breather of all, but its final edition came out on 10 July. Murdoch, in a bid to avert the hacking crisis, shut the paper, like a veterinarian who takes one look at your boisterous, nippy, but otherwise healthy mastiff and puts it down.

This barrage of print has one overriding effect: in Britain, you cannot hear yourself think. You never really notice this until you leave the country, whereupon the white noise suddenly stops. The noisiest paper, without doubt, was the *News of the World*, which resounded with three continuous notes. The first and most defensible was sport; last year, the paper laid bare a match-fixing racket in Pakistani cricket, a bigger and more

lucrative deal than it sounds. Then there were television performers, who furnished an astounding proportion of the paper's
stories. (When historians come to measure the age of Murdoch,
that symbiosis between media will loom large.) Last and most
cacophonous, there was the assumption, or the ardent hope,
that somebody, somewhere, was having sex with somebody he
should not be having sex with. Viewed from outside, what this
fixation suggested was a giggling braggart, fidgeting in the
school playground and pointing at girls with whom he would
never stand a chance.

The resulting product was the bestselling newspaper in the
country; make of that what you will. Murdoch certainly did. He
bought the paper in 1969, acquiring the *Sun* later that year and
both *Times* titles in 1981. The *News of the World* had been alive
since 1843 but, at the time of Murdoch's approach, it had not
been kicking for some while. In 1950, its circulation stood close
to eight and a half million, an astonishing command of the reading public, but had since fallen to around six million. This was
in line with a general subsidence; as Kevin Williams explains in
his book *Read All About It*, 'the decline of the mass Sunday newspaper is attributed to the incorporation of its values into the
mainstream daily papers. The reader did not have to wait for the
sleaze, scandals, and sex that up until the 1960s had only been
available on Sundays.' Lurking somewhere behind this is a sul-
furous inversion of religious practice: it's not enough to confess
your faith on the Lord's day; you must go out and live it every
day of the week.

One of the last people to inveigh, with any effect, against that
heresy was Cardinal Heenan, the Archbishop of Westminster,
who took Murdoch to task, in 1969, for having bought and
splashed, or resplashed, the memoirs of Christine Keeler in the
News of the World. She was the woman who had enjoyed simulta-
neous affairs with the secretary of state for war, John Profumo,
and a Soviet attaché – a grave security risk and, by any standards,
a superheated news story. But that had all happened six years
earlier; Profumo had resigned and devoted himself to work
among the poor in the East End, and the saga had grown cold.
Murdoch was warming it up again, because his instinct, as keen
as ever, told him that the will to forgive is weaker, in the

communal conscience, than the urge to drool. He was reported as saying, 'People can sneer all they like, but I'll take the 150,000 extra copies we're going to sell.'

Nonetheless, he apologised to the cardinal, thus setting a pattern that persists to this day. Murdoch would preside over an exclusive, reap the reward and, if necessary, express contrition, while his underlings readied themselves for the next scoop. On 16 July of this year, as the hacking scandal bloomed, News Corporation placed full-page advertisements in several newspapers – including, with some panache, the *Guardian* – headlined 'WE ARE SORRY' and adding, 'Our business was founded on the idea that a free and open press should be a positive force in society. We need to live up to this.' That is a direct descendant of a statement that Murdoch issued in 1995: 'This company will not tolerate its papers bringing into disrepute the best practices of popular journalism.' The fault, on that occasion, was a story, in the *News of the World*, about Victoria, the troubled wife of Earl Spencer, Princess Diana's brother. Included were photographs, described by the paper's editor, Piers Morgan, as 'evocative,' of Victoria Spencer on the grounds of a private clinic. The matter was referred to the Press Complaints Commission, the invertebrate body that oversees the misdeeds of British newspapers. 'That press complaining thingamajig,' Murdoch called it, according to Morgan, when they spoke a few days later.

Morgan owes much to Murdoch. He ran 'Bizarre,' the showbiz column at the *Sun*, before taking the helm at the *News of the World*, in 1994, at the age of twenty-eight. From there, he left to edit the *Mirror*, the *Sun*'s enduring – and traditionally more left-wing – rival, from which he was sacked in 2004, having published photographs of British troops abusing Iraqi civilians. The front page showed a soldier urinating on one of his victims. It was more than possible that such images could stoke retaliation against British forces, and Morgan soon had a fresh problem: the pictures were fakes. (He has said that he is still uncertain of this.) For anyone who wishes to learn how the cycle of contumely and pardon – or simple forgetfulness – spins in England, note the consequence. Morgan went on to become a judge on *Britain's Got Talent*, on ITV, and on *America's Got Talent*, on NBC, before ascending to the throne of Larry King, on CNN.

Morgan's diary, published as *The Insider* in 2005, is a tour guide to the freakery of life among the red-tops. What stands out is not the crowing thrills, or the major foul-ups, but the run-of-the-mill assumptions on which the tabloid press relies; they are the secret of the Murdoch mill. In the *News of the World*, on 13 November 1994, Morgan ran a photograph of Spike Milligan, once a harebrained figure in British comedy and now, apparently, whittled to what the caption called 'a shadow of his former self.' The picture, it turned out, was not of Milligan at all, but, as Morgan reassured himself, 'Spike will see the funny side, I'm sure. He's a comedian.' Four days later, when a letter arrived from Milligan's lawyer, expressing a grievance and requesting compensation, Morgan wrote, 'I genuinely cannot believe how prickly Spike is being over all this.' Such is the quintessence of the tabloid: to bruise and bully, and then to back off, exclaiming, Come *on*, we're only having a laugh. Can't you take a joke? The British sense of humour is both an invaluable broadsword and an impenetrable shield.

The most thickly armoured warrior, in this regard, was Kelvin MacKenzie, who edited the *Sun* from 1981 to 1994. When it comes to ethical discrimination, MacKenzie makes Morgan look like Ronald Dworkin. Students of the period should consult *Stick It Up Your Punter!*, by Peter Chippindale and Chris Horrie, much of which is consumed by MacKenzie's reign. Here you will find, for instance, details of the interview with Marica McKay, the widow of a British sergeant who died in the Falklands and was honoured with a posthumous Victoria Cross, the highest British award for gallantry – an interview compromised by the fact that she never actually spoke to the *Sun*. Or there was the mission to out Peter Tatchell, the Labour candidate for the London constituency of Bermondsey, who was finally snared by the headline 'RED PETE "WENT TO GAY OLYMPICS."' MacKenzie was informed that Tatchell had not, in fact, attended the Gay Olympics in San Francisco, but, undaunted, the editor simply inserted the claim between quotation marks and ran it anyway. It suited MacKenzie's bellowing homophobia, which, in turn, was consonant with his racial fears. 'Botha has said the days of white power are over in South Africa. What he doesn't say is what's going to happen when the darkies come down from the trees,' he said. That was reported in the *New Statesman*, in 1985, by Peter Court, who had briefly worked as a graphic designer for the *Sun*.

When *Stick It Up Your Punter!* first came out, in 1990, it was hailed for its comic momentum, and the back cover of the paperback is strewn with snippets of admiring reviews from, among others, the *Economist*, the *London Review of Books* and, yes, the *Guardian* – the well-bred visitors laughing at the tabloid zoo. Read now, it seems less amusing, and what previously felt like a string of high jinks comes across as a tireless parade of emotional cruelty. Court had a colleague in the art department who was instructed by MacKenzie to 'do us all a favour, you useless cunt – cut your throat.' According to Matthew Engel, in *Tickle the Public: One Hundred Years of the Popular Press*, a news editor was discovered whacking his skull against a wall, in an effort to pre-empt what he thought a raging MacKenzie would do to him later.

All of which suggests that the seeds of the current crisis were planted long ago. If your attitude toward the lives of others is that of a house burglar confronted by an open window; if you consider it part of your business to fabricate conversations where none exist; and if your boss treats his employees with a derision that they, following suit, extend to the subjects of their inquiries – if those elements are already in place, then the decision to, say, hack into someone's cell phone is almost no decision at all. It is merely the next step. All that is required is the technology. What ensues may be against the law, but it goes no more against the grain of common decency than any other tool of your trade. This has been confirmed by Paul McMullan, a former deputy features editor at the *News of the World*, who started by blowing the whistle on phone hacking and now appears, for the hell of it, to have switched from a whistle to a trumpet. Questioned on the BBC on 5 July, he said that, having pondered the matter of Milly Dowler's messages being hacked, he has come to view it as 'not such a big deal.'

McMullan cuts exactly the figure that one would hope: the stained white suit, the tie askew, the despairing beard, the eruptive complexion and the hair that no comb would dare engage. Yet, at present, he is perhaps the only player in this drama who speaks without a trace of caution – cheerfully confessing to what he hardly perceives as wrongs, and manfully struggling to grasp those moments when even he may have exceeded his brief. On BBC radio, he spoke, with a fuddled melancholy, of Jennifer Elliott – no celebrity, but the daughter of the actor Denholm Elliott, who was in *Trading Places* and *Raiders of the Lost Ark*. He died in 1992. She had a drug problem, and McMullan wrote about her in the *News of the World*, in 1995, alleging that she was a beggar and a part-time prostitute. Just to coarsen things, he admitted that the tipoff came from a policeman who had taken payment from one of his colleagues. Jennifer Elliott later hanged herself. Asked by the BBC, 'Do you think that decision had anything to do with what you wrote and what you did?' McMullan replied:

> Yeah, I totally humiliated and destroyed her. It wasn't necessary, she didn't deserve it. She was having a bad time after her own dad had died. Yeah, I went a step too far. And it was based on a now criminal act, and so you gotta sometimes question, well, in some cases, criminal acts perpetrated by journalists aren't always justified. And in this case, not only was it not justified, it was downright wrong, I sincerely regret it, and, again, if there was anyone to apologise to, I would. But they're all dead.

*

If you want to track down a forebear of McMullan, try George Flack:

> That's about played out, anyway, the idea of sticking up a sign of 'private' and thinking you can keep the place to yourself. You can't do it – you can't keep out the light of the press. Now what I'm going to do is to set up the biggest lamp yet made and to make it shine all over the place. We'll see who's private then!

Flack was a fiction – a journalist dreamed up by Henry James for his 1888 novel *The Reverberator*. To pass from the author of *The*

Golden Bowl to the *News of the World* is to range from one end of the human pH scale to the other, yet James detected the note of pure threat, and wondered how we might cower beneath it. Fear and loathing of the press is as old as the press itself, and the press would argue that the mighty in their seats have much to be fearful about; but the British tabloid press, in particular, spends much less time on the mighty, from day to day, than on the lowly, the lecherous and the foreign. The *Sun*, 4 July 2003: 'Police swooped on a gang of East Europeans and caught them red-handed about to cook a pair of Royal swans.' The Press Complaints Commission found that the newspaper 'was unable to provide any evidence for the story.'

Yet the story ran, deftly hardening the readers' xenophobia, though its primary purpose, in the land of the grey sky, was surely to dispel their clouded gloom. As one scans the history of Murdoch's rise, this mission to entertain assumes far more importance than his political agenda. Unlike Rothermere and Beaverbrook, he relishes not the orotundity of power ('It is the duty of newspapers to advocate a policy of optimism in the broadest sense,' Beaverbrook said, in 1922) but the more subtle power of suggestion. (When Murdoch was angling to buy the *Times*, he entered a committee room 'like someone visiting a friend in hospital' – the recollection of Harry Evans, who was about to cross over as editor of the Sunday paper to editor of the daily paper.) Murdoch is not prone to intellectual nicety, and his support for any given government has been determined, more often than not, by its willingness to strike the fetters from the market; once the Conservatives chose not to refer his takeover of the *Times* and the *Sunday Times* to the Monopolies Commission, it was easy to guess where Murdoch's fealty would lie. But if one had to isolate an instant, in the thirty years of his ownership, that best portrayed the Murdoch touch it would be the dictum that he issued, over the phone, on the evening of Saturday, 23 April 1983. The *Sunday Times*, poised to publish Hitler's diaries, had hit a wrinkle; the historian Lord Dacre, who had verified their authenticity, was having second thoughts. Stop the presses, or forge ahead? Over to Murdoch, in New York: 'Fuck Dacre. Publish.'

That is a sheer tabloid instinct, in a broadsheet world. It paid off, too; the diaries were soon exposed as forgeries, but, as

William Shawcross explains in his 1992 biography of Murdoch, 'the circulation of the *Sunday Times* rose 60,000 while the controversy raged, and 20,000 of those readers stayed with the paper.' Shawcross admires Murdoch, with reservations – more so than detractors like Evans, who noted a 'bleak hostility,' or Evans's successor, Frank Giles, who found Murdoch 'intemperate and disagreeable.' Then, there is Michael Wolff, who, throughout *The Man Who Owns the News*, his 2008 exploration of Murdoch, is openly fascinated by the elusiveness of his prey: 'He uses his newspapers to change *himself*. It's as though he can't express himself without one.' This notion of an Australian chameleon is not easy to accept, especially for those who prefer to label Murdoch a cantering rhino, yet on one thing all the commentators, warm or frosty, are agreed: the guy likes newspapers, or at any rate the rough business of newspapers. Less has changed than Wolff proposes, perhaps, in the years since Murdoch bought the *News of the World* and declared:

> Since a paper's success or failure depends on its editorial approach, why shouldn't I interfere when I see a way to strengthen its approach? What am I supposed to do, sit idly by and watch a paper go down the drain, simply because I'm not supposed to interfere? Rubbish! That's the reason the *News of the World* started to fade. There was no one there to trim the fat and wrench it out of its editorial complacency.

That could be Margaret Thatcher, acquiring an equally faded Britain ten years later. Fat-trimmers, like all diet obsessives, understand one another; in the words of Charles Moore, Thatcher's authorised biographer, 'they were both trying to do something against the status quo; what's happened since is that Murdoch has become the status quo.' He is hardly the first outsider, or upstart, to make that switch; like a *News of the World* reporter writ large, he loitered on the doorstep of the British establishment, then muscled his way in and decided to hang around. Whether he likes the look of the joint, after all these years, is far from certain. America suits him better. Britain, for its part, has never really liked the look of Murdoch, thus confirming the prejudices of the youngblood who turned up from

Australia in the 1960s and found himself tussling with bishops. Spurned by the British as a colonial, from an uncouth continent, he exacted the perfect revenge: he colonised their imagination.

That is why witnesses at the House of Commons Select Committee for Culture, Media and Sport, which summoned Rupert Murdoch and his son James to appear on 19 July, were so taken aback. Almost the first move of the father, as the session began, was to cup his ear toward an interlocutor and, with that tiny gesture, he broke the spell – the wicked charms that he had wreathed around the United Kingdom for decades. Here was no beast, no warper of souls or glutton for companies; here was an oldster, tortoise-slow on the uptake, with head drooping, shoulders slumped, rousing himself now and then to make a point by slapping the table before him. Though meant to sound decisive, the slap reminded some viewers of a grumpy grandpa asking when his Jell-O would be served. What ensued was equally bewildering, for Murdoch's answers to the committee denoted at once a Kane-like power ('The *News of the World* is less than one per cent of our company. I employ more than 53,000 people around the world') and minimum control, as the chief executive officer declared himself scandalised by events, while also appearing ignorant of what many of those events were and when they had occurred. Even the fact that News Corporation had paid the sums of £725,000 (US$1.2 million) and £1 million (US$1.6 million) to two victims of phone hacking in an out-of-court settlement seems barely to have flickered on his radar.

Seasoned Murdoch watchers, who have pursued the man since he appeared on the cover of *Time*, in 1977, clambering towers in the guise of King Kong, were not convinced. He may have voiced his belief, before questions began, that 'this is the most humble day of my life,' and he may have deflected many of those questions onto the Prince Kong who sat, alert and in possession of the facts, at his side, but might this not have been the greatest impersonation of semi-senility since Harold Pinter performed *Krapp's Last Tape* in London, in 2006? Could it be that Murdoch, once the quizzing was done, had leaped into a limousine, cracked open a beer with his teeth and started barking orders into half a dozen phones? He could even have paused, despite himself, to applaud the efforts of the *Guardian*, which, in its doggedness to unveil illicit dealings in the labyrinths of those who rule and police the nation, is doing precisely what the younger, keener Murdoch had in mind. To make trouble for an Etonian in Downing Street: nothing would have been sweeter.

*

Whatever the case, the last laugh has been his. Murdoch knows something that his assailants will seldom concede, and that renders their call for radical change, in the rapport between governance and the media, both tardy and redundant. The change has already happened; culture, media and sport are not in Murdoch's pocket, but the British, not least in their yen to watch soccer and cricket on Sky, have reached into *their* pockets and paid for his feast of wares. The country is in uproar just now, but outrage en masse functions like outrage in private: we reserve our deepest wrath not for the threat from without, which we fail to comprehend, but for forces with which we have been complicit. The British press has long revelled in the raucous and the irresponsible; that was part of its verve, and it was Murdoch's genius, and also the cause of his current woes, to recognise those tendencies, bring the revelry to a head, and give the people what they asked for. He reminded them of themselves.

Look at an average copy of the *News of the World*, from 27 March, well before the latest outcry. There are only scraps of news here, and almost nothing of the world. No woman in the first six pages wears anything warmer than lingerie. An entrant from a televised ice-dancing contest is granted a double-page spread to muse upon his newly transplanted hair. And the column on the op-ed page is by Fraser Nelson, the editor of the *Spectator* – a respectable weekly journal, loosely tied to the Tories, with a strong showing in arts and books coverage. Over the course of four decades, under Murdoch's approving gaze, the lowbrow has paid no more attention to the highbrow than it ever did, while the highbrow has paid both heed and obeisance to the low – submission, in the weird wrangling of British class consciousness, being preferable to condescension. The most telling piece in the *Guardian*, in the wake of the hacking scandal, came from a former editor of the paper, Peter Preston, who analysed

ANTHONY LANE

the sales figures and showed that more ABC1 readers (that is, those with better education, employment, and pay, and thus close to advertisers' hearts) read the *News of the World* than the *Sunday Times* – more, indeed, than the *Observer*, the *Sunday Telegraph* and the *Independent on Sunday* put together. Murdoch must have closed the *Screws* with a pang.

The front page of the 27 March edition bore an archetypal story, in that it was barely a story at all. The headline read 'JORDAN DROVE ME TO SUICIDE.' Now, this could not literally be true, unless the paper's foreign desk was even more foreign than we knew. Rather, the lucky survivor was Alex Reid, a professional cage-fighter, and formerly the paramour of Jordan – the defining, improbable deity of the past ten years, acclaimed for her volcanic breast implants, for her crowning appearance on a jungle-based reality show, *I'm a Celebrity, Get Me Out of Here!*, and for the five bestselling novels that she engendered but did not actually write. In short, like other personae in the Murdochian drama, she scarcely exists outside the appetites of the tabloid press – and there, you might expect, she would remain, as safe a standby as Christine Keeler was. Should you wish, however, to delve into all that Jordan means, and the reasons for her reign in the jungle that is Great Britain, there were two lengthy, in-depth interviews published last year, one with her and the other with Alex Reid. Both were in the *Guardian*.

The New Yorker

The Trial of Mary Bale

M.J. Hyland

It's Saturday, 21 August 2010, a clear, warm summer's evening in Coventry. A woman, dressed like a nun on casual day, is walking home. Her grey hair is cut short and dry and her skin is pale but looks fresh, healthy; the skin of a non-smoker. She's spent the afternoon visiting her father in the critical ward at Walsgrave hospital, but she seems to walk lightly, without burden or purpose.

In Bray's Lane, she stops outside a pebble-dashed house. There's a cat on the low garden wall next to the bins. The cat isn't a kitten, but it's the kind of cat that will always be small. The woman looks at the cat and then she looks away, a quick glance down the street. She pats the cat, but there's something strange about what she's doing. This isn't an affectionate rubbing. This is a vigorous and unnatural attention and, after a moment, as though she's changed her mind, she lifts the lid of a wheelie bin, grabs the cat by the skin of its back and throws it in. When her hand parts with the cat, she lifts her fingers as though out of filthy water, then she walks away, her pace quicker than before, a little nervous, excited. She's going home now to the terraced house where she lives alone, three streets away.

Later that evening in Bray's Lane, a young mobile-phone repairman and his wife begin to wonder where their cat, Lola, has gone. The couple go to bed and hope she'll be back in the morning. But on Sunday morning there's still no sign of Lola.

After breakfast the man goes outside to begin searching. It's another warm day, and since he doesn't have to go to work, he has time to search in the alleyways and across the road in the wholesalers and among a pile of tyres outside the tyre shop. But there's no sign of his cat, and he gives up.

At midday, the couple decides to drive to a nearby café for lunch. It's hot, so they wind their windows down and, just as they're about to leave, the man hears a cat mewing. He gets out of the car and hears the crying coming from inside the wheelie bin, so he opens the lid and there she is, Lola, covered in her own mess.

While Lola eats her first meal in fifteen hours, served on a white dinner plate, the man and his wife check the footage from their closed-circuit video camera – the camera they rigged up themselves a few months earlier to deter vandals. And then, on the CCTV footage, they see what happened. The man and his wife decide that they're going to find out who the woman is. They waste no time posting the security footage on YouTube and setting up a Facebook page, 'Help Find the Woman Who Put My Cat in the Bin.'

Within hours, the woman is identified by users of the website 4chan. Although 4chan is principally a forum for posting and discussing manga and anime, it has become infamous for the internet vigilantes who use the site's anonymous '/b/ board' to track down and persecute 'wrongdoers.' There is no moral code governing the use of the /b/ board's pages, which the *New York Times* has called 'an obscene telephone party line,' and the *Baltimore City Paper* 'a collection of kids with butterfly knives and a locker full of porn.'

It's Sunday night, and the woman's details have been unearthed online and are freely available for the internet's smorgasbord of scorn: her name, her address, her place of work and her home phone number. Her name is Mary Bale and her trial by internet and social media begins. Death threats are made and hate pages on Facebook such as 'Death to Mary Bale' attract a mob. Somebody writes, 'She should be repeatedly head-butted,' and 'She should be flogged to within an inch of her life, the evil bitch!'

*

23.08.10

On Monday 23 August I was in a hotel room in Edinburgh, where I was staying as a guest of the festival. It was about midday and I was sitting on the bed preparing for a panel discussion. I was hoping to catch an update on the Chilean miners who had been trapped underground since 5 August and I had the TV tuned to Sky News. Reports had reached the surface that all thirty-three miners were alive, and were surviving on a sip of milk, two teaspoons of tuna fish and half a biscuit each every two days.

I don't have a television at home. My news comes from Radio 4, the BBC World Service and the *New Yorker*. But when I'm in the same room as a TV, especially a big flat-screen TV like the one in that hotel room, I tend to leave it on all day and night and gawp, or fall asleep with it on, just for the sound of company. On 23 August, as I sat on the king-sized bed, I put my notebook away and watched. A new story had broken: a woman had put a cat in a bin; she'd been caught on surveillance tape and had been hunted down by vigilante internauts.

I was fascinated by the making of the story and the determined malice of Mary Bale's hecklers. I agreed that she'd done something stupid, but I was floored by the scale of the fallout. I knew that I'd one day write the story, but I also knew I'd have to wait a while.

*

24.08.10

The next day, Tuesday 24 August, the *Sun* and the *Mirror* both pick up the story and TV crews begin to swarm: BBC 1, BBC 2, ITV News, Channel 5, Channel 4, Sky News and Fox News take it in turns to interview the cat's owner, whose name is Darryl Mann.

Darryl is in his twenties. He has fair, cropped hair and a tattoo with thick black lines and swirling dots that snake down to his hand. In one of dozens of TV interviews, he sits on a plastic chair in his concrete yard. A rusty barbecue has been moved to make room for the cameras. 'I know people are angry,' he says. 'We was angry at the time.'

Another TV camera, another journalist, and this time they want Darryl to stand outside his house, with his back to the front door. Next they want him to stand behind the wheelie bin, cradling Lola in his arms, her head held gently against the Ocean Pacific logo on Darryl's T-shirt.

'I don't know how anybody, you know, could go to sleep at night,' he says to the camera, 'knowing they've locked a cat in a wheelie bin.'

Darryl's wife Stephanie is also interviewed, though less often than Darryl. In an interview for an American news channel, she sits on the settee stroking the cat. Stephanie is pretty, with silky black hair, which she wears tied back. A microphone is clipped to her cardigan. When asked how the cat was found, she says, 'We got out of the car and Darryl heard a painful meow … and there she was, sat in the bin.'

Stephanie is asked to respond to the news that Mary Bale is suffering from depression, and that her father is terminally ill. She says, 'It's terrible that her dad's in hospital, but to be totally honest, it's not my cat's problem … I don't like [Bale], but I don't want her to get hurt.' Photographers and journalists from the *Sun* arrive at Darryl and Stephanie's with gifts for Lola; a cat bed, a scratching post, a hamper of cat treats and a new 'Pampered Pet' cat dish.

*

25.08.10

The next morning, Wednesday 25 August, the *Sun* runs its 'exclusive' on the front page under the headline 'It's a Fur Cop.' Inside, under a picture of Lola licking her lips, is the caption, 'Happy – Lola with *Sun* treats yesterday.' In an interview on CBS's *The Early Show*, Darryl sits on his leather armchair and watches the CCTV footage on his laptop. On the left arm of his chair, there's a packet of cigarettes, a full ashtray, car keys and a mobile phone.

Meanwhile, Mary Bale and her mother are fighting their way through a crowd of cameras and reporters outside Walsgrave hospital. Mary is driven home by the West Midlands police. There are three female officers and one male, all wearing flak jackets. When they get to her house, one of the female officers opens the car door for Mary and another guides her from the squad car to her door. They do what they can to shield her from the mob of cameras and journalists.

Watched by millions, the CCTV footage of Mary Bale's unbidden malfunction lasts a mere one minute and twenty-seven seconds, but it contains all the essential elements of a viral classic. It's perfect YouTube length, with an ideal slapstick narrative shape. Much of its drama comes from the old *Candid Camera* staple: the startling and surprising image of somebody getting caught out, doing something naughty in private. But unlike *Candid Camera*, there's no laughter softened by recognition and sympathy. Most viewers of the cat-in-the-bin footage make narrative and dramatic sense of what Mary Bale did by deciding Mary's impulse was cruelty. And if she's cruel, there must be glory in showing the world on Twitter and Facebook that you know it to be so; that you are offended by what she did because you love animals and could never do such a thing; you are one of millions in secure and guaranteed agreement; you are superior and right.

If Mary had been a teenager, a welfare-sponger or a lout with a crack habit, there'd be no story. This is a professional, intelligent, middle-aged, middle-class woman surprising the hell out of us. And how she was caught is as important as what was caught. The meta-elements of the story are enthralling. There's a suburban house protected by surveillance cameras erected by its owners; there's their technology-savvy response, which sets off a high-speed chain of events governed not by journalists and media professionals but by a homemade news-making posse. People are mesmerised, not just by what Mary did, but by the role of Facebook and the shadowy 4chan in the almost instantaneous tracking down of the perpetrator.

Mary Bale had no prospect of a fair trial. The extent of the spread of the footage and its devastating fallout wouldn't have been possible a decade ago. A tiny event became international headline news because, like excited and compulsive children, we're so keen to play with our new internet toys that we press on without restraint, without comprehension of the real harm our play might cause. The power of the internet to prosecute within hours of somebody being caught 'red-handed' seems to have weakened our ability to respond with proportion and compassion. Online and anonymous, we attacked Mary with the same impulsiveness and lack of inhibition that made her our target in the first place. In the liminal space of Facebook and Twitter we post comments as though the words aren't quite real, as though they have no real-world consequence: as though we're not ourselves. And if we're not ourselves, not quite real, then the targets of our campaigns can't quite be real, either. We behave as though we think the pain caused in the virtual world isn't real pain.

*

19.10.10
On Tuesday 19 October, Mary faces her first court hearing for charges of animal cruelty. Her father has died the Thursday before. Outside Coventry Magistrates' Court, the pack of journalists waits. She walks into the court's foyer looking beaten and tired, her head bowed. The journalists shout their questions and Mary tries to shield her face from the cameras.

A significant part of the prosecution case against Mary uses the interview she purportedly gave to the *Sun*, and Mary and her defence counsel spend a good part of the day refuting the things she reportedly said. The prosecutor argues, 'The defendant says she didn't intend massive distress to the cat and she didn't know why she did it. That doesn't fit with what we see. She plainly looks to see if anyone is watching, which clearly indicates she is aware of the moral position she is in.'

The judge says, 'I accept that you were in a stressful situation at the time but that's no excuse for what you did.' Mary is fined £250 and ordered to pay more than £1000 in costs. Outside, TV cameras and microphones, tripods and zoom lenses point at Mary and more journalists ask, 'Mary, can you explain why you did it, Mary?' 'Are you sorry, Mary?' 'Have you got anything to say, Mary?'

Mary Bale says nothing and returns to her mother's house to hide.

*

28.01.11

On 28 January 2011, I found Mary Bale's phone number and address on BuzzFeed.com – 'the best place for launching viral media' – but the number had been disconnected. So I decided to write to her instead. In a page-long handwritten letter I told her that I was on her side and that I'd understand if she didn't feel able to trust me. I explained that I was a novelist, and that my most recent book, *This Is How*, is about a man who murders another man in a boarding house: a split-second act that puts him in prison for life. I asked her if I could interview her by email, by phone or in person; whichever suited her best.

Mary replied by email a few days later and thanked me for my letter. She still needed to think about whether to give an interview, but she wrote a few paragraphs describing her recent days: circumspect and understandably cautious, and yet longing to get it out. In that first email she said that the day before she received my letter she'd been at the job centre. After three months of living at her mother's house and being signed off for anxiety and depression, she'd decided to look for work. While she was waiting to be seen, 'The gentleman sitting next to me tapped me on the shoulder and expressed sympathy for my situation ... He was genuinely supportive and considerate.'

That same day, she'd been approached by a representative of a TV production company asking her to take part in a documentary to put her side of the story, something which she was not prepared to do. 'They seem to think that now I've been unemployed for some time, I would be more receptive to a sum of money being waved under my nose ... I have never intended to make any money from this situation and have rejected many offers from the *Sun* in particular ... that is not my style.'

Two days later, Mary sent another email agreeing to an interview by email or phone, and 'if you feel a further meeting is required then we can arrange to meet face to face.' I wrote back and said that I'd be happy, for now, to begin the interview by email. The next day I sent sixteen questions. And then, silence. I worried that I'd messed it up but two days later her email arrived, apologising for the delay and answering my questions. She signed off, 'I hope that helps.'

I was happy to have her answers, but I needed more. I wanted to write a meticulous account: Mary Bale's experience is not only strange, but it's strange in a new and peculiarly modern way. Millions, online and by way of 24-hour news, watched her do the worst thing she's ever done and millions laughed. Mary Bale became internationally infamous as 'Cat lady' and 'Cat bin woman' and yet nobody had heard the particulars or intricacies of this phenomenon's effect. A few days later I sent another email, asking more than a dozen new questions. Over the course of an email exchange lasting two weeks, Mary answered. And from her answers I was able to piece together her story.

*

Mary Bale's story: 23.08.10
On Monday 23 August, Mary had returned home from visiting her father in hospital at around 5 p.m. There was a message on her answer phone from her boss at the high-street bank where she worked, asking her to call him urgently. She rang him straight back, but he was on another call. As she wondered what the missed call might have been about – she had taken a week's leave and thought it could be about the handover – the phone rang. She assumed it was her boss, but it wasn't; it was somebody saying they were from Norwich Union, and asking for her by name. Mary was confused: 'It's not a convenient time to talk,' she said, and put down the phone.

A few minutes later, there was a knock on the door. It was a man Mary had never seen before but 'he claimed to be looking for a neighbour.' Over his shoulder, she saw 'a man crouched behind a car taking photographs.' She demanded to know what was going on, and 'the man admitted he was from the *Sun*.' He showed Mary an image taken from the CCTV footage: a picture of her putting the cat in the bin. He wanted to know if she'd 'been in that street at that time,' and he wanted to know why she'd done it. Mary shut the door on him and as soon as she was inside, her boss rang.

'Is it you?' he said. He'd seen the footage and he knew what Mary had done. She told him about the reporter at the door and that she needed advice, but there was no time to talk. There was another loud knock at the door. 'I have to go,' she said. Her boss told her he would call back soon.

Mary opened the door. It was the same reporter. Now she was in a bind: she had signed a contract with the bank that included strict undertakings that she would not do or say anything that might damage the bank's reputation, but she had to say something and the reporter wouldn't go away. He asked her why she did it. She said, 'I told him there were much bigger and better things to be writing about … like the war in Afghanistan … it's only a cat.' She also told him that her father was gravely ill, that she'd been to visit him in hospital on Saturday and that was all she wanted to say. She shut the door and went back inside. The phone rang again. It was another man, who said he was the news editor at the *Sun*. 'He told me it would be all expenses paid in a hotel if I gave him my story.' But she refused and hung up. The phone rang again; another reporter from the *Sun*, even more aggressive than the first. 'He was trying to scare me with ideas of being besieged by reporters etc., to try and get his exclusive.' She put down the phone.

Mary couldn't concentrate; she couldn't rest and she couldn't eat. She was 'climbing the walls.' On it went: 'There was an element of good cop/bad cop as they tended to alternate their calls … and the phone rang every half-hour or so.' But she didn't want to unplug the phone because she was still waiting for her boss to call.

At around 9 p.m. the police rang. They told her that this was a matter for the RSPCA. And yet they said, 'We'll be placing a patrol car outside the house as a precaution.' Mary didn't see why she needed protection: 'It didn't sink in at this stage that I was in any real danger.' She had no idea that the story was all over the internet. She didn't know that there was already a hate page on Facebook called 'Death to Mary Bale.' She hoped the phone calls would stop and, if they did, she'd get a chance to speak to her boss. But the calls didn't stop. At 10 p.m. there was another knock on the door. Mary looked through the living-room curtains and saw that it was another reporter. She didn't answer the door. She wanted only to go to bed and get some rest. At 11 p.m. the phone rang again and it was the first reporter. He told Mary that even though she'd refused to do an interview, they'd be running a piece in the morning. She went to bed at midnight.

*

24.08.10

On Tuesday morning, Mary woke early. 'I had a very sleepless night and left the house early in the morning (6 a.m.) to avoid the press.' There were no reporters outside but she was afraid there would be. Mary was still on leave and decided to go ahead with her plans for the day. She had booked a ticket for the Royal Shakespeare Company's *Morte d'Arthur* in Stratford-upon-Avon, and because she was a Friend of the Royal Shakespeare Company, she also had a ticket for the filming of a trailer for which the RSC needed audience members. She got into her car, drove to Stratford and 'called at a petrol station and checked a copy of the *Sun* and sure enough there I was.' Mary called her mother right away but her mother was at the hospital and she told Mary that she should go ahead to Stratford and then stop by later that evening.

Mary didn't yet know that her story had become international news. She didn't yet know that Sky News was playing the CCTV clip in an unstoppable loop. She didn't yet know that reporters on Sky News were saying, 'Terrified four-year-old Lola is learning to trust again,' and, 'People in Coventry are disgusted by what she did ... a nation of animal lovers is appalled.' She didn't yet know that the CCTV footage had gone viral, or that the internet court had got hold of her by the scruff and thousands of people had set out to see her punished.

Mary was in Stratford watching the RSC's performance 'when the press furore really started, and if you believe the *Sun* I was giving them an exclusive interview, and if you believe the *Mirror* I was holed up in my house ... I was actually in Stratford, enjoying the sunshine, the filming, having a meal between performances ...'

During the intermission, Mary called her mother. She had been 'besieged by reporters who refused to believe that I wasn't there. The press had tracked down my mum's phone number and address, my sister and sister-in-law's address and phone numbers and they all had calls and visits from reporters.' Mary agreed to be at her mother's as soon as she could.

When Mary drove past her own home, there was a horde of reporters outside, so she decided to drive straight to her mother's. But when she got there, more reporters and photographers were waiting and she had to fight her way through. She decided to sleep there, 'but even at my mum's house the phone rang and rang.' At last Mary understood just how much trouble she was in, and that things were going to get worse.

*

25.08.10

On Wednesday morning, when Mary and her mother faced the crowd of cameras and reporters outside Walsgrave hospital, Mary had felt furious and saddened. 'They had no humanity about them. They behaved like a pack of animals.'

The West Midlands police 'were great. I had two officers escort me to my house on two separate occasions to collect clothes and check mail.' On Wednesday, when they were inside the house, one of the officers picked up the hate mail from the hallway carpet and while they were there, more messages were left on Mary's answer phone. One of the messages said, 'I've lost my cat, meow, meow.' The police were 'amazed by the number of press on my road and the difficulty we had in getting to the house.' They decided to take her answer phone back to the station to screen for death threats.

*

For the next month Mary lived at her mother's house, until the police were 'happy for me to move back home.' She was grieving, depressed, broke and unemployed (she had resigned from the bank). 'That was a time when I thought I was going to lose everything, and that I wouldn't be able to pay my mortgage and I worried quite a lot about damage to my house, like bricks through the windows. But none of that happened. It was just the hate mail.'

But in her first email to me, after she'd described the sympathetic man at the job centre, she'd also told me that when she was leaving the job centre, she'd been followed by a couple in their late teens, singing, 'Mary Bale puts cats in bins' to the tune of 'There Is a Tavern in the Town.'

On 22 February, I wrote to Mary to ask if she would be willing to meet me. I said I could come to Coventry, perhaps on the weekend. Her reply came by email: 'Sorry but I don't see the point of a face-to-face meeting – I am not going to be around this weekend, and can only see it as a waste of your time and mine.'

I wasn't surprised. I had already asked her more than two dozen questions and she'd answered them all, and we'd also had a conversation on the phone. She had nothing more to say. But I worried about the bluntness of her refusal so I sent another email asking if she was annoyed that I'd asked to meet her.

She wrote back, 'No, I'm not annoyed … I am understandably wary about anything being taken out of context (and I don't mean to imply that you would be anything like the people that hounded me at the time), but I don't feel comfortable with a face-to-face meeting. I have turned down other offers of interviews on this basis, and felt that your offer to deal by email and telephone allowed me to tell some of my side without being thrust too much back into the spotlight – somewhere which I have never wanted to be … Best wishes, Mary.'

Mary Bale still doesn't know why she put the cat in the bin and there'd be little point in me asking again. Besides, her insistence on not knowing makes sense to me, and it's one of the things that most fascinated me about her story in the first place. A few weeks after the story broke, my friend Ian McGuire said, 'She was putting her father in the bin,' and he was attempting to get at the kind of thing writers of fiction work hardest for; the thing Ian McEwan recently called the 'fine print of consciousness.'

When the first reporter on Mary's doorstep asked, 'Why did you do it?' she told me that she didn't – in that moment – remember doing it at all. 'I challenged them and then they said they were from the *Sun*,' she said, 'and they showed me a photo of the cat being put in the bin.' She doesn't say, 'the photo of me putting the cat in the bin.'

Her words keep her away from what she did. When I first asked her to tell me exactly where and when she put the cat in the bin, she said: 'The house where the incident occurred is on that route between mine and my mum's house … the incident took place according to the CCTV on Saturday 21st August at around 8 p.m.' Mary says 'according to the CCTV' and 'the incident' but she can't say, or won't say, 'I put the cat in the bin.'

It doesn't matter whether Mary can remember or not: the proof of the CCTV footage tells us that, on 21 August 2010, Mary Bale looked over her shoulder before throwing a small cat into a bin. What it doesn't tell us is that her mind was stuffed with the bother and sorrow of her father's sickness; that her act was an irrational and spontaneous expression of pain, anger, frustration or sadness, accompanied by thoughts she'll never remember having or, conceivably, that she acted with no thought at all.

The Financial Times

A Handful of Thoughts Before the Dust

Craig Sherborne

I do inside jobs. It is not an endearing feature. You can draw your curtains on the neighbours. You can shut the door on busy-bodies from across the road. But your own flesh and blood in your lounge room? Your lover in your coital bed? Each of us has been listening in on other people all our lives. Watching them. Smelling them. Loving them or not. To write about what we have witnessed is to break faith with life. It is to betray the most inti-mate, sacred code.

If you don't break that code, why bother writing? Fiction with-out autobiography in it is a mere mind game such as sudoku. Historical novels keep the world at a convenient moral distance because it is not our world. We can judge the distant past smugly, sentimentalise it, pity it and criticise it, feeling flush with supe-rior values from the high ground of the twenty-first century. Long dead people can be reimagined as scum or hallowed. The facts of their real lives used as a base resource for developing into book life.

We're not squeamish about doing that if it's old history. We're comfortable with the following equation: real life + imagined life = new life. It's the literary equivalent of adverse possession, the quirky property law that allows anyone to take ownership of land where the title is dormant.

Current or recent personal history is another matter. The title is not dormant. This history is presumed to be fenced off against trespassers. There is unease when authors shed their dignity in the service of art. Anger if they shed other people's to create their characters. A writer can argue until they're ink-blue in the face that the shedding is being done to express what it is to be a human being in a particular place at a particular time, enduring particular circumstances.

They sound disingenuous, pompous, full of lame excuses. The writer has the advantage of being the writer. Therefore writees can only ever be sublimated, exploited, shafted. Writing really isn't all that important if it's likely to give offence or hurt someone's feelings, is it?

Yes of course it is. It's where the new-life equation can be most relevantly applied. The great public events of our epoch may frame our lifestyles, but the small drama of our individual existence and that of those our lives get tangled up with, the little fate of single souls, comprise the very essence of our being. Not to write that is not to write anything worthy of a word like truth.

I've always loved the poem 'Epic' by Patrick Kavanagh. It starts out: 'I have lived in important places, times / When great events were decided.' The poem is not referring to more than a boundary dispute between two farmers, but Kavanagh reminds us that to most people their local epics are what count to them. The vast sweep of time may render a person insignificant in the scheme of things, our lives will very soon break down into dust, but nothing is more important to each of us than our own tiny epics. That is where the real stories of humanity are found. It is the bedrock of literature. As Kavanagh put it:

> *Homer's ghost came whispering to my mind*
> *He said: I made the Iliad from such*
> *A local row. Gods make their own importance.*

Thus, we are all gods. And the god who writes about it is a god-thief, stealing back from obscurity the narrative of our small time on earth. Ancient cultures left handprints on cave walls to do the same: I am, they were saying. I was here. I don't know why but I was.

Inventing the written word 5000 years ago allowed us to say it ever more complexly: While the great world was churning I was happening. Wars were happening, politics, disasters, but I was happening too. The people I loved were happening. The people I hated. The ones I honoured or dishonoured, we were all happening. We were the centre of the world, our world.

I've done outside jobs: journalism. I learned not to mistake a journalist for a god-thief. Journalists' theft is a very different kind of stealing. They press in from outside someone's life, often at a time when a person is most vulnerable, gate-crashing grief or triumph. They exploit that person's narrative purely for commercial gain, providing content for their employer to justify their own salaries. This may require feigned empathy and sympathy or even a cash payment to the person exploited.

In the process, the most valuable possession that person has, their life's narrative, is bleached of nuance and complexity for the purpose of mass consumption, rendered down to the nearest cliché.

By my count there are a dozen categories of cliché in journalism, victim or villain being the bookend examples. Fiend, thug, hero are obvious others. I can't think of a worse way to treat someone's life than to strip it down to one of those clichés for the sake of the ephemera of news and entertainment. To pretend to speak with authority about a person's life when you may have met them for a day or less, maybe only half an hour, or not even that, and in the artificial lung of an interview, is fraud. Yet this is considered to be in the public interest, an ethical, useful activity.

Even the most researched 10,000-word profile for the *New Yorker* can do little more than relay tics and quirks. What they looked like, their clothing, their hairstyle. Where they lived. What the gossipers would have us believe about their behaviour, or the courts. They have not been that person, lived in their skin or had the vantage point of being many years around them to get a good enough look at their unique core.

Better to do inside jobs. Not to do it would be to say that in our time people were not worth writing about in any serious way. Our tiny, solitary epics were too trivial, puny. Or we had so perfected ourselves as a species it was beneath us to bother with more than outside jobs.

The Australian

Out of Bounds: Sex and the AFL

Anna Krien

When seventeen-year-old Kim Duthie told *60 Minutes* last month that she had lied about being pregnant to a St Kilda footballer, it was as if she lifted a spell. Almost everyone, from the mainstream media and radio breakfast shows to devotees of online footy forums, Twitter, blogs and YouTube, had found themselves caught up in the teenager's life since she became the subject of an investigation into St Kilda Football Club last year.

Proclaiming to be speaking on behalf of all women mistreated by footballers, she had in January attended St Kilda's first training session and thrown flimsy placards on the ground reading 'St Scandal,' 'HU$H,' 'AFL (All Fucking Lies)' and 'RESPECT. AFL can you please spell that for me?' Female columnists wrote about her 'chutzpah,' while older journalists reported wide-eyed on her ability to text, tweet, film and take photos on her assortment of mobile phones. When the seventeen-year-old set a 'honey trap' for a dodgy 47-year-old player manager, releasing audio and video footage of their alleged affair and his coke-snorting habits to the media, she was applauded. 'You're amazing,' gushed radio host Kate Langbroek on Nova's *Hughesy & Kate* breakfast show. 'We salute you.' Miranda Devine called her 'an avenging angel' in the *Daily Telegraph*. The teenager's Twitter feed grew to over 20,000 followers. On radio, men fought over whether she was a child or not, and whether it was illegal to sleep with her. Each time the AFL urged the media not to feed on the teenager, the governing football body was accused of sweeping the girl under the carpet. Journalists just couldn't help it. They were addicted to her, and she to them.

Then Kim Duthie appeared on *60 Minutes* (Channel 9 is believed to have paid a five-figure sum for her appearance) and told reporter Liz Hayes she had never been pregnant. 'I don't know why I did it,' she said. 'I was a stupid immature little teenager.' The convincing photos she had put of herself on the internet – holding her pregnant belly – were fake. In one photo Duthie's eyes are wide and she has her hand over her mouth in mock horror. She is wearing a bra and St Kilda footy shorts. *Oops*, her expression says, *look who got me pregnant!* It now appears that she made herself look pregnant by blowing air into her very elastic abdomen. The media lapsed into an uneasy silence. To make matters worse, the AFL's chief executive, Andrew Demetriou, subtly chastised the press when he revealed he had been aware something wasn't quite right about the girl's claim. 'I was led to believe through some of our other investigations that that may have been the case but as you know … there has been a number of occasions whereby this young girl has said things that have proven to be incorrect and that's why we've chosen all along … to act responsibly and not play this out through the media,' he told radio 3AW. In a style best described as 'numb,' Duthie's revelation was duly reported, but the opinion pieces on her own and the footballers' behaviour now became scarce. The clamour to write the definitive piece on 'the St Kilda schoolgirl' was over. The spell had been lifted and everyone was naked, muddied and a little bit ashamed.

But questions persist: just because she lied about being pregnant, does it mean footballers are off the hook? If anything, the lie was a placebo test and the boys failed dismally. Faced with the accusations, Duthie says one teammate told her to 'fuck off, you slag'; another player allegedly sent her a text message, when there were fears she was suicidal, saying, 'You slut. Die.' She also says the club's management coached her on what to say to police, who were investigating on behalf of the Victorian Department of Education whether players had acted inappropriately at a leadership clinic conducted at her school. Kim Duthie was never going to be a heroine for women's rights for taking on the big boys at the AFL. What is interesting is how much the public wanted her to be. Duthie became the weapon for other people's misgivings about a certain vein of schoolyard misogyny that has persisted in spite of the AFL's own attempts to graduate.

*

The AFL is big business. Over seven million spectators entered the stadiums last year. State governments and local councils across the country injected $650 million into the league, while its revenue amounted to $335.8 million. The once working-class game is now flanked by Queen's Counsels and professional advisers, and supporting a major-league football club is not as straightforward as might once have seemed. Instead of going towards the game, members' money and taxpayer subsidies may end up paying for court trials, settlements, even private detectives to follow and build up a file against an alleged rape victim.

Of the 800 AFL players, on average seventy-five are newly plucked from a draft of a thousand young men each year. At Collingwood Football Club annual meetings, new draftees are introduced to members. Eddie McGuire, the Magpies' president and former CEO of the Nine Network, reads out their names, followed by height, weight and sprint speed. Lined up, they are the club's latest investments. Each has passed the closest thing to a quality assurance test. An assortment of fitness tests, medical examinations, potential injury analyses, family background and psychological checks has occurred; even their drop-punt kicks have been filmed and studied in slow motion.

The final touch for the draftees is a photograph. Each recruit is to stare in steely fashion into the camera lens. They are coaxed to flex their muscles. Often a player will grip a red leather ball with one hand (handspan, by the way, is also measured). This photo is perhaps the first inkling that players are entering into more than a simple contract to play ball. The flash of the camera is as searing as a brand. Some players, stars in their country towns and schoolyards, are already naturals at handling this kind of attention, but if you look closely at these early images, you may still glimpse the ghost of a boy, not yet rendered invisible by pounds of meat and muscle.

Although on the verge of adulthood, these footballers are about to enter a state of prolonged adolescence. For most of their peers the social world is set to expand, but for these select few their already insular existence has just contracted. They will be expected to live, eat and train with their team, as part of a single organism. Recruiters have scoured their personal lives for distractions, hidden vices and interests that may later demand priority over the game. Supportive families are great, clingy ones not so good. As the former footballer Tim Watson wrote in the *Age* in 2005, defending then Carlton player Nick Stevens's decision to play footy instead of attending his brother's wedding:

> You can say to your brother: 'I will do my best to attend your wedding but if, by chance, we make the final of the Wizard Cup, my priority has to be to play for Carlton. I am a professional football player; it is an occupation I get well paid for and I have sworn an allegiance to the playing group that I am a part of whatever it is we do as a group.'

(Stevens's allegiance to his football 'family' was curiously reciprocated that same year at the Brownlow Medal afterparty at Crown Casino, where it was reported someone had slipped a Rohypnol into his long-term girlfriend's drink. Perhaps this was simply a 'prank' played on Stevens, albeit via the medium of his girlfriend.)

Young draftees will be subject to diets, curfews, lectures and punishments, which will sit awkwardly alongside storytelling nights of initiation into a clique of in-jokes, nicknames, bets and dares, when humour and humiliation control the power dynamic, and veterans wax lyrical about the debauched adventures of Thommo, Johnno and Stevo.

Distil all that and transfer it into the body of a young man – this conflicting state of entitlement and responsibility – and you may well have a very confused soul.

*

'The game has changed.' Whoever you talk to in the Aussie Rules football world says as much. For some – such as Indigenous players – that's a good thing. Since implementing its anti-racial and religious vilification policy in 1995, the AFL can now boast that more than 10 per cent of players are Indigenous, vastly more, proportionally, than the Indigenous 2 per cent of the larger population. But for others, well – football just isn't like it used to be.

In a recent *Herald Sun* Q&A column, the sports journalist Jon Anderson and the former Carlton player David Rhys-Jones bemoaned the passing of the glory days. 'In many ways I feel sorry for today's players,' says Rhys-Jones. 'OK, they get the money, but do they have the fun? No way.' Back then, he says, journalists rolled around in the 'same drip tray' as the footballers. Anderson chips in with a memory: remember when someone let loose with the fire extinguisher at Brian 'The Whale' Roberts's pub? Sigh.

If the shift in footy culture can be pinpointed, it was in 1993, when the Saints' Nicky Winmar responded to racist abuse by lifting his jumper and pointing to his black skin. The photographic image of that event is now famous. This defiant act, said former footballer Andrew McLeod at a recent United Nations forum on racism in sport, 'made the AFL sit up and take notice.' Two years later, a policy 'to combat racial and religious vilification' was rolled out across the league and then extended to every Australian Rules football competition in Australia.

While the new rules soon became a source of pride for the brand, they also signified the disinheritance of a certain type of football subculture. Dyed-in-the-wool types viewed the policy as a slippery slope to political correctness – and, to be fair, the league does at times seem to be taking itself too seriously. The $2000 fine imposed on Richmond player Matthew Richardson when he gave the finger to abusive spectators and the schoolmarmish posturing when the controversial Ben Cousins did the same to a TV camera in the Richmond Tigers' changing room seem over the top. Cousins was fined $5000 by his club's leadership group for the incident. When CCTV footage of Brendan Fevola taking a piss in a shop alcove is aired on Channel 7 and results in his club fining him $10,000, it is not hard to conclude that the AFL has put itself at the mercy of a highly strung and righteous media.

However, when the football personality Sam Newman impersonated Nicky Winmar by 'blacking up' on *The Footy Show* in 1999, it also became clear that something much darker and malicious was rebelling in the world of footy. Six years later the AFL rolled out its Respect & Responsibility program, aimed at shifting attitudes towards women and girls, and *The Footy Show* responded with another 'harmless' prank in 2008. On live TV, Newman staple-gunned a photo of the football journalist Caroline Wilson to a mannequin's head. The mannequin was wearing only a satin bra and underpants.

'I tell you what, she's a fair piece, Caro,' he said, standing back to admire the dummy. As he held up items of clothing, fumbling around its breasts, one of the show's hosts, Garry Lyon, laughed and wrung his hands.

'You getting nervous about this?' enquired Newman, as he approached Wilson's teeth with a black texta. 'Garry, can I just say something, Garry?' he continued. 'We're only having fun … and I know you're getting nervous about it, but we're only having fun. If you're on our show, you're on our show …'

'We are!' yelped Lyon, shifting around uncomfortably on his seat. The TV audience was whooping and cheering for Newman. '*We are!*' Lyon repeated.

Consciously or unconsciously, Newman's gag and many like it are designed to pull down this new moral code. He tested Lyon's loyalty on air. Newman later defended the gag as a kind of compliment. It was, he said, a sign that *The Footy Show* culture, aka Sam Newman, accepted her. This appears to be the definitive problem with football. Not just AFL, but rugby, American football, European soccer – hell, turn the ball into a puck, put a stick in each man's hands, and it's a problem in ice hockey. The problem is not the game per se, but the macho culture of humiliation that tends to shadow and control it.

*

The German word *schadenfreude* translates as the pleasure one receives at the suffering, misfortunes or humiliations of others.

In the world of professional football, winning and losing are the only possible outcomes, and the very basic motivation to win is part and parcel of the sport. To win is to see someone else lose. Empathy is a handicap.

Off-field, *schadenfreude* can become complicated. It can cleverly disguise itself – particularly in the context of threatened inferiority – as banter, initiation, gags and 'just a joke.' Be it fending off intruding females or reinforcing your ranking in a team by humiliating new members, taking pleasure in another's degradation has a seesaw effect. They go down and you rise up.

In Kim Duthie, football's dark tendency towards *schadenfreude* met its match. And this is what the St Kilda Football Club has repeatedly failed to understand in its dealings with the teenager. Duthie was a top athlete when she first met the St Kilda players and, while she was flattered by their sexual attention, she wanted more than simply to sleep with footballers. Duthie wanted to *be* them. When she was cut off from the team, this highly competitive teenager had her first inkling of the limitations of her sex – and so she broke the rule that bonds all football players: what happens on the footy trip stays on the footy trip.

*

The 2010 Grand Final was a draw. It was an unfathomable concept for the players and spectators – how do you party when there are no winners and no losers? Then, to the delight of publicans, merchandise sellers and sausage manufacturers, the AFL announced a rematch between Collingwood and St Kilda.

The Pies beat the Saints and the city of Melbourne was still cloaked in night when the story of a pack-rape by celebrating footballers began to surface. By morning, police confirmed that they had confiscated bedsheets from an apartment in South Melbourne and were preparing to question two Collingwood players. 'Yet another alleged girl, making alleged allegations, after she awoke with an alleged hangover and I take it, an alleged guilty conscience,' retired footballer Peter 'Spida' Everitt announced on Twitter, and followed it up with 'Girls!! When will you learn! At 3 am when you are blind drunk & you decide to go home with a guy IT'S NOT FOR A CUP OF MILO!'

Kerri-Anne Kennerley picked up the thread, sympathising with players, saying that footballers 'put themselves in harm's way by picking up strays.'

Then, just days before Christmas, Duthie posted online the now-famous photographs of three St Kilda footballers. The captain, Nick Riewoldt, is naked and shrugging comically as a younger player, Zac Dawson, holds a condom wrapper close to his penis. It looks like a photo with a 'before' story but at a press conference Riewoldt solemnly assured the public that he had just woken up and was snapped as he got out of bed. In the second photo, midfielder Nick Dal Santo is lying on a bed, holding his penis as if in preparation for a wank.

Although the teenager claimed she had taken the photos herself, it was said – and later confirmed – that the players took the photos of each other on a footy trip in Miami. Ross Levin, a lawyer and the club's vice-president, threatened to tie the teenager up in litigation for the next fifteen years of her life.

Few observers acknowledged the eerie familiarity of the teenager's choice of font for her Christmas e-card. Over the images she had typed, in red italic font, 'Merry Christmas, Courtesy of the St Kilda School Girl!' thereby referencing a viral email that had circulated through the AFL Players' Association, present and past footballers, footy staff, various government departments, law firms and police officers several months earlier. Attached to the first email was a photo of Duthie taken from her Facebook page. She is wearing black leggings and a St Kilda jumper cut off at the midriff, with 'The Saints Girl' typed over the top. Also circulating was a digitally altered movie poster for *Three Men and a Baby* with the actors' heads substituted for the players believed to have slept with her.

With her counter-strike, the internet suddenly became Duthie's schoolyard. 'I was not sleeping for days on end,' she later told the *Age* journalist Peter Munro. 'I would just sit up on my laptop reading article after article about myself. I was just so obsessed with wanting to know what the world was saying about me and trying to defend myself at the same time.' When she posted the photos, Duthie was holidaying with her parents in a Gold Coast motel room. By the time her parents settled in front of the TV for the night, their daughter was on the evening news, bizarrely in a room that looked exactly like the room they were in. Scores of Australians watched as Duthie spoke to her laptop, manically tossing her long brown hair and answering her mobile phone to torrents of abuse. 'OK,' she says feverishly, leaning into the video camera on her computer, 'so everyone wants to know what I'm fucking really feeling like. I can't even explain it. Do you know how fucking angry I am with everyone? Oh my God, I could fucking *scream*.'

When Duthie flew into Melbourne Airport, a media scrum was waiting. Her parents, she told the reporters, had taken the bus home and she was not welcome to join them. She was dressed in a black blazer over a short dress, shiny black heels, and had a tattoo on the inside of her wrist like an entry stamp into a night-club. It was as if Kerri-Anne Kennerley had conjured up a 'stray.'

*

'We used to have the Downlows,' recalls Craig Dermody, who played amateur football in Gepps Cross, a rough part of Adelaide. The Downlow was the Gepps Cross club's equivalent of the AFL's 'best and fairest' Brownlow Medal and it went to the club member who did the most debauched thing on the end-of-season trip. The first Downlow that the then sixteen-year-old witnessed was at a seafood restaurant with the team and coach. 'The owner was getting drunk with us and our coach took the owner's tobacco pouch out of his front shirt pocket, pissed in it and put it back in the man's pocket.' Everything that could be drunk was drunk that night in the restaurant, recalls Dermody. The wait-ress, the owner's daughter, screwed in the corridor. When I ask if they at least paid the bill, Dermody shakes his head. 'Nah, the owner loved us. He wanted to be one of us.' For his 'pissing in the tobacco pouch' gag, the coach got the Downlow that year.

Another gag the Gepps Cross Rams liked to do was take a piss while standing at the bar as the next round of pints was tallied up. (When St Kilda player Fraser Gehrig did the same thing in 2004 and accidentally urinated on the woman standing beside him, the media had a field day. Gehrig later claimed it was 'splashback' that had got her.) Gepps Cross, like many other clubs, survived on its bar and pokies earnings. Its punters were also its players and a high level of tolerance was required in order to maintain this symbiosis. 'Pie and porn night' is a community club mainstay, as are strippers. In Melbourne's southeast, Prahran Football Club hired a stripper to rev up its players in the changing room before a match. They lost. In a world like this, as a minion or a top player, it would be easy to start perceiving women as service providers.

You have the mothers who cheer from the sidelines, drive to and from games and training, cook carbohydrates the night before, volunteer in the canteen, get the grass stains out of uniforms. There's the female support staff tending to the players' injuries, massaging their hamstrings, studying their eating habits and micro-managing their media image. In the past five years, the AFL has made a concerted effort to have women directors and commissioners but in some quarters the presence of women in powerful positions has strengthened the resentment of females intruding in what is a male domain, especially when they speak up. 'They serve very little purpose at board level,' said Newman on *The Footy Show*, after five female club directors had written to complain about the episode that humiliated Caroline Wilson. 'What do they do? I'm not knocking women [but] for very little input they demand a lot of clout.'

On a big night out with the 'boys,' women are there to make the men feel closer to one another – not only at strip clubs and brothels, but at bars and nightclubs and even on the sidewalk. They bond over a girl's body – be it checking her out together in a bar, leering out of a taxi window and yelling at her on the street, watching their mate have sex, or even passing a girl between them. One of the problems of watching porn together, particularly with the gang bang as common plot, is that the further detached from reality a group is, and the more entitled they feel, the more they might start to expect a shared porn experience. And then, finally, you have the WAGs, the tail of the dog, otherwise known as 'wives and girlfriends' of footballers.

In online photo galleries, WAGs are ogled; 'Sports stars not only rake in the big bucks and travel around the world doing what they love most, they also get some of the hottest women in the world. Here are some of Australia's sexiest sports WAGs,' writes *FHM* magazine. In the *Herald Sun*: 'Every sport has them, their stars wouldn't perform as well without them. They are the wives and girlfriends, or WAGs. Take a look.' On radio: 'Triple M makes a calendar of Melbourne's hottest WAGS!' Not only are these lucky women service providers, they are trophies. Amazingly, Wayne Carey (suitably nicknamed 'The King')'s fall from grace in the AFL was not when he grabbed a woman's breasts on a city street after drinking with his teammates for twelve hours straight and said to her, 'Why don't you get a bigger pair of tits?' Nor was it when it came to light that his North Melbourne club had negotiated a $15,000 settlement with a woman who claimed to have been sexually harassed by Carey and another AFL player. No, Carey hit an all-time low in the popularity stakes in 2002 when he shagged teammate and vice-captain Anthony Stevens's wife in a bathroom at a party. Touchingly, the Kangaroo players publicly linked arms around their vice-captain and Carey was shunned. But the issue wasn't about morality – if it had been, Carey would have been shunned years before. It was about being cuckolded by a teammate.

Back at Gepps Cross, Dermody never got the sense club members had a limit to their tolerance of bad behaviour until Adam Heuskes arrived to coach them. 'A few people left then, but not many. He was a former AFL player and a poor club like ours was considered pretty lucky to get him.'

Heuskes was twice accused of raping young women in front of, or with, his teammates, in 1999 and 2000. One incident, on an oval across the road from the Adelaide nightclub Heaven, saw friends take the alleged victim to police immediately after locating her. She said three AFL footballers including Heuskes, who had been drinking in the nightclub, raped her. Police charged Heuskes and another AFL player but the charges were dropped six weeks later when the then South Australian Director of Public Prosecutions, Paul Rofe, advised the police they had insufficient evidence. Without witnesses to the incident, the allegation, like so many, boiled down to a stalemate of 'he said, she said.' Two years later, the three footballers reportedly paid the woman $200,000 in an out-of-court settlement, effectively gagging her. Some years later Channel 7's *Today Tonight* raised the issue of Rofe's own connections to the game, as a director at the Adelaide Football Club (and former player) at the time of the rape investigation. When the tarnished footballer came to Gepps Cross, Dermody said his interest in the club and footy was waning – but he did play a few games under the notorious footballer. 'He was a pretty charismatic guy,' he says. 'And he was quick, always had a comeback. He could humiliate you in a second.'

*

In Aussie Rules, 'sledging' is seen as a legitimate way of taking down the opposition. It involves getting in the ear of the opposition and baiting them about their social shortcomings, which used to include being 'a faggot,' 'a girl,' 'a monkey,' 'a black bastard' or 'a towel-head terrorist.' Recently one footballer was even sledged for being 'selfish' for leaving his critically ill child to play footy. Spectators like to join in the sledging, female fans included – who, in footy, make up almost half of the crowd – calling players 'girls' and 'poofters' when they duck out of a headlong crash. With the introduction of vilification codes, the Respect & Responsibility program and so on, acceptable social shortcomings for use in sledging are getting harder to come by. But as a result of media scrutiny, players are now getting sledged about their scandals. In 2008 St Kilda's Nick Riewoldt was overheard on an umpire's microphone saying to Essendon player Andrew Lovett, 'You bash your fucking missus.' Lovett had just been fined $500 after he was found guilty of breaching an intervention order taken out by his ex-girlfriend. Less than a year later, Lovett was traded to the Saints.

Then, after a night of drinking, a girl accused the 'dark one' of raping her at one of the St Kilda players' apartments (Lovett is Indigenous). When the players were questioned by police, they said they had crowded around Lovett after the distraught girl left, trying to find out what happened. In court St Kilda ruckman Adam Pattison testified, 'I remember Fisher saying, "Did you chop her?"' and Lovett said, "Yeah, I did, but she had no problem."'

Then there is Stephen Milne, also a Saints player and the most notorious on-field sledger. Since rape allegations in 2004, Milne is now called 'rapist' by his opposition and is booed by spectators. Neither of these creative spins on sledging appear to be moral judgements – rather they're perceived as weak spots, something to make a player see red and lose sight of the ball.

In 2004 the American writer Robert Lipsyte, an award-winning sports reporter and columnist for the *New York Times*, dropped a bomb at an American Psychiatric Association general meeting when he suggested that 'psychiatry has not taken enough interest in jock culture as a window into other American pathologies.' By dismissing sports 'as all fun and games,' he said, analysts were ignoring 'the values of the arena and the locker room [that] have been imposed on our national life.' This is a far cry from the idea that sport brings people together and is the great leveller. It is also noteworthy that the two teenage gun-men of the Columbine High School massacre in 1999 pre-empted their killing spree by demanding all 'jocks' to stand up and declaring: 'Anybody with a white hat or a shirt with a sports emblem on it is dead.' In the aftermath, much of congressional and mainstream debate sought to place the blame for the shoot-ings on violent video games, movies and the internet. But a task force set up to examine the Columbine school environment believed there was more to it. 'I don't think any one thing drove them to this,' task-force member Joyce Hooker told *Washington Post* writers Lorraine Adams and Dale Russakoff. 'But I think we need to say, "Whoa. Why did they focus on athletes?"' The reporters went on to draw a parallel between the teenagers' rage, their endless humiliation in pranks and the reign of the 'jocks' at their school:

> Dozens of interviews and a review of court records suggest that Harris's and Klebold's rage began with the injustices of jocks. The pair knew of instances where athletes convicted of crimes went without suspension from games or expulsion from school. They witnessed instances of athletes tormenting others while school authorities looked the other way. They believed that high-profile athletes could finagle their way out of jail.

Australia is not America – but this quote has an awfully familiar ring to it. In the past two years, a series of allegations of special treatment of footballers by the Victoria Police has emerged. In 2010, the Milne rape case (in which teammate Leigh Montagna was implicated) resurfaced despite the two players being cleared. The detective and sergeant leading the investigation had since left the force and the silence around the case came to the attention of Channel 9. Former Senior Detective Scott Gladman said that the investigation had been seriously hindered by other police and that the alleged victim's statement was leaked to the club. 'She's just one of these footy sluts that runs around looking for footballers to fuck,' one officer allegedly told Gladman, urging him to drop the case. Unauthorised photocopies of transcripts were made, a missing page being found on a police photocopier. Recordings of the player interviews vanished from Gladman's desk for up to seven hours. 'We were told that if things went well, consider yourself a Saints person for life,' Gladman told the TV station. The former cop's claims were backed up by Mike Smith, who had also worked on the case in 2004. Smith said one cop associated with the St Kilda Football Club was very interested in the investigations. This particular policeman is now widely believed to be Senior Sergeant Hans Harms, who had been a trainer at St Kilda for seventeen years. A Saints insider told 3AW that Harms had travelled with the players to games and knew them well. 'He gave massages, did training, strapping, game preparation and [ran] water bottles during the game.'

These allegations have since triggered an Office of Police Integrity investigation into Brighton Police Station, which is around the corner from Khyats Hotel, where both St Kilda players and off-duty police are regulars. A raid on the station revealed that witness statements, Gladman's reports and a master tape of interviews from the case are missing. 'They wanted to be seen to be more important in their eyes to the club,' Mike Smith had said of the officers. 'Anything they could do to help the club they would do.' Then, in July 2010, a freedom of information request filed by Australian Associated Press came through. The police document was largely blacked out but the gist of it was clear: it was a memorandum of understanding struck between Victoria Police and the AFL, a contract which formalised the sharing of files, photos, videos and evidence on people involved in the AFL. The police were required to let the AFL know of any investigations into the league's players and staff, and would contact it before making any public comment. The formality of this intimacy between police and football looked plain ugly to outsiders. It was one thing to hear about certain police officers undermining investigations because of their fanaticism for a football club, but an official document such as this reeked of conspiracy. And now there's Kim Duthie. The *Age* reported last month that over eighty police officers have accessed and read her file on the Victoria Police database.

*

What Kim Duthie now aspires to is a mystery. When she was fifteen, she was the youngest mountain runner selected to represent Australia in Italy, and she became the under-eighteen national champion. An interstate competitor for hurdles, long jump, high jump and running, she was a naïve schoolgirl who ate, trained, studied and slept. Now she lives in hotels paid for by the St Kilda Football Club as part of a deal struck by the two parties on the condition that she delete the photos she posted on the internet. Duthie issued a statement asserting that the players involved with her met her socially following a match and not at her school. In the past eighteen months, she has tested and stretched the plastic tape of child protection around her and, like a hatchling just out of its shell, she has encountered predators quick to detect her nubile vulnerability. Player manager Ricky Nixon has photos on his mobile phone of Duthie in her underpants; he claims he took the photos to protect himself when she arrived drunk at his office and started to strip. Last month Nixon checked himself into rehab. He is forty-seven years old.

'I'm already sick of it,' replies my neighbour when I say that footy season is about to start, aware he is an avid AFL fan. As we stop to commune over our green bins, the mention of the game makes his face sour. Football never stops now and his discontent does not stem solely from the handiwork of an angry teenager. The collusion by the AFL and the press that footy is more than just a game has taken a toll. Last year, Carlton's captain, Chris

Judd, won the Brownlow Medal. Known as an all-round good guy, he looked uncomfortable as he accepted the award at the televised black-tie affair. On stage, he answered questions delivered by the event's host with the usual 'not really saying anything' air of a role-model footballer – then suddenly, Judd did something different.

'I think footballers and Brownlow medallists get put up on pedestals ...' he said, in response to the host's question about what it meant to win the award. 'Football, if you like, is sort of make-believe. It's like a self-indulgent pastime where you go out each week and announce to the football public the type of person you and your mates are. It's not real.' Struggling to articulate himself, Judd clung to the example of former player Jim Stynes, now Melbourne Demons club president, a philanthropist and youth worker, as someone doing valid work in the real world. When Judd paused, the room erupted into applause. But it felt like a smother. And then, seemingly as quickly as he could, the host moved on: 'You touched on it earlier: how tough was it to leave the West Coast Eagles?'

The Monthly

Can We Be Heroes? Chris Lilley and the Politics of Comedy

Peter Conrad

In Chris Lilley's *Angry Boys,* the mother of the Sims twins – disadvantaged slackers from the bleak South Australian bush town of Dunt – breaks some bad news. Dan has volunteered to donate an eardrum to help restore the hearing of his deaf brother Nathan. But the procedure fails: there's no chance, their mum glumly reports, of implanting a cochlea. Lilley, playing 'Nath,' scowls fatalistically, perhaps not having heard the prognosis; playing Dan, he chuckles with unholy glee. Why is he laughing, his harassed mother demands.

Why indeed? Laughter is instinctive, and what it conveys is a flushed awareness of superiority. But there is more to it than one boy's enjoyment of the other's distress. Dan, for the most part droolingly inarticulate, in this case consents to explain his amusement: he's laughing, as well he might, at the word cochlea. Penis-obsessed like all Lilley's male alter egos, he finds a crazy hilarity in the notion of a cock lodged somewhere inside your ear. He might have been even more delighted if he'd known that the word refers metaphorically to the spiral shell of a snail. What would you sooner have in that orifice on the side of your head, a phallus or a slug?

The absence of a laugh track – the chorus of mechanised glee that makes American sitcoms so convivial and so unthreatening

– leaves us fumbling to decide for ourselves whether we find Dan's reaction funny. The misanthrope will chuckle, as I did, and the wit will rejoice at the little specimen of linguistic exotica that Lilley has held up to view. Someone more compassionate will be shocked at the crude, cruel breach of social and moral decorum. The eighteenth-century essayist Horace Walpole reckoned that 'this world is a comedy to those who think, a tragedy to those who feel,' which is why 'Democritus laughed and Heraclitus wept'; however, the choice between the two options is never easy because we all think and feel simultaneously. Lilley, who plays both the joker and his victim, can get away with being Janus-faced, at once wickedly sardonic and tenderly sympathetic, and his twinned characters share this ambiguity. When do-good social workers recommend transferring Nath to an 'educational facility' in Adelaide, Dan is dismayed. He protests, and not only because he will lose his whipping boy – the inferior half of himself, whom he can punish with impunity. Unable to change the situation, he storms out into the backyard where he paces up and down, quietly sniffling. 'Daniel's crying!' screeches his little sister. Raillery and ribaldry were always the cover for a brotherly love that could not be openly avowed.

A great comedian has to be a theorist of comedy, aware of its rules and its ethical scruples in order to test or defy them, as Lilley so dangerously does. A great comedian is also a philosopher *manqué*, since the constant concern – which preoccupies Lilley whether he is anatomising the aspirational try-hards of *We Can Be Heroes*, examining the lethal nastiness of adolescence in *Summer Heights High* or surveying a wider world of ravaged innocence and corrupt, commercialised dreams in *Angry Boys* – is the odd, contradictory business of being human. One way of defining our species is to say that we are animals that laugh. But to be human is to exist in an indeterminate, middling state: our laughter can be humane and generous, the acceptance and enjoyment of common imperfection, although it can just as well aim to dehumanise and playfully destroy its object. Mirth is affectionate, yet anger – which fuels many of the characters in Lilley's new series, just as it provokes the rampages of Jonah the Tongan bully in *Summer Heights High* – has a righteous ferocity that takes no prisoners. Comedy can be a mode of aggression, the acting-out of a violent resentment or the satisfaction of a grudge, and when Jonah trashes the school from which he has been expelled the spectacle of so much baffled disappointment and such raw hurt is hideous to watch. A cello emotes, and the other pupils look on in misery. Even so, the animal that laughs remains a beast and, at its most primal, the comedy of *Angry Boys* relies on bodily functions that express hostility more succinctly than any witticism could. A horde of surfies in one episode challenge a rival tribe to combat by pissing on their sandy turf from high on a cliff. In another, Nath squats on the hood of a police car and shits to make clear his opinion of the law.

Lilley doesn't just want to make us laugh; his plan is to tickle us illicitly until we do, then reprimand us for being so heartless. After the joke disintegrates or is neutralised by our unease, it's hard for comedy to recover its guiltless composure. Ja'mie, the North Shore princess sent to slum for a term at Summer Heights High, circulates a text message to her cronies mocking the bogans she has befriended at her new school. She calls one of them 'a Clearasil "before" shot,' while another is 'a Housing Commission whore.' Both phrases owe their brilliance to Lilley, who of course plays the odious Ja'mie: the first has a catty epigrammatic finesse, the second is gloriously fantastical, as if the Housing Commission were responsible for assigning resident hookers to the proletarian dormitories it builds. But neither characterisation pleases the girls in question, who receive the text by mistake. When they object, the unapologetic Ja'mie drawls, 'Guys, just learn what a sense of humour is, OK?' As always, Lilley is challenging us from behind the character's mask: we enjoy hurling barbs at others but can we tolerate the pain when they rebound?

Australian humour has always been hard-bitten, shamelessly abusive, formed by the competitive antagonism of a frontier society. In early America men gunned their rivals down; our Australian forefathers mocked those they disliked or feared, which achieved the same result while causing a more permanent injury. Lilley is unmerciful, and – like Dickens joking about wooden legs and severed heads – he refuses to accept that anything should be out of bounds. The surgical boot of the would-be athlete Pat Mullins in *We Can Be Heroes* generates much chortling merriment. *Summer Heights High* has its platoon of 'specials,' kids confined to wheelchairs or suffering from Down syndrome: they are treated like village idiots, our excuse for taking pride in our own supposed normality. Comedy has traditionally backed away from disability, preferring to ridicule vices that are optional and corrigible. William Congreve, explaining the critique of affectation in his 1700 play *The Way of the World*, said there are people whose afflictions ensure they remain 'rather objects of charity than contempt'; when the Old Vic in London recently revived Georges Feydeau's farce *A Flea in Her Ear*, a pious reviewer lamented that the play made fun of a character with a cleft palate (which did not deter me from splitting my sides at the actor's baffled efforts to enunciate sentences without consonants). To his credit, Lilley is not so squeamish, whether he's confronting physiological or political embargoes. He is determined to offend: as the Chinese nerd who blacks up for the Dreamtime musical in *We Can Be Heroes*, he managed to outrage two Australian racial taboos at once.

One of his new personae in *Angry Boys* is Gran, a detention-centre dominatrix who is also the grandmother of the Sims twins. Her charges are a posse of juvenile offenders, whom she proudly describes as 'the worst boys in the state'; organising team games in the flyblown prison grounds, she encourages the players by heckling them as 'Negro' and 'Abo,' 'faggot' and 'poof.' They beam with gratification, basking in her tough love. Like every other comedian portrayed by Lilley, Gran enjoys exploiting her power and can't help experimentally pushing its limits. Hence the gambit she calls 'Gran's Gotcha,' a particularly evil form of practical joke. A tearful boy is told that his sentence has been quashed on appeal, helped to pack his paltry belongings and ushered to the gate, where he is told his mum is waiting to collect him and take him home. Of course the gate remains barred: Gran has got him and she gloats as she marches him back to his cell. Could Iago have devised a more sadistic wheeze? It's her Australian way of fortifying her charges, instructing them – as if they had recently disembarked on the fatal shore, their chains clanking – to abandon all hope as they enter this brutal place.

Yet Gran is a grim disciplinarian with a squashy interior; she hand-embroiders superhero pyjamas that she distributes to her charges and brings her favourite guinea pig to cheer up a catatonic teenager serving a term for the grubby crime of dog-wanking. How do we respond to a scene that appeals to facile snobbery (the guinea pig after all is called Kerri-Anne), risks mawkish sentiment as Gran cradles the boy while lightly hinting at sexual abuse, and never lets us forget that what's being punished is a silly and sordid act of bestiality with which the law probably ought not to bother?

All of this is messily ludicrous; then, Lilley introduces death as the ultimate reproach to comedy. Gran reminisces about her fondness for a previous internee, a boy on the isolation ward who ended by hanging himself. 'A little bit heavy, isn't it?' she murmurs, daring us to snigger. Comedy has no compunction about wounding its victims but it seldom slays them. Lilley, however, massacres characters wholesale in the interest of frustrating comedy's scheme to engineer happiness. The gallant Pat Mullins in *We Can Be Heroes* has a sudden recurrence of liver cancer and dies before she can begin her quixotic roll to Uluru; her husband blubs real tears in remembering her, and we're as shiftily embarrassed as if we were witnessing a friend's breakdown. Random casualties pile up in *Summer Heights High*, calling a halt to the fun. A pupil at the school is killed by an ecstasy overdose, and most of the Sudanese villagers who receive patronising sponsorship from Ja'mie are wiped out by a flood. Mr G's yapping chihuahua, Celine, scampers into traffic and is reportedly flattened. In a fortuitous twist, the obnoxious dog is resurrected, which challenges us to admit that we were secretly delighted by the accident: as Oscar Wilde remarked, only someone with a heart of stone wouldn't laugh at the death of Little Nell.

And once we have observed a minute's mournful silence, what happens next? Comedy resumes, heedlessly resilient, instantly overcoming hurt and loss. At the end of a Greek tragedy, the amphitheatre was invaded by satyrs brandishing stiff, goatish phalluses, who stirred up a festive pandemonium. Lilley, too, is riotously priapic. Phil Olivetti in *We Can Be Heroes* leers about his hefty endowment, and Jonah in *Summer Heights High* draws bulbous penises all over the school buildings. *Angry Boys*, which exposes the strutting imposture of masculinity, is even more obscene.

Or is it? Once again, Lilley delights in creating discomfort, with qualms about inadequacy undercutting the fertile riot we expect. Dan Sims brands a mongrel dog a 'fag' because its hindquarters wiggle as it shows off its testicles; he chastens Nath's frantic wanking, and tries to dent his brother's erection by hurling a shoe at it. One of Lilley's new creations, a Los Angeles rapper called S.mouse, brags about his 'motherfucking dick' and his 'big black balls,' though it is all loud, empty braggadocio, as his discontented girlfriend hints.

Back home, a beach bum called Blake Oakfield – played by Lilley as a sad pseudo-Californian wannabe, a surfer, who, like Mishima's sailor, has fallen from grace with the sea – is actually a gelding. His balls were amputated after he was shot in the groin during a pub brawl, and he claims to be investigating the possibility of acquiring a decorative prosthetic pair to plump out his Speedos; meanwhile, he needs daily testosterone supplements and relies on a sperm donor to beget his kids. He seems to be wishing his own emasculation on others, since he initiates new members of his surfie gang by tying chunks of bleeding meat to their genitals and sending them out beyond the breakers to attract sharks.

The most fiendishly penis-fixated of Lilley's personae is a woman: this is the ambitious Japanese matriarch Jen Okazaki, who forces her teenage son Tim to pretend he is gay to boost his career as a skateboarding champion. 'We know you love cock,' she tells the wilting lad, coaxing him to ogle the pendulous nuts of a pin-up in a porn mag. Jen is a castration complex in human form. For her, the male organ is a merchandising opportunity and, to exploit her son's popularity, she manufactures a line of fleshly pink fetishes for a gay clientele – a cock-shaped whistle that enjoys being blown, a penile drinking bottle that enables you to rehearse fellatio while hydrating, a disciplinary scrubbing brush with a bristly phallic knob, a dildo that somehow doubles as a dispenser for grated cheese. Unlike Sir Les Patterson's frisky trouser snake, the members Jen sells have all been chopped off the body and rendered harmless, feminised by the anaphrodis-iac household tasks they perform.

Despite their swagger, Lilley's angry boys all turn out to be detumescent: what, he seems to be asking, could be funnier than a penis? If comedy is about lying and self-deception, how better to define it than by thinking about that puffed-up append-age, so briefly imposing and so easily deflated? We are even treated to a close-up of Blake's empty ball sack, as sorry a sight as a pair of popped and shrivelled balloons.

The sense of impotence is national as well as sexual, which makes *Angry Boys* additionally uncomfortable. Although it seeks to capitalise on Lilley's fame overseas, its American and Japanese storylines actually measure the estranging, intimidating dis-tance between Australia and the rest of the world. Nath is a fan of S.mouse and Tim Okazaki, so Dan invites them to a party held on the scrubby farm before his brother's departure for the deaf school in Adelaide; a family reunion of all Lilley's disparate personae can be expected in the final instalment of the series. But Steve, a laconic and discouraging bricklayer – the boyfriend of the twins' mother – reminds them of Australia's isolation, or its banishment to a nether realm: 'Celebrities aren't gonna want to come here,' he says, surveying a vista of derelict sheds, unplanted paddocks and a muddy puddle that the boys call a dam.

This meagre local reality can't accommodate the wish-fulfill-ing fantasies of Americans, who assume life will make their dreams come true (and often indignantly take hostages or open fire on passers-by when they discover how wrong they are). In *We Can Be Heroes*, Ricky Wong's musical *Indigeridoo* contains an uplifting gospel song that intones 'Your Dreamtime is here' and in *Summer Heights High*, as Mr G drills his students to perform Cole Porter in the school gym, he explains: 'I'm teaching them to dare to dream.' This being Australia, Icarus soon plunges back to earth. Ricky wistfully renounces 'dreams that might not come true'; Mr G resigns in a tizz, saying, 'Shoot me for wanting to dream.'

In *Angry Boys*, Lilley looks at those dreams from the other side of the Pacific and jeers at their falsity. His monsters, unlike Dame Edna or Sir Les, know they are phoneys: S.mouse is a

bourgeois brat who masquerades as a ghetto gangsta and Tim
Okazaki is both an American teenager passing himself off as
Japanese and a straight boy claiming to be gay. The motive for
their deceit is commercial. As S.mouse complacently yawns, 'All
I'm doing is trying to deliver the shit the fans want.' Switched
into reverse, this might be Lilley's cautionary admonition to
himself: don't pander to the fans; irritate or insult the audience
rather than satisfy its expectations; and, above all, don't let yourself be co-opted by America. 'That's not disruptive, that's entertainment,' says one of the ruffians in *Summer Heights High* when
accused of misbehaving. But Lilley would rather think of himself as a menace to public order and a disrupter of the received
wisdom than as a slick, cozening entertainer.

Angry Boys is what William Empson called a version of pasto-
ral, contrasting two worlds – one complex and modern, the
other bucolically simple – that are separated by the gaping
vacancy of the Pacific. It regrets the loss of innocence and of
childhood, both of which were preserved by Australia's isolation.
Sentenced to house arrest in Los Angeles, S.mouse gathers
around him the battery of electronic appliances that complicate
our lives and compel us to live at second-hand. In Tokyo, Jen
Okazaki beams at the tacky, kinky gadgetry she sells.

Perhaps the Sims brothers are lucky to have so little: Dan is
furious on Nath's behalf when their mother says that, if he consents to be sent away to the deaf school, she'll get him an iPhone.
Against the technological swank and cushioned affluence of
Japan and California, Lilley sets Australia's drab tedium – the
single dusty thoroughfare called Main Street that the Sims boys
enliven with wheelies or the outback railway station where they
listlessly wait for a train that never comes; the encampment of
shacks where Blake Oakfield and his washed-up mates while
away the rest of their lives. Against success on the American
model, Lilley sets Australian failure. The Sims twins are dead-
end kids, and Blake is a shiftless has-been. But they are harmless, and have found a kind of happiness simply because they
don't fanatically pursue it.

Can we be heroes? As Lilley contrasts his ignominious homeland with those brighter horizons across the ocean, he seems to
be saying we can't, and adding that we shouldn't want to be.

Anyway, Australia has always preferred antiheroes. There's just one problem with that down-in-the-mouth, ironically defeatist conclusion: Lilley's genius as a writer and a self-multiplying performer proves it to be wrong.

The Monthly

In the Pines: A Girl Skulks Along Memory's Edge

Inga Clendinnen

There is a lot of talk these days about childhood memories being the fountain from which we replenish our unique but depleting adult selves. This generates even more talk about the reliability of memories. What follows is constructed out of irreplaceable, indispensable, unreliable memories, the only corrections being those insisted on by my brother David Jewell, who played for Newtown and Chilwell Cricket Club (Senior Matting) over many years.

Remembered: a cricket ground at Queen's Park, Geelong. A beautiful ground ringed by a white line to mark the boundary, a white fence for leaning on, and an outer ring of storm-green pines. The sun is high at 2 p.m. when the game begins; the shadows lengthening, the sounds of bat and ball more distant as the sun slants and the game moves to its close at six. For me the cricket is always sunlit, perhaps because on wet or blustery or blistering days I find something else to do. The players in their creams and streaked white boots lounge on matted pine needles or in the natural armchairs of pine roots polished by years of exposure and a couple of generations of human bottoms. Someone – the one-legged opener? – is sitting, rather grandly, on a deck chair; beyond him, Captain Morry's 1932 Chevy. Its handsome red grille noses the fence. A shadowy someone is in the passenger seat: Mrs Morry? No other women. Wives are present only in the gleaming cream of cricket shirts and pants. And I have my first puzzle: how was my recalcitrant mother persuaded to fuss over cricketing creams in the clatter and steam of her huge Monday boil-ups? My brother tells me that afternoon tea used to be served by the home-team ladies during the twenty-minute break, but now, at the close of the war, there is no afternoon tea and minimal fraternising with the opposition: they have their own strip of boundary, their own pine trees, their own little cluster of spectators. In our cluster there's some moments of clapping, some peaceable ribbing – to a player back after the second ball has spread his stumps, 'Couldn't bear to leave us, Charlie?' – but mainly we watch in silence, and when it is over everyone goes home for the meal we call 'tea.' My family eats at six, but on cricket nights my mother has the meal on the kitchen table at six-thirty sharp. Talk and analysis, if they happen, happen elsewhere.

All this is sixty-plus years gone, but in the wide-open eye of my mind it is yesterday, as luminous, as indisputably actual, as a Manet. But this Manet is framed not in gilt but in swirling vapour trails ...

In those petrol-hungry days cars were work vehicles, used frugally, but surely Carson Carroll's ute was usually there, picking up a couple of other players along the way? Morry always brought the Chev. He'd collect my brothers and their gear where they waited at the corner of Noble Street and Shannon Avenue. As for me, I walked: up to Noble Street, left turn, past the last of the houses and their yodelling dogs, along the bony path scalping the bald hillside, then down the gravel-skid to the river flats, the bridge, Queen's Park, the oval. Those names. 'Geelong' was a peculiar word – I had no notion where it came from – but our street was named for Lord Shannon, our river was the 'Barwon,' and 'Queen's Park' belonged to the dumpy queen with the big feathered hats. In the second half of the '40s Geelong was a small town laced together by sporting clubs which often had a church in the background, not that it mattered. My second brother played under-15s cricket for 'St Matthew's Church of England' without seeing the inside of a church. The Catholic–Protestant division ran bitter and political, but while the purest

Protestants played only between themselves, 'The Catholics' fielded teams in the general senior competition, and when Newtown and Chilwell won the premiership in ... 1947? 1948? ... it was a Catholic team they beat (my older brother making an elegant seventy-plus). Most of the people in the team, like most of the people I knew, seemed to profess nothing beyond a cheerful secularism.

There were no visible class distinctions, either. Pastry cook, dairyman, schoolteacher, clerk, chemist, railway worker, carpenter, cobbler – the team's string of occupations reads like an old-style nursery rhyme. Captain Morry was foreman at the local ropeworks; the ropeworks manager-owner played under his strict captaincy. Carson Carroll, a small, dark, gentle man I suspected of being sweet on my dashing big sister, ran a dairy farm at Fyansford; my big brother's best friend's father ran a pub (the lovely name comes echoing across the river flats: 'The Ocean Child'). Then there were the schoolboys from Geelong High or the Gordon Tech recruited by one of our eager army of 'spotters.' The clubs were short of men by war's end. My big brother, six years older than me, was one of the team's star batsmen when he was still at school, going in at one or two down, often scoring better than fifty and (to my mind) always beautiful to watch. I also remember my scalding envy when my other brother, a mere three years older than me and still wearing short pants, was urgently called to the crease towards the end of a tense match (had someone been hurt?). He can't have been much more than twelve, but he made three, carried his bat, and a handful of years later was one of the club's steadiest batsmen. There was also a long relationship between the club and Geelong College. Even in those days the 'private' schools were their own world of cricket coaches and Saturday matches, but boys from the College (the Hassetts, later Ian Redpath) played for Newtown and Chilwell whenever they could, before they decamped to Melbourne for a more glamorous destiny.

'Hurt.' In those days when, say, a batsman crumpled, everyone came running, then huddled unhappily while a privileged few helped the wounded one from the field and into more expert care. I simply can't get used to the fish-eyed indifference projected these days, with even the men closest standing like logs and everything left to the pros. As for sledging! As for a captain whingeing at an ump's decision! Back then, decorum ruled and umpires were a tribe apart. They might chat briefly with Morry (if they'd met him in the street there'd be handshakes and shoulder-clasps) but at the ground their aloofness protected their authority, which was absolute. There might be lip-tightening at a decision, but never an audible murmur of dissent. Nor do I remember any altercations between players (that would have brought calm Morry running) and no swearing, either, on field or off – or did I, even a junior female, haul an invisible no-swear zone around with me?

Watching, I'd be freshly astounded, as I'd been through season on season of impromptu beach cricket, at the male passion for inventing rules and then for passionately honouring them. The women I knew were infinitely more ... flexible? Devious? They might offer lip service to a rule or a principle, but verbal protestations would adjust comfortably to circumstance. Meanwhile the men would be actively cherishing not only the diamond-cut rules but the thickets of protocols and customs and sanctified memories grown up around them. This was a most durable form of sacred men's business, being produced locally through shared ceremonial action in a specially sanctified space, and consolidated into lore through the slow drip-feed of talk, time and repeated experience, with all this happening inside a democratic male tribe where hierarchy depended a little on age, more on character, and most on God-given talent.

Yet there were, it seemed to me, moral oddities. One example: when our one-legged opener peglegged out to the crease, the opposition would bring on their slow bowler so he couldn't just prop back and whack 'em (he had a great eye) but would be forced to use his mismatched feet. And I worried: was this a fair tactic to use against a man with a wooden leg? Yet it never raised a murmur. Yes, he had only one leg and was therefore allowed a runner, but he fielded usefully (in slips) every week, and every week he earned his place. Of course they should bring on their slow. Anything other would indicate lack of respect.

And now I have to face Mrs Morry. A dear friend of mine insists that her vivid, detailed, emotion-drenched earliest memories are camera-accurate, and I believe her. But I discover some of mine, however vivid, however cherished, are fantasy. I have cheated Mrs Morry. I have evaded or blurred her, when at every match there she would be, sitting very upright in the passenger seat of the Chevrolet, watching the game through the upright windscreen – and keeping immaculate score. As I now know. As I now (almost) remember. What I remembered until yesterday was that I was the one who kept score, but now that my brother has 're-minded' me, I can see her, faintly wavy behind the glass, obdurately there. Perhaps my false memory rests on some crisis occasion, when she was ill, or away, and I was assigned the only female role in the ballet? No. Remembering harder (blinking into the smoking crystal) I see Carson Carroll sitting beside me, a little away from the main group, repeating the numbers, watching my pencil, praising my exactitude. His wrist is in a cast. Carson is the fill-in scorer. Carson is also being kind to a droopy ten-year-old female hanger-on who happens to have a pretty sister. I was never the scorer, not even once – and a private, secret source of self-pride shreds, and whisks away. I think I managed my lonely childhood by imagining myself to be socially invisible: the watcher unwatched, the never-participant observer. Decades too late, I burn with shame to know I was not only seen, but managed, pitied ... But there is no one to complain to. Kind Carson has been dead for years, and my brother has been putting me back in my box for what seems centuries.

The worst of it is that memory once 'corrected' is like fraying silk or a disintegrating ice floe: losing existential integrity, it is opened to decay. 'The Cricket' I loved – my luminous Manet – is diminished now, as a detail flakes away to slither into an undifferentiated past too featureless for human use.

*

There are some enduring legacies. The cricket gave me a safe perch to observe a weekly march-past of ideal ways of being male, from calm reliability through eruptive power to glancing grace. I could assess the attributes desirable in a mate quite as directly as if the pines had been palms and the men in their creams had been leaping and stamping with plumes on their heads and bones through their noses. Cricketing creams are as

elegant a masculine display rig as I've seen, and instead of dancing I was offered a quiet walk to the wicket, the taking of guard,
a light tossing of a red ball, a tensing – and then an intense
concordance of fluent and magnificently unpredictable action.

Somewhere beyond and above us hovered the Australian Test
team, every player a deity with his own distinctive attributes. I
had chosen mine: small, dour Lindsay Hassett, once a useful
bowler, now a middle-order batsman capable of opening if he
had to (I liked him to open). He might seem an improbable
choice, given the presence in the team of, for example, tall, handsome, narcissistic Keith Miller, but my devotion never wavered.

It was based, in part, on delusion, as devotion so often is. I
had somehow persuaded myself that a bat my older brother used
and which I spent many hours grooming had belonged to, had
even been used by, the great Hassett. (I was so solitary and secretive a child I could manage to believe almost anything.) I now
think, or my other brother thinks, that it must have been a
'Hassett bat,' not Hassett's personal own. But I know I went
through the delicate, sensuous business of maintaining it believing it to have been his: oozing on the golden oil, tap-tapping it
tenderly into the silky wood, testing with my fingertips the fine,
tough cord close-wrapping this brave, worn, wonderful, history-
drenched object through which a glorious past sang. I could not
have loved it more had it been wielded at Thermopylae. I think
it was Hassett's dourness, his tenacity, his intense privacy which
lay at the core of my devotion to him. I saw him as a man of
Thermopylae: gallant, isolated, ready to sell his life, but at the
highest price possible.

This heroic identification was reinforced by the vocal theat-
rics of that celebrated cricket commentator, Alan McGilvray, on
that most intimate and insidious form of public communication,
the radio. During my infanthood 'The Cricket' had been a jubilant squawk of 'Rickety Kate!' from the warm brown Bakelite
radio with its warm brown Bakelite smell: a cry unintelligible to
me (I thought 'Kate' must be some kind of jointed doll who fell
over a lot) but instantly meaningful to everyone else – a wicket
had fallen. My brother tells me that when Geelong High School's
end-of-year ball and debutante presentation happened to co-
incide with an overseas Test match, the Palais was wired for

sound, and that when 'Rickety Kate!' came booming out over the dancers the dancing (or the clammy circular shuffling, as I remember it) would stop until the squawk was interpreted, the news digested, the mood adjusted.

I also remember from those days, with access to radios limited, the mournful cry that would come echoing from passing trams, along empty corridors, between houses and gardens: 'What's the score?' And sometimes, just sometimes, an answer, jubilant or glum: 'Four for a hundred and forty-eight, and MILLER'S GONE!' A year or two later and I was a radio addict: *The Mask of Dimitrios*, *The Green Hornet* and (heard vaguely as I ran around and around the outside of the house, banging my palms on my ears to confuse the sound waves) *The Phantom Drummer*, of which the introduction alone – a distant drum, throbbing – reduced me to jelly. And – skulking along the very edge of memory – another marvellously mysterious one: a sahib voice, declamatory, 'I will build my house here!'; a non-sahib voice, tremulous, 'But Sir, the Great Bull Elephant walks here!' … and then some almighty crashings and squealings. The Great Bull Elephant had, presumably, walked.

These were private, close-to-secret pleasures, just me and my radio. 'The Cricket,' turned low to sibilant undulations to appease my unappeasable mother, was communal worship, with four heads bowed before it: my father's shining pate, my brothers' gilded ripples, my lank mouse. Alan McGilvray instructed me why I should love Lindsay Hassett by representing him as the ultimate in reliability and moral poise – 'at the wicket all day, scoring twenty, just what Australia needed, a captain's knock' – yet capable of moments of heart-lifting grace: 'And it's short and Hassett is dancing down the wicket and he's cracked him through the covers for four, glorious shot, glorious shot!' And from the dozens of photographs and the handful of newsreels magically animated by that voice, I would see him dance.

Then came 1948, with 'The Invincibles' touring England, Hassett vice-captain to Bradman and therefore leading the team whenever Bradman was 'resting,' therefore subjected to constant vociferous appraisal. His public elevation saw an end to my private devotion. It is true I also turned fourteen that year. Were strategies for the hunt beginning to replace moral and aesthetic contemplation? Possibly. I confess to a dawning interest in the Geelong College cricket team (through the mists I summon the impassive Easter Island image of the taller opener). But my cricket-forged ideal only went underground. Years later (after, I admit, marrying a non-cricketer) I would name my second son 'Richie' for Richie Benaud's imperturbable possession of self.

I remember those afternoons, and those men, with love. I don't know what scars they bore, because when they were playing cricket they set them aside. I think it was their best selves who played there at Queen's Park, and that is how I remember them.

Today I picked up a DVD from the 'Recently Returned' rack in the local library. It is titled *Classical Footy* and it promises me 'the ultimate collection of footy highlights set to classical music'; 'the greatest marks, goals and physical clashes' of the last thirty years. Only thirty years. No Chicken Smallhorn? No Lindsay White? The cover invites me to use it as 'a marvellous mood-setting background.' A background? I will watch it alone, tonight, with proper formality, and the gods will return, dancing.

Will someone do that for the cricket? Please? I need to see Hassett dance.

Australia: Story of a Cricket Country

In the Rat Room: Reflections on the Breeding House

Gail Bell

For two-and-a-half years, between 1969 and 1971, I spent eight hours per day – minus weekends and holidays – in voluntary confinement with hundreds of caged albino rats. I knew nothing useful about rats before taking the job, very little about vivisection and had not yet begun my student life at the University of Sydney, which owned and operated the animal breeding station. It wasn't until I was older and slightly more switched on that I asked myself the difficult questions that hasten a confrontation with the ethics of playing God.

In many ways it was the perfect job for a young recovering panic merchant. Geographical isolation, hours alone with non-speaking mammals, a heavy door between me and the other primates and a routine to learn and master at my own speed. Nominally, I was a laboratory assistant in a facility that had no lab. The training on offer was of the passed-down-from-wiser-heads variety and I could hope for no piece of paper at the completion of the probation period. Not that I was staking a future in rat wrangling; everyone has to start somewhere and I had my eye on the distant gleam of scientific discoveries. My first sight of the facility and the overwrought fantasies it evoked in my nineteen-year-old self were incentive enough. Like the princess who loves the ugly toad for reasons known only to the wised-up reader, I gazed down on the dark building at the end of a pretty country road and thought: Yes, I can do that.

*

The animal house lay at the base of a rolling down, a corruption of conjoined ox-blood brick buildings as dark as a pre-revolution factory and crowned at the furthest reach by two chimneystacks. Not even the ripening wheat in the adjacent field could offset its graveside gloom.

Feeling stupid in my best frock and shoes and mouth-breathing against the smell, I followed the director along a pathway to the business end of the operation. At the sound of our feet, guinea pigs fled to the safety of bunched-up straw. Closed doors and electrical humming gave a sense of people hiding nearby, of breathing synchronised to footfalls. When the director spoke aloud, he was answered by a sudden chorus of noise, the place waking up to his alarm-clock presence and all that a visit from the man in charge implied. A door swung open anticipating the knock and there was Old Jack ready and beaming. The director handed me over and that was that. I was in.

Jack ran the mouse rooms and knew all the tricks.

'Rodents is rodents,' he said. 'Think of it this way, a rat is just a big mouse.'

Once the director disappeared to the cool privacy of his office, Jack rapidly lost interest in me. After a quick tour of the mouse kingdom he passed me over to Maureen, who was in charge of rats and needed an offsider.

'Better get yourself a pair of skates,' she said, looking down at my shoes. 'No end of orders coming in.' Rats were the big-ticket item that year. I would have my own rat room, my own colonies and my own quotas. Even if the science of animal husbandry flowed like a silent river beneath the work in front of me, I was now a member of the animal-house fraternity and, on the inside, science was a dirty word. Science was what the dills at the university practised. Science was a head-trip. Out here real people did real work.

The other staff were mostly dour men in their twilight years, loners who chose to work in a place where you could keep yourself to yourself and not be bothered by outsiders – a situation favoured by the layout of the enclosures, the locked rooms, the silent corridors, the pens and the open runs. It would be months before I ventured into unexplored territory, turning off one pathway onto another, following the strange hooting sounds that were nothing like those of rodents.

I was too busy acquainting myself with the rat room. Before the introduction of plastic boxes, my rats lived in wire cages stacked in aisles, floor to ceiling, in a windowless room kept at a constant temperature. They chattered and rustled like my father's pigeons, going about their rat routines in the best way they could manage through the wire grilles and barriers to physical contact. I doled out compressed food pellets, filled their water bottles and took away their excrement. For company I played a small portable transistor radio tuned to a top-ten-hits station. It never occurred to me that rats might like classical music, just as it never occurred to me that they might appreciate having their lives enriched by toys or games. These guys were headed for the scalpel if they were lucky, and the torture chamber of drugs or electrodes if they weren't.

On cleaning day I worked my way up and down the aisles, sliding out the trays under each cage, heaping the shit and sawdust into a wheelbarrow using a scraper. And I didn't always avoid tipping the sloppy mess onto my feet. The sweetish fetid smell got into my pores, my hair, my mouth, and never left my clothes. 'Fat lot of good your posh education is in here, eh, lass?' Old Jack liked to say. No amount of trying to set the record straight worked against Jack's idea that I was a stray silvertail landed in the wrong part of town.

The cycle of life plays out quickly for lab rats, with longevity usually only granted to the population kept for reproduction. The breeding males with their disproportionately large testicles had the easiest time of it, sitting out their sullen isolation until the boredom was broken by a fresh virgin dropped into their laps. The females popped out litters after three short weeks, nursed the tiny pink jellybean pups to weaning age, grew protective and worried when their babies were snatched away, then quickly forgot them as a new pregnancy evolved.

We bred Wistars and Sprague Dawleys, both white, both red-eyed in appearance but importantly different in research terms. Mixing the breeding lines was the first thou-shalt-not commandment I learnt. Any rat that hit the ground, no matter how quickly retrieved, was dead meat. Maintaining the integrity of these albino freaks was what we lived for in the rodent rooms. Researchers need clones, not mongrels with idiosyncrasies that can't be factored into their experimental design. Once rats have cycled through twenty generations of brother–sister inbreeding, each individual is 98 per cent the same as the next; after forty cycles the percentage nudges 100.

Six months into the job, the wire cages were dismantled and replaced by plastic boxes. Our rooms became less humid, less smelly, and we agreed that the rats seemed happier. Of course we judged the index of happiness by our own standards. That an animal as social as a rat might prefer mixed company to cleanliness never entered our heads.

I avoided any behaviour that seemed overtly cruel, even though my orientation (as dictated by management) was ruthlessly eugenic. I killed the weak and the lame, the underweight, the crooked of tail, the surplus to needs and the odd aggressive biter. Maureen taught me the 'lift and snap' technique for rat killing, a brutal but effective use of superior human body mass. We cracked their necks as matter-of-factly as breaking eggs during the business of filling an order for twenty Spragues of a certain exact weight for the never-seen professor who transmitted his requests by telephone. The dead bodies went into a box to be collected by Dudley, the taciturn disposer of corpses. Occasionally we had to exterminate a whole bay of rats because of disease or injury or the whim of a superior, and these creatures were thrown into a bin outside the door. When sufficiently full, we poured undiluted chloroform into the tin, clamped on the lid and waited for the scrambling to stop. Dudley told me they burnt quicker with a bit of chloroform to kick things along.

Perhaps my knack for snapping necks without a pang of guilt came down to me in the blood. After his tour of duty in the atomic-bombed ruins of Hiroshima, my young father, needing funds to marry, heard there was work in the killing sheds at the Homebush abattoirs.

The way he tells it, he adapted quickly to the implacable momentum of the slaughterhouse. He hoisted squealing pigs onto upward rising conveyor belts, cut tendons, slit throats, slipped and sloshed in ankle-deep blood. Two thousand pigs on a good day. Once in the gut sheds he chopped the end of his little finger clean off at the first joint. As children we used to hold up the stunted digit and marvel. *How did it happen? Was there a lot of blood? Did you scream?*

My father killed with great dexterity, like an Easter Show woodchopper. Vets were banished from our house in my growing-up years. If the family dog was in the throes of tick-bite he would wrest the animal from our clinging arms, ignore our pitiful cries of 'please, Daddy, don't' and carry the limp pet off down the backyard. In the morning we'd put flowers on the little mound of dirt and despise him for his black heartlessness. On his retirement farm in the high country he had a special shed where he killed and dressed sheep for the table. 'You eat lamb,' he'd say. 'Where do you think it comes from? Outer space?' Good slaughtering was a skill. There were no shortcuts, and never any excuses for cruelty. 'Blokes in a hurry at Homebush,' he'd tell us, shaking his head, 'cut into a beast before it was dead, just to speed up the line. No need for it.'

*

During my years at the animal house, Peter Singer was gestating his 1975 book, *Animal Liberation*. The shift away from disregard for the subjective experience of experimental animals to today's acknowledgement of animal rights (with the accompanying hog-tying grip of ethics committees in tertiary institutions) had everything to do with the movement started by Singer. Once researchers believed that the smaller animals felt no pain; some still hold that belief. But where in nature do we see creatures giving up their lives or limbs with no show of protest? The mouse imperfectly caught in the trap squeals. The fleeing rat struck by a stick cries out in distress. The spider or ant reels and struggles like a drowning person after a whiff of Mortein. Even the fabled lemming tumbling to its death scrabbles its paws at clean air. 'The experimenter who forces rats to choose between starvation and electric shock to see if they develop ulcers (which they do) does so because the rat has a nervous system very similar to a human being's, and presumably feels an electric shock in a similar way,' wrote Singer.

The tenets of 'speciesism' as described by Singer were unknown in the animal house. We bred them, fed them, then shipped them off to the university in a truck, where anything could happen to them and usually did. If rats weren't the ticket for a particular experiment then a few dogs would do, and if dogs failed the criteria then we had (from time to time) gibbons, sourced in Sumatra.

My time at the breeding station was not an Orwellian Room 101 experience. The 'worst thing' in my world had already happened at the hands of some unknown troublemaker who had fired a gun at me one night on a lonely road. Rats presented no threats to my physical or emotional wellbeing; it was strangers and loud noises and cruising cars that excited my adrenaline, not the rustle of tiny feet in sawdust. I enjoyed my work and gave no thought to the active part I played in facilitating the sacrifice of rodent lives to the engine rooms of science.

However, I was affected in a very different way when I ventured out of the cocoon of the rat room. At the far end of the animal house, behind doors, I discovered a chamber of horrors: dogs brought back from the university dental and surgical departments, sad creatures, sadder than pound dogs, with strange additions to their natural morphology. Skin grafts shaped like handles sewn to the torso between their hips. Missing teeth. Misshapen throats. Some went back and forth to Sydney until they were no longer wanted or suitable, and then they were euthanised – that soft, seductive word implying a gentle roll into sleep. From the dog pens, the carcasses went straight to the incinerators. The smell on the wind could make you sick to your stomach.

In the same valley as the animal house the university had an agricultural outpost. When the killing and the burning flesh got too much, I'd take my lunch break outside and watch the undergraduates in dungarees move along the rows in what looked like some version of hippy heaven, stopping to do the graceful work of spreading an ear of wheat on the palm of a hand to take its dimensions. In the way that compartmentalising allows us to entertain both sinister and benign views of the same predicament, I would finish my sandwich, take a last wistful look at the sun-baked fields then go back to the rats.

When I picked up my studies again and handled rodents in pharmacology practicals in the early 1970s, I participated in what I now see were unnecessary demonstrations of superior firepower to prove outcomes that were already known. Classes of clumsy students wielding syringes (some intent on cruelty; some not meaning any harm but effectively prolonging the agony with repeated timid pokes) lunged at defenceless mice as part of their training, purely to confirm information that had been on the record for centuries. Morphine dulls pain. Diuretics make you pee. Digoxin slows heart rate.

I freely acknowledge a case of retrospective guilt here. At the time I was trying to get my grade average up.

*

With age comes reckoning. And more, if we are to believe findings published in a recent edition of *Psychology and Aging*. 'Emotional intelligence' peaks as humans move into their sixties. Older brains appreciate the 'sadness' of sad situations because the 'detached appraisal' switch that was employed in youth breaks down. This is interpreted as an evolutionary uncoupling of pathways and network systems that were built up in the storms of shaping a life out of the materials to hand and that are now largely redundant. Without battles to fight, the 'brain on ice' (Lenin's words) begins to thaw out.

I come back to a winter memory of my father tethering his kelpies in the overturned shell of an old water tank, the high country wind cutting through the holes like frozen spears, the dogs huddled, flat, my father contradicting my city-girl fussing with a farmer's-wisdom counter-attack about how working dogs *expect* to be left out in the cold. Now in his eighties, Dad has a fox terrier (traditionally a ratting dog) permanently on his lap. He spends $800 on vet bills, wraps the dog up in various coats when a cloud passes over the sun and thinks I'm hard for fending off its yappy, heel-nibbling carry-on each time I visit.

He remembers me bringing home mice from the animal house. Boutique colours created on the quiet by Old Jack. He remembers them breeding 'like rabbits' and escaping into the neighbourhood. Maverick exercises like that would never play today. Ethics committees employ an animal welfare advocate to argue the case for lab animals. Rodents are given enriched environments, toys, the opportunity to forage, to socialise, to play. The numbers of small mammals (millions) in research projects are being steadily reduced. Compromises have been struck. Welfarists (who regard a primate to be as important as a mouse) challenge old assumptions about the perception of pain in animals at the same table as scientists who make the point that, while lab animals cannot give consent, it can at least be said that being purpose-bred is a superior starting point to being shipped in from shelters or pounds. More effort is made to add analgesics to the list of ingredients in an experimental design. And, not before time, science is embracing alternatives: fruit flies, locusts, mathematical modelling, computer simulations, tissue cultures.

*

Occasionally, a bush rat will climb up to the high platform of the bird feeder at the bottom of my garden to nibble at the husks of seed left out for wild birds. Its agility is astonishing. Up a tree trunk, out onto a thin limb that sways under its weight, a leap, a grasp, an acrobatic upside-down twist and there it is, hoovering up the leavings of the last pair of lorikeets. At night, possums do the same thing. If we have guests we turn on the floodlight to watch and smile at their 'caught in the act' expression. But possums are one thing and rats are another. My father, no lover of rats, puts out baits, which he knows I hate. He has no sympathy for my argument that tricking an animal into swallowing a slow, painful poison is worse than a quick execution by trap.

I rarely get worked up about wild rats. They know how to play the game; their ability to operate successfully under the radar of human domination is legendary. They shadow our lives like thieves and panhandlers, foraging in the foodstores and drainage systems of human settlement, silently stalking the grain tiller, the harvester, the storeman, the cook and the disposers of kitchen slops. And that's the good part.

Where I see red is when unnecessary exploitation of lab rats is pushed under my nose. Recently on the TV news two scientists from the University of Sydney smiled into the camera and broke a good news story, which boiled down to something like: we have produced a batch of happy rats by giving them oxytocin, a feel-good cuddly drug that makes them more social, and more responsive to each other. The impetus? The rationale? To then trial the drug in humans with social anxiety disorder. I was struck by a kind of fury at the way the message was lobbed into my living room. Social anxiety disorder? The Big Pharma–invented condition that only a drug can cure? 'Creating' rats who like to be with each other, want to touch, stroke, circle around each other like uninhibited kids with energy to burn and no one to set limits? Rats do that anyway, without being injected. No need to pump a new mother rat full of oxytocin. She's making her own. She's soaking in it. Rats are social creatures. Even lab rats under artificial lights will call to each other.

I divert the conversation with my father away from Ratsak to the ever-expanding horizons of science. It's true that the drugs that keep my parents (and me) going were developed in labs, and that, necessarily, animal sacrifices were made. My father wonders how I can argue against research when we need to get on top of diseases but, of course, I am not making that argument. I am pleading for better research based on better science. Badly designed experiments reflect badly on us all. I once listened, transfixed, to a discussion on 'ethics and advocacy – insights into animal experimentation' on ABC Radio National, paying particular attention to a revelation made by Mike Calford concerning a meta-analysis undertaken at the National Stroke Research Institute: 8500 animal studies into the effectiveness of particular drugs in the treatment of ischemic stroke arrived at no useful outcome due to bad design. 'That's a lot of research energy and a lot of animals wasted, isn't it?' asked the host, Natasha Mitchell. To which the professor replied: 'It certainly is.' The sweetener in this story was the willingness of the scientists involved to go back to the drawing board and rethink their methods.

Montaigne's essay 'On Cruelty' has a sentence that presses on the sore point at the heart of animal experimentation: 'I ... cannot bear to hear the hare squealing when my hounds get their teeth into it, even though I enjoy the hunt enormously.'

'Science is about the hunt,' I say to Dad.

But the hunt need not be the blood sport it was in the past. If scientific research is lionhearted enough to spare the rat in favour of the tissue culture when such a choice is viable, then why not speed up the approval of alternatives and respectfully exit the rat room?

The Monthly

Death and Distraction

Helen Elliott

Her subject is distraction. She's written a book about it, published by one of those intimidating American academic houses. She's American and has that attractive twangy accent I can never place. South coast? Boston? With her, though, it's not about the accent. She's very, very smart and the Radio National interviewer is very, very taken with her.

So am I. Google my name and 'distracted' will be riveted to it. I was about to do some reading when that twang lured me across the kitchen tiles, nearer to the radio. Witty, that capacity to morph into your subject. But she's not just a witty snare; she's saying fresh things about a scrappy and infinite topic. I unscrew the still hot one-cup espresso machine, empty the grounds into the compost and, despite my recent swearing off at two, make my third coffee for the day. While I wait for it to spit and gurgle at me I empty the dishwasher. I can't rush out with the overflowing compost, because I'll miss what she is saying and already I don't want to miss a word.

She's making the interviewer laugh. *Oh-oh-oh-oh!* He has an elegant lilt and black lines of T.S. Eliot slide down my peripheral vision. Was it *The Waste Land*? How many years since I've read that? I still have my original copy. I think.

They're talking about language, about the anachronistic meaning of the word 'distraction,' the way it was used for around

300 years. Not so long ago it meant being *pulled away* or being *pulled in pieces*. That's what she says. Yes! I remember! I can even see the book, *Latin Roots*, with the cracked cover in a weird black-green colour that made my mouth dry. That book was in some shape when I got it third-hand, after two boys. The Latin root *distrahere* means to pull asunder.

There was, she says, a recent American survey of people working in offices that attempted to track their attention spans. What? The results must be wrong. I tear some paper from the roll and wipe down the bench. After seventeen years it never looks clean. The survey indicated that workers are interrupted every three minutes. Every three minutes? And if they're doing something that requires detailed attention it might take as long as twenty-five minutes to get back into it. Workers spend 28 per cent of their day being distracted.

I'm the cartoon cat that's fallen on its head. Twenty-eight per cent? Exclamation marks bounce off my eyeballs. Companies are interested in this study, because the time their workers waste costs billions every year.

Then there's this: she says – or the interviewer, who seems to have read her book, says – that it isn't just outside interruptions that cause these minor bleeds every three minutes. The workers distract themselves. Their email pings; their mobile drums; they need to look up a result or Facebook, or monitor an online discussion.

She's set me off like a metronome. How right she is; concentrated work is not possible in offices. I know this because there have been times in my life when I've had to work in those glass and steel cylinders that shimmer on the horizon when I take the freeway from my snug little suburb into the city. As I get closer they take shape, looming like independent colonies. One of them has pointed ears *à la* Batman, and every time I near the end of the freeway I expect an image of Jack Nicholson playing the Joker. He's an actor I dislike. Still. People who know about architecture tell me that the Batman building is a fabulous example of creative architecture.

That's what they tell me, but I'm cautious about rushing to admire the newly made buildings we live and work in, especially these public buildings, facades agitated with bling, angles calculated against serenity. When I'm in them I don't feel awed or uplifted. Disconsolate and nervy, more like it.

If I think about all the people who work in these buildings, all these individuals going about their one precious life as ardently as I go about my one precious life, I feel a distant but glacial prick. It's closely related to that stupefied panic I have whenever I've watched archival footage from World War II, where lines of people are standing on the edge of trenches waiting to be shot. Or being shot. *Bang. Oblivion.* Each separate soul. Just like me. Who were they? What were they feeling, thinking? Disbelief? Acceptance? Distraught? The word that used to be an alternative to distract. These days I can't look at anything violent.

I was thirteen when I read Anne Frank's diary and it left an invisible tattoo. I turned sixteen, seventeen, eighteen, sometimes delighting in myself and in the world, just as she did, so sometimes I thought about Anne and about how she never knew what it was to turn sixteen. How could this happen? That there was once a girl exactly my age, just as dazzled with life, expecting to live just as I expected to live … and then she didn't. *This happened.* I knew Anne Frank. I knew what she was feeling but, despite my empathy, my *famous* empathy, I'll never understand what she faced. That's like trying to pocket the wind.

What luck that I can work from home, where no one can distract me every three minutes.

I turn off the gas and pour my coffee into a small white bone-china cup that has gold laurel leaves, handpainted, winding around the rim. It's called Golden Laurel and was made in Derbyshire when dishwashers were a pair of slim hands in pink rubber gloves. She's using the word *hopscotching* to describe how we navigate the new, technological world. *Fragmentation, sound bites, split-focus* all sound lumpy compared to *hopscotching*. Hopscotching cascades with images: children, barelegged, short tartan – tartan! – skirts flying as they leg across the pattern to wherever the tor has landed. I used to love the chance and the exhilaration of that game.

The interviewer just called her Maggie, but I missed the introduction and have no idea who she is, other than that she has written the distracting book they are discussing. The interviewer is galvanised by the subject, so much so that he forgets himself, and the whole thing threatens to dissolve as he shambles in like an intellectual elephant just as she's starting to say something. *Oh-oh-oh-oh!* Do shut up. He's a brilliant and learned man, but I've listened to him for years and I know his patterns of thought and I know – and mostly agree with – his opinions. (We're both calcifying.) Because of this I'm always tolerant of his foibles, but today I'm sailing towards impatient. Maggie has only twenty minutes. Let her speak!

I bang my cup down in its saucer and the golden laurels threaten to crack.

She starts speaking about intellectual restlessness. Her thesis, as far as I can gauge, is that while technology is amazing and helpful (*tonic*, she says – lovely), the way we use it is changing the physical capacities of our brains. As she speaks my own brain highlights in mercury. Neuroscientists are coming to believe that our constant hopscotching may be physically altering wedges of our brains in such ways that we are no longer capable of reflection or of the deep thinking that results in difficult problem-solving. She cites two things that cause my brain – currently in a humming state of orange alert – to skid to a halt. One is that fifteen-year-old American children rate very low on critical thinking (although, hooray! Australian children perform far better) and are lining up for huge doses of adult ADHD medications. The other is that a high percentage of longstanding internet users in America did not realise that paid content is common online.

She means, I imagine, marketing, advertising masquerading as independent scholarship, something I expected people automatically assumed every time they read on the net. I never trust it face-up, particularly the first arrival from Google, but she is saying, what? No! Over 60 per cent of people, of *educated* people, read everything without scepticism, without doubting what the professional, visually attractive text says. But I suppose that in a world in love with the image, the text *is* the image. So if a piece of text looks attractive it has a greater chance of being believed.

Like people? What about all those studies done confirming that pretty people of both sexes do better in every way in the world: rail against it if you like, but it seems we're hardwired for prettiness.

When I was a child I believed everything I read. Print – black marks haunting white paper, transforming themselves into indelible truth – was my daily miracle-in-progress.

As I listen I'm trying to get a mark out of the kitchen bench with an organic cleaner that is worse than useless on seventeen-year-old white laminate. Was it the raw beetroot I grated last night? I'm going to use more raw beetroot because I read some-where – or maybe I heard it somewhere? – that it is one of those foods. You know. Foods packed with all these as-yet-unidentified antioxidants and enzymes that prevent or cure cancer. My friend has cancer. Should I mention raw beetroot? Everyone gives her advice. I think she might die of advice. Or goji berries. I saw them in the supermarket today. My sister-in-law's sister reckons goji juice saved her life, but she didn't have cancer. She had ennui. You don't turn your face to the wall and die of that these days.

Lobotomise? She, Maggie, said that? My shoulders slump. Is she, too, becoming a cliché: Jack Nicholson again, this time just crazy, as in *One Flew Over the Cuckoo's Nest*? (Why is Jack Nicholson embedded – *embedded!* – in my head like a sinister ectoplasm?) Maggie is saying that by switching tasks constantly, by this inces-sant mental and even physical movement, we are in danger of lobotomising our brains. A lobotomised world is lying in wait. Another dark age.

She's not talking about one dark age, nothing one-dimen-sional about this, but about all the dark ages through history that were often brought about by an intense technological revo-lution. Our cultural habit, as we lose literacy, is to turn to more technology. What did she just say? Collective forgetting?

The art historian (and endearing snob) Kenneth Clark says that the hallmark of civilisation is its claim to permanence.

I'm listening hard because, despite the cliché, what she says is exhilarating. I feel like a code-cracker. Bletchley, here I come. I hadn't even known there was a Greek dark age. Of 500 years. Five hundred? I try to screw that down into memory as I rub at the beetroot stain, which I now see is going to remain a memory for as long as the house is standing.

Maggie believes – and she has excellent research from the best universities, to back her up – that our new skimming habits of mind are destroying and undermining brain function at this deeper level. We no longer have the ability to wrestle with texts and finally will not be able to solve complex problems. She is speaking about the architecture of the brain, of how it requires a keystone and then careful building. The keystone she calls attention. As she speaks, I see it exactly. ATTENTION. In rich, uppercase orange.

The neuroscientists who have been studying nothing but attention for the past decade believe that it is an organic thing, in the same way that our circulatory or respiratory systems are organic. They have isolated three separate but interacting networks – mental processes – at the centre of their subject.

One is focus, the spotlight on whatever is at hand; the second is awareness of the details of what it is; and the third, and most important, is an executive cortex, putting into action the learning. After each learning activity the brain alters physically.

I am curved across the bench, chin resting on hands, head drooping close to the radio. Listening. Last time I listened like this it was to hear the fistula doctor working in Ethiopia, Catherine Hamlin, the only contemporary woman who could be a saint. She shook me up so much that for months after I wanted to offer up my silly life to some higher cause. That was a few years ago. I never give the radio all my attention. If I am in the kitchen, the bathroom or even the bedroom and want to listen to the radio, I always make the most of time, *make the most of time!* and do something practical. Cleaning in the kitchen and bathroom; taking the clothes from the chair and folding them away if I am in the bedroom. I enjoy order.

I used to listen to the radio as I cooked, but for the past few years I've noticed that the concentration required means that I only half-hear the radio. Now I listen, half-listen, to music. I've accepted that multi-tasking, or as Maggie calls it, multi-skilling, is admirable. In a complicated and teeming life I took for granted that it is the only way to be effective – unless, of course, living in squalor doesn't worry you. Multi-tasking is a way of controlling time by layering it. Making the most. But in the layering ATTENTION starts to crumble.

What's this? Connectivity soup? Now there's a metaphor that sings. It seems that although we're more connected than ever, we're more isolated than ever. The critical points Maggie pursues in her book are the need to pay attention to our intellectual selves and to our relationships. She suggests that if we cannot think deeply, we cannot relate deeply. With email and Facebook, with this instant capacity to connect electronically, we're no longer interested in the less thrilling but deeper, and perhaps calmer, relationships. Round and round we swim, twinkling our little lights at one another, in love with the noise and exhilaration of the moment but disabled when we find we want to explore more profound places. She touches on the lack of physicality in relationships and I think of the fractional chill whenever I come across one of those smiley faces in an email: antidotes to emotional intelligence.

Maggie's twenty minutes are up and the interviewer parachutes into the next topic, which sounds like yet another exposé of American nefariousness over the past decade. I'm sure it's all true and I'm sure I'll agree with whoever is doing the exposing, but I don't want to listen. I just don't want to *know*. Being righteously outraged is exhausting.

I rinse my cup. Do I pay enough attention to living?

Griffith Review

On Not Writing

Morris Lurie

Hergesheimer needs a haircut. A previous barber boasts bad breath and a shouty manner, let's not even enter the area of artistic incompetence, Hergesheimer suffering such scissors for three even four foolish years, not to give offence, you understand, concern for the feelings of others imbibed at the mother's knee, decency, duty, an overflowing sensitive heart, maybe habit and laziness also to somehow factor in, except finally enough, goodbye and good riddance, an alternative barber engaged, a brother of the first, as it happens, plus his son operating the adjoining chair, nice kid too, from either or both you'll get a guaranteed good job, never mind it's a far-flung suburb to put it mildly from where Hergesheimer now entrusts his head.

Wait.

The story hasn't even started yet.

And it's not about the barber anyhow.

Either of them.

Any of the three.

Because what we've got here is the device of Hergesheimer being made to travel a certain road on as it happens a particular hirsute pursuit so that his eye may chance in passing upon a certain building, a particular house.

Of split-second optical occupancy only its sufficient requirement.

Done.

He's stung.

Here it comes.

In full wide-screen Proustian retrieval and reminder.

The whole story.

Bang.

Just like that.

But let's have our Hergesheimer take his seat at the barber's, pretend an interest in football as the clippers do their work, eyebrows? yes please, nice to see, as he stands up, finished, cover cloth whipped away, shoulders whisked, he can still produce a creditable amount, the barber going for the broom, nothing to be ashamed of there.

And he could of course refresh or reinforce that initial optical occurrence on his way back home but he doesn't need to.

Once is plenty.

What's to study?

More than enough.

*

Hergesheimer, you may have surmised, our Hergesheimer, you might have appreciated, my Hergesheimer is a writer.

Two hundred stories.

For adults and children.

Three dozen published books.

The *New Yorker* used to have a rule about not having stories about writers, maybe still does.

You had to make them artists or architects or acrobats.

Well, this is not a story.

Nor is Hergesheimer really Hergesheimer.

Regard him, if you will, as naught but a necessary veil.

Of flimsiest transparency.

Avoid direct sunlight.

Cool iron only.

Wash as wool.

I trust I have made myself clear.

In that respect at least.

*

So he comes home.

Sits himself down.

Feels inside himself, in growing excitement, that unmistakable buzz.

Watches his brain pushing it this way and that.

Weighs phrases.

Tests sentences.

Road-tests alternate openings.

Can barely sit still such is the jumping blood inside him.

Maybe even begins to scribble, on whatever paper, in pencil, in pen.

As suddenly to stop.

Naah.

What for?

I don't need to do this.

I've given up writing.

I've done it enough.

I don't write any more.

*

Let's call him Zeigler.

A Mr Zeigler.

Couldn't make a go of it, whatever he tried.

A wife, a child, mouths, expenses.

A brother, however, in America, he said, at last, at least, a ray of possible light.

It had to be better, how could it be worse?

He would sail himself first, he would see, he would bring over then his wife, his child.

So he sailed.

And a minute later he was back.

A rich man.

*

So here for your edification is a certain summer night, a particular Sunday; I am somewhere around ten years old.

Don't worry about Hergesheimer, he doesn't exist yet, there isn't yet the need.

Where we live, my mother, my father, my grandfather (Dad's father), my sister and me, is in a little rented maisonette – now there's a cute word if ever – with a low brick front fence you can sit on and a street light directly outside.

Friends of the family are visiting, have gathered, got together, assembled, dropped in, have had tea inside, now they're sitting on the front fence, some of them, some on our kitchen chairs my mother has carried out.

Moths dash around the street light.

Mr Zeigler is holding forth.

A poverty! he cries. A darkness! Where his brother lives in two black rooms, you look up through bars, the feet of people in the street walking on your head!

Not even in Europe you saw such a thing.

And every night my brother falls to his knees, prays to God, his boss should live another day, he will still have tomorrow a job.

Mr Zeigler, not a smoker, lights a cigarette.

Exactly what manner of business the brother's boss operates I can now only speculate, it must have been mentioned, whatever, a factory, into which Mr Zeigler by his brother is successfully pleaded, is employed there for five minutes, work it out for yourself, a ship one way, by aeroplane the other, here he is back.

His wife, a small woman, by a fur coat wrapped around.

Their child, his daughter, in the best school enrolled.

A house of latest style ordered and built.

Should we worry about the brother?

Back in America.

What happened to him.

*

All that.

Imagine.

All that.

Naah.

And quietly, quietly, the buzz dies away.

Except it didn't.

Because I wrote that story.

Land of Opportunity.

Excellent title, if I say so myself.

Written by me, you understand, not by Hergesheimer.

Hergesheimer not yet even imagined, certainly in no way required.

This is the me living in London in the so-called Swinging Sixties doing egg and chips in a ratty bedsitter writing stories every second minute trying to stay somehow alive.

Which I did.

As you can see.

My seven expatriate years.

To come home then.

And drive to have a haircut down a certain road past a particular house to remind me of that story my London literary agent of that time had advised me was unsaleable which naturally I believed and so immediately threw away.

No copy kept.

Possibly foolish.

Whatever.

Bedsitter days.

Done.

So to imagine that story in resurrection now, its subsequent history if not actually included would howsoever skirted inescapably cast its besmirching shadow on in many ways an otherwise quite sterling chap.

And deeper.

On a complicit community.

Blacker.

On, even, my own mum and silent dad.

*

A lie must be endlessly reiterated, the truth need be stated just once.

Discuss.

*

Let's lighten up here, let me give you a little history, a sort of slide show, if you will, an illustrated for-instance, a happy example of a gratefully accepted, eagerly bowed-to beneficial buzz.

Something to do with computers is how it began, I recall, the initial glimmer, the instigating throb.

Something to do with robots.

Something to do with I'm not quite sure exactly what.

A boy in a tree?

A furious father?

A rarely seen tropical bird?

Which I pushed around, all these vague imponderables, for the better part of maybe a month, if not longer, could be even two.

Which don't see as frustrated.

Or imagine as flummoxed.

Certainly in no way stalled or stymied or vexed.

In fact, quite the opposite.

Exactly the reverse.

Paper in the typewriter.

A heading.

What I Know So Far.

Was it enough?

Was I ready?

Actually, the opposite.

Quite the reverse.

Impossible now not to begin.

So here's a boy in a tree imagining himself in the deepest jungle suddenly sighting a believed-extinct exotic bird which, for the benefit of all mankind, he is about to shoot with a tranquilising dart, and just as he lifts the blowgun to his lips (the cardboard inner of a toilet roll), his mother calls him in to tea.

And he's just starting on his spaghetti when his writer father comes in all furious because his computer has just gobbled the best page of writing he's ever done in his whole life and the last thing he needs is to see his son eating spaghetti in a disgusting way, go to your room!

And?

Well, the boy falls asleep, never mind injustice, never mind no tea, and the next thing he knows there's a single-eyed shiny silver robot standing at the foot of his bed demanding something which the boy doesn't linger to discuss but is out the window in a flash, the robot in hot pursuit.

And?

What happens then?

I haven't got the faintest idea.

I've been sitting here writing since nine in the morning and look it's five o'clock.

I need a walk.

Which I take.

Here I go.

And somewhere on that walk, maybe even just five steps from the front door with the walk not even properly started yet, I suddenly know exactly what's going to happen in the next chapter.

As again the next walk.

And the next walk.

And the walk after that.

Wait a minute.

Is this just some made-up-as-you-go-along nonsense I'm writing here?

A boy in his pyjamas running in the night pursued by what exactly?

The boy knocks on doors.

An old schoolteacher gives him a piece of chalk.

The village junkman gives him a meal.

A girl from school hands him a flower.

And still the robot comes.

What to do?

Where to go?

How to hide?

It's five o'clock.

Time for a walk.

Here comes the next bit.

Here's the boy climbing the stairs to the room above the garage where he's been strictly forbidden to set so much as a single toe.

KEEP OUT! it says on the door.

GO AWAY!

NO CALLERS OR VISITORS WHATSOEVER!!

NO INTERRUPTIONS BROOKED UNDER ANY CIRCUM-
STANCES!!!!

THIS MEANS YOU!!!!!

Yes, this is it.

The most secret space.

The most private place.

His father's writing room.

Where the boy, pursued by his father's fury, to cut to the
chase, wishes to offer his leaky fountain pen, if that's of any use,
to his computer-bound dad.

Fury?

Or should that be envy?

The child the father of the man and all that?

I'll leave you to unravel the symbolism.

I wasn't aware of any myself.

I was just abuzz.

*

I find a publisher.

I sign a contract.

The book comes out.

I fully expect it to change the world.

How can you write a book not believing that?

Why would you bother?

*

*If you sing a song a society wants you to sing, you will clank with med-
als to your foul grave.*

Write on one side of the paper only.

Neatness counts.

*

This is a suicide note.

Joseph Hergesheimer was an American writer of great popularity who fell from favour, couldn't understand it, didn't know why, bellyached about it endlessly to his pal Mencken, refused to go gently, if you like, into that good night, is quite forgotten now.

I appropriated his name to pass unnoticed, as it were, amongst you.

Oh, I see! an ex-mother-in-law once unmasked me, I think when I was bellyaching about such-and-such a book of mine not being published. Everyone's out of step but our Johnny!

I took it as the highest of praise.

Or I'm lying on my shrink's couch and bellyaching about a children's book I've written which says the world is a welcoming place and no one will publish it and there are nine million books which say the opposite and I don't try to stop them so why do they stop me? and my shrink says, Because your book makes their books wrong.

You can see why a writer might need a disguise.

Enough bellyaching.

My first book was grabbed by the first publisher who saw it, read and accepted, three days flat.

My most recent fretted for fourteen years before it was allowed entry into the public sun.

Excuses, both of them.

Or that this story took an hour to write, one draft, perfect, didn't need to change a single word, that one eight buckets of sweat and four reams of paper, the better part of a year.

So?

I've worked stricter than office hours, dawn to dusk, midnight and beyond, months and years, no days of rest.

Blocks.

Stoppages.

Fallen beyond fallow into arctic silence.

Even said, finally, Hey, I've quit.

Do you believe that?

Do I?

It's possible?

The irritation, that defining singularity that makes a writer, a writer of salt (and God help me I don't want to know and certainly not talk about any other kind) can be made to just go away?

Get serious.

A writer is writing even when he's not writing, maybe even more then, even if he never writes again.

Got it?

Class dismissed.

Meanjin

The Whisperer in the Jungle

Maria Tumarkin

A man with money, tenure and an embarrassment of literary and academic prizes, still young and almost good-looking – by the standards of academia – whose books have been translated into more than twenty languages and whose equally accomplished wife is resolutely by his side (she would be ready to take the bullet for him in the second-last act), initiates what should be his own swift downfall. The man's moral incontinence and the jealousy he feels for his peers (who, if anything, are trailing behind him in this imaginary race that never lets him rest), together with the illusion of safe anonymity that the internet provides for those not inclined to concern themselves with its basic mechanics, provoke him to go on a rampage of sorts. His instruments are blunt; the turns of phrase he uses to savage his peers would be shameful for most, let alone for a man who holds himself in forbiddingly high regard (and no, not without reason) as a writer. In some other time, his self-addressed evocation of intellectual immortality on Amazon.com – 'I hope he writes forever' – would have haunted him for what would feel like forever.

But not in our merciful day and age. Instead the man sends his supercharged lawyer out on a quick reconnaissance mission, and when that fails he puts his wife forward (or let's say she willingly goes forward, best not to assume too much here), and then when *that* fails he makes his confession ('Yes, it was me') and blames his behaviour on the latent powers of Stalin, the all-powerful antihero of his latest work, diagnosing himself with vicarious trauma by osmosis. Not even six months later, with unspecified damages paid out and a few months of 'sick leave' allowing the man to momentarily excuse himself from the spotlight, he hits back with another book, a book that makes enough people in the right places remember he is 'one of the finest historians of our age,' until the whole humiliating 'incident' begins to feel like a slip-up, a regrettable lapse of conduct and judgement, the kind of thing that could, at a stretch, happen to the best of us …

*

The first and only time I saw British historian Orlando Figes in person was at the Melbourne Writers' Festival in 2008. He was in town to promote *The Whisperers*, his just-released and already much lauded big book on people's private lives under Stalin. Wisely, the festival organisers paired him with Robert Dessaix, Australia's most accomplished Russophile. A writer I admired (Dessaix) in conversation with a historian I was intent on liking (Figes): this had to be good. I dragged along a friend of mine, a Russian Jew like me, too familiar with Figes's subject matter not to be sceptical about the value of going along but prepared to be worn down by my protestations. 'It will be worth it,' I promised, basing my certainty on – what? I cannot tell you now. But I must have been sufficiently convincing, or excited, or desperate for her company.

Melbourne is a place where you notice well-dressed people, and that afternoon a disproportionate number of them were seated inside the Capitol Theatre on Swanston Street, which was as close to full as I had ever seen it. Not far from us a man in his seventies wore a bow tie, a reminder that it was still possible to feel a sense of occasion at a writers' festival, no matter if they are as commonplace now as sales at struggling department stores. And there was, I had to admit, something deeply appealing about the idea of looking at a stage with two men on it – two middle-aged men without dancing shoes, with no swaying back-up singers, with not a baton between them – and feeling yourself ready to be blown away.

Up on that Capitol Theatre stage, too big and well lit for a conversation, the youthful-looking professor of history sat like a man who did not expect to get even remotely uncomfortable, leaning back in his chair with his legs crossed leisurely, well beneath the knees, as if they'd need never go hard and flat on the floor in search of firmer ground. Next to Figes, Dessaix seemed barely to occupy a third of his chair. There was an alertness about Dessaix, an axis of concentration connecting his eyes to his body, as if he knew deep down that every public event, however well groomed, has a kernel of chaos inside it and he was ready for chaos, looking forward to it even. I closed my eyes, not wanting my mind to be distracted by Figes's maestro pose, wanting only to listen. But the voice – so clearly habituated to hearing itself in a room of awestruck silence – that voice was equally disconcerting.

On a small table beside Orlando Figes was what looked like a glass of white wine. (My memory, most likely unfairly, omits a picture of a similar glass by the side of Robert Dessaix.) Maybe it wasn't wine, but the glass certainly looked the part, and in the course of that afternoon session Orlando Figes would bring it slowly to his lips, appearing to savour its contents, and I'd feel – virtually every time this happened – a small stabbing in my heart. Figes was talking about a book he'd based on the life stories of 500 Soviet families who had endured a monster of a century. Yet he had the air of the star guest at a dinner party, and I could see no sign of a man, not on that stage at least, whose soul was aching for the country he had spent decades thinking and writing about or for the people who had let him deep into their hearts and homes, into all that was devastating, heroic and unspoken in their family histories.

After ten minutes I reached out and put my hand on my friend's hand. I was afraid to look her in the face.

My friend and I, just by virtue of having been born in the Soviet Union, knew that the sweeping statements being hurled with overwhelming certainty from that stage were crude, conveniently mangled and phrased cheaply for effect, but it was something else that made us ill, a question. How could a person write a book about *this* kind of history and not have his heart even a little bit broken? Dostoyevsky's 'the soul of another is a dark forest' is a warning not to assign any facile transparency to the interior lives of others, and it is a warning I have always taken to heart, but that does not stop me remembering clearly what I saw that afternoon – Orlando Figes talking about the people whose lives he'd described in *The Whisperers* not as fellow human beings remarkable and heartbreaking for what they had witnessed and endured, but as curious creatures exhibiting fascinating behaviours under freakish socio-historical conditions. The book itself, whatever its flaws, does not have that anthropological tone. Yet the man, more naked on that stage than he imagined himself to be, showed no deep species affinity for his subjects. I struggle for the word to describe this Figesian quality, and if arrogance is indeed the word, then it is the sort of arrogance that extended well beyond the subject matter, well beyond Robert Dessaix (every bit Figes's equal) and that Capitol Theatre audience. It extended to the practice of history-writing itself.

There was something uncontained about this arrogance, something that could not be kept in check, a compulsion to show off that was adolescent in its thrusting look-at-me-ness quality and decidedly unprofessorial. 'Zhenya,' he said, when conversation turned to the much-admired writer Evgenia Semyonovna Ginzburg, survivor of eighteen Gulag years, half a century Figes's senior and dead three decades. In Russian, you use formal first names and patronymics when speaking of adults with whom you do not have a close personal relationship, particularly if they are older or deceased, especially if they happen to be a distinguished public figure such as Evgenia Semyonovna Ginzburg. Yet Figes called her Zhenya – informal, familiar Zhenya – as if he were an intimate of any Soviet intellectual of his choosing, dead or alive. People in the audience were, on the whole, unfamiliar with Russian language conventions. But when I turned to look at my friend, there was a flame in her eyes.

Towards the end of that session, Orlando Figes mentioned the all-night conversations he'd had in Russia – the kind of conversations you never get to have anywhere else. It was a moment of humility and tenderness. He took it back almost instantly, throwing in at the very end: 'Maybe it's all the vodka.'

The audience laughed. My friend stared at the floor.

'Well,' said Robert Dessaix, 'I don't drink. And I have never had conversations like that anywhere else.'

*

Do you want to know what my problem is?

We have created a monster – and there are many more out there with no shortage of chairs from which to hold forth in public and no shortage of publics ready to drink in every word. The man who had it in him cowardly to attack, bully, threaten and then hide behind others, pushed not by desperation or personal misfortune but by some kind of existential greed, was already there on that Melbourne stage a year and a half before the scandal broke. He was there fully formed, that anonymous reviewer who would haplessly, as if by half a fig leaf, cover his identity with the pseudonym 'Historian' and then rip into the books of his peers, or his direct competitors, if you do indeed accept the premise that public intellectuals think of their subjects the way drug dealers think of their street corners:

Robert Service, history professor at the University of Oxford: 'Awful … curiously dull.'

Rachel Polonsky, who a few years before had unfavourably reviewed one of Figes's earlier works: 'The sort of book that makes you wonder why it was ever published.'

Kate Summerscale, winner of the Samuel Johnson Prize (for which *The Whisperers* was short-listed): 'Oh dear, what on earth were the judges thinking?'

Orlando Figes, history professor at Birkbeck College, University of London: 'Leaves the reader awed, humbled yet uplifted … A gift to us all.'

*

Ever since the story (the scandal, the row, the controversy) spilled forth in April 2010, these words have proved irresistible, to the British media in particular. They have been printed and reprinted countless times. I feel no hesitation in repeating them here once more. Let them stand. Let them be read more times still.

I am digging this story up again because to this day it feels large to me, not merely the incongruous straying of an academic at the peak of his powers but more like a sweeping epic befitting the Russian nineteenth-century literary tradition that Figes sought to capture in *Natasha's Dance*, the book that preceded *The Whisperers*. (Was the humourless arrogance of that earlier book's subtitle – *A Cultural History of Russia* – a warning of things to come?) I am digging this story up because I think it is a different story to the one that's been told so far.

What happened, after all, is not the intellectual world's equivalent of screwing someone in a cupboard at a boozy Christmas party. I refuse to think of this as a trivial story about intellectual arrogance and technological ignorance, about a cutthroat world of academic rivalry in which the smaller the stakes – and the stakes, as famously noted, are mightily small – the more frenetic the bloodlust. Nor, it strikes me, is this merely a tale of the internet unleashing the behind-the-back savagery that the print media's ban on anonymous reviewers has traditionally kept in check, although the laying bare of what Norman Lebrecht calls 'the shady pseudonymous culture of Amazon reviews' is surely one indisputable good to come out of this story.

No, my feeling is that in front of us is a much bigger story, one symptomatic of a particular kind of public culture that is able to absorb certain transgressions but not others, a culture that has a bigger problem with the stain on Monica Lewinsky's dress – such is this culture's fixation on the thousand variations of sexual impropriety – than with, say, the ostentatious abuse of intellectual power. It is a culture that is forgiving, indeed encouraging in some of its quarters, of a certain intellectual psychopathology notable for its indifference to three key human emotions: empathy, shame and remorse. (In the case of Figes, it was not shame or remorse that paved the way for his post-Amazon rehabilitation but Financial Dynamics, a public relations firm he hired.)

In his 2008 article 'The Disadvantages of an Elite Education,' William Deresiewicz notes an implicit acceptance by universities of the Anglophone world of an equation that says intellectual worth equals moral impeccability – an equation unlikely to have eluded Figes, with his double first-class degree from Cambridge and his diagnosable God-like aspirations.

One of the great errors of an elite education, then, is that it teaches you to think that measures of intelligence and academic achievement are measures of value in some moral or metaphysical sense. They're not.

They're not. Except, somehow, this substitution of 'intellectual' for 'moral' has become so common as to appear utterly unremarkable. How else could the university professor who didn't get away with it magically get away with it – and not be compelled to serve time in exile from his readers, his peers, his students? How else could it seem perfectly acceptable for a man to behave shamefully yet to feel no shame?

Sick leave is about ducking and regrouping, not shame.

*

In an email circulated among colleagues, and written before Figes's 'Yes, it was me' confession, Robert Service observed the bitter irony of someone (he and Rachel Polonsky were pretty sure it was Figes, but in no position to say so explicitly) engaging in the practice of anonymous denunciations when anonymous denunciations were a ubiquitous part of life under Stalin. *The Whisperers* has quite a lot to say on the culture of 'mutual surveillance and denunciation,' which, while not entirely a Soviet invention, was certainly at the beating heart of the Stalinist world. Figes describes a 'mad scramble for denunciations.' 'In the climate of universal fear,' he writes, 'people rushed to denounce others before they were denounced by them.' For the anonymous denouncer, nothing was at stake; for the denounced, everything. Countless families were destroyed.

Stalin died. People began returning from the camps. They encountered – sometimes deliberately, often by chance – the individuals who'd denounced them. Figes quotes the famous words of the poet Anna Akhmatova: 'Now those who have been arrested will return, and two Russias will look each other in the eye – the Russia that sent people to the camps, and the Russia that was sent to the camps.'

A remarkable characteristic of these two Russias was the forgiveness many people showed towards those who had denounced or informed on them. Figes recalls the historian Irina Sherbakova's story of a woman, a survivor of the camps, pointing out in the crowd, with not a hint of hatred or contempt, the informer who'd sent her there. Sherbakova quizzed the woman. The woman replied with a quiet, detailed account of how the man must have become an informer: the sequence of fateful events, the virtual inevitability of it all, the repression of members of his own family, the fear.

Such forgiveness was predicated not on religiosity or some particularly stubborn strand of morality, but on the realisation that what happened in that country was a tragedy shared by all decent, thinking people – not only the repressed but also those who were made into the instruments of repression. One way or another (and no, not all ways are equal) everyone was broken, violated, diminished. This is not an argument for moral equivalence. There is, indeed, no moral equivalence. What there is, though, is a shared, comprehensive tragedy – a moral catastrophe that no one chose and everyone had to face. Lest one is tempted to moralise, especially from the vantage point of today, here is Nadezhda Mandelstam, and there lived few more uncompromising witnesses of Soviet totalitarianism than she:

> If any brave young fellow with no experience of these things feels inclined to laugh at me, I invite him back into the era we lived through, and I guarantee that he will need to taste only a hundredth part of what we endured to wake up in the night in a cold sweat, ready to do anything to save his skin the next morning.

The Soviet experience teaches us that fear – total, long-term (twenty-nine years of Stalin, seventy years of 'the dictatorship of the proletariat') and institutionalised fear – can indeed create the necessary conditions for a society in which most of the people, at least some of the time, feel compelled to behave as if they are in a jungle. How, then, should we regard the prominent historian of this precise experience who attempts to recreate a version of that jungle in the cosy confines of the British public sphere, ostensibly to sell more of his books? A rhetorical question, you understand.

On a visit to the Moscow branch of the Memorial human rights and historical society a few years ago, I asked about *The Whisperers* and its author, knowing – and this is something Figes acknowledges readily and with suitable gratitude – that a team of Memorial historians had carried out the bulk of the book's research. It was a straight question and I got a straight answer: 'The man is the biggest self-promoter we've ever met.' It made sense that the people at Memorial would think impolite thoughts about the eminent populariser of Soviet history. They come from a research tradition antithetical to the culture of self-promotion. Their work – preserving historical documents, collecting oral-history accounts of Stalinism – does not tend to carry their names. It does little, I imagine, for their sense of professional self-importance. Memorial historians go about their business with the urgency of military field surgeons, knowing all the while that the current Russian government is on a mission to rehabilitate the Soviet regime (which is doing exceedingly well, thank you) and that without their work all truth and memory in their country would be lost, extinguished, vandalised. They know, too, that the last of the eyewitnesses of Stalinism and the Gulags are dying, and that the clock is ticking madly.

*

A new book by Orlando Figes, *Crimea: The Last Crusade*, came out in October last year. Considerable enthusiasm greeted its publication. Particularly instructive was the hurried footwork of the book's reviewers. Clearly the author's moment of self-promoting madness had to be mentioned, but the sooner it could be put to bed (usually in the first paragraph) the better. Virtually every reference to his 'foolish errors' (Figes's words) had the feeling of an unpleasant chore the reviewer had to take care of. Not one review carried a single original thought on why a conversation about intellectual integrity may be relevant and worthwhile, especially not now that the toad was on its way to becoming the prince again.

Angus Macqueen, in the *Guardian*: 'I have no idea what got into Orlando Figes earlier this year when he started posting anonymous reviews attacking fellow historians while praising his own work. I can only report that this fine writer and ambitious historian is back doing what he does best ...'

Anne Applebaum, in the *Spectator*: 'First, a disclaimer: this review will not touch upon some recent, odd behaviour of this book's author, Orlando Figes, because I can't see that it's relevant.'

Dominic Sandbrook, in the *Telegraph*: 'What was lost amid these absurd antics was the fact that Figes is a first-class historian, as his splendid new book, an epic account of the Crimean War of 1853–56, amply demonstrates.'

Oliver Bullough, in the *Independent*: 'In the tsunami of bad publicity that has swamped Orlando Figes this year, it has been easy to forget that he is a star: one of the finest historians of his age.'

If such intelligent and diligent reviewers as these have unanimously signed up to the game of disassociation between Figes the Leading Historian (whose books you review in serious broadsheets) and Figes the Flawed Man (whose behaviour you have fun with in tabloids), then where and how can we speak of both Figeses together? Where and how, more to the point, can we address the disjuncture between the integrity of our intellectuals and the power – books, tenure, grants, students, media exposure – we let them amass?

The truth is we have been having this conversation for centuries. Orlando Figes, when considered in the long tradition of intellectuals behaving badly, is actually pretty small fry. If anything, his misdemeanours (unless you happen to be Robert Service or Rachel Polonsky) are borderline farcical. Yet still we are none the wiser. No one (really) knows what to do with you – and not just you, Professor Figes, but all you celebrated writers, artists, scientists (you know who you are); you bullies, cowards, hypocrites and cynical opportunists; you filmmakers who forced your little selves inside other people's children; you philosophers who abandoned your own children to orphanages; you eminent scholars who proudly headed university departments in book-burning, people-eating dictatorships.

What are our options? To not read your books? To not watch your films? To unlearn your discoveries and remove your paintings from museums? We are impotent, as you know full well.

Do we condemn you, publicly shame you, boycott you, excise you, ignore you, send you to re-education camps, burn you like witches on the metaphorical fires, make you wear 'Traitor' signs, engage you in Socratic dialogues? If we know our history (twentieth-century totalitarian societies will do), we know all of that's been tried before.

And so we are impotent twice over.

*

I know these things come and go, but at the moment, to my delight, my four-year-old son is particularly fond of the fairytale about the fisherman and the little golden fish. Not the way the Brothers Grimm tell it, mind you (the brothers are so very dry), but a magnificent version by Alexander Pushkin on which generations of Russian-speaking children have been raised. A poor fisherman catches, by chance, a little golden fish. In what is a first for the fisherman, the little fish speaks to him, in a human voice, promising him the fulfilment of any wish if he lets her go. True to his nature – unassuming say some, unenterprising say others – the fisherman asks for nothing. He simply throws the fish back in the water. His wife, on learning what happened, scolds him for such idiocy (they are dirt-poor after all and utterly desperate) and sends him back to the sea to ask for a new washtub to replace their broken one.

The old man goes hesitantly, embarrassed. The little golden fish greets him kindly. She tells him not to worry and to go home with a light heart. At home the new washtub is already waiting, just as the little fish promised. Next to it stands the old woman, sour and agitated, more ready than ever before for some speedy wish fulfilment.

That first modest wish gives way to more and more ostentatious demands, delivered without hint of an apology. The old man is no longer the woman's husband, not in any real sense, but a lowly messenger between her and the little golden fish. With every new request, the little golden fish grows less and less patient. Finally the old woman, having wished for all she can think of, demands to be made Empress of Land and Sea and for the little golden fish to be at her service. A line is crossed, the sea grows stormy and dark, the old fisherman trembles, my son holds his breath … And it all comes crashing down. The little golden fish does not come out of the sea. The old man returns to the old, broken washtub and to his old, ugly wife, who without the accoutrements of wealth and status granted to her by the little golden fish looks even older, even uglier, more disfigured still. (Pushkin, bless him, leaves the story at that, but the Brothers Grimm insert some improbable 'be grateful for what you have' tirade from the old man. I bet he just goes and has a quiet drink, mightily relieved.)

'Why could not she stop?' begs my son. 'Why did she have to ask for more? More, more, more.'

My son runs around the room, mocking the old woman. He demands that I tell him why. I look for words to explain greed, that sense of entitlement that some people grow into so quickly, the incontinence that can afflict a human soul. For some reason (and perhaps this is a developmental thing), of all the many lessons imparted by fairytales – do not eat fruit offered by strangers, check your grandmothers carefully for signs of wolf hair, carry breadcrumbs in your pocket at all times – the lesson of greed is the one my son understands most readily. He realises the utter inevitability of the little golden fish closing the shop on the old woman.

We raise children to see the invisible lines that should not be crossed and for hundreds, thousands of years we have been telling stories about these lines, handing down warnings from generation to generation about what happens when we lose our mind and push too hard, want too much, demand and expect without measure, until the little golden fish, once so patient, so eager to listen, wants nothing to do with us any more.

*

The story of the man who had everything but wanted more still and was implicitly encouraged by the world around him to think that his sense of entitlement was right and justified is about to be forgotten. It is already hollow and old. To tell it anew feels gossipy and gratuitous and like something in bad taste. Yet the man in the tale is not an aberration. He is a logical conclusion of certain forces in our world: of post-moral meritocracy at our academic institutions, of the disappearance of empathy and remorse from public intellectual life, of the way it has become possible to be a professional historian yet learn nothing from history. It is the kind of story we should find a way to pass on with care and seriousness, the story of how he fooled us all – and how we are fooled no more.

Meanjin

On Self-Knowledge: A Ring and Its Keeper

Andrew Sant

On my left index finger is a ring that fits snugly. It's been there for a decade. I began to wear it several years after my father died. Then, a few days ago, I was washing my oily hands in hot water – I'd been cooking a fish dish – and the ring slipped off. This had never happened before. I'm staying in lodgings in London – though they go by some flashier name – and the basin I was using lacked a plug, the metal sort you manipulate up and down via a lever behind the central hot and cold tap. The ring shot straight down the plughole.

It is a gold band joined in a buckle, known as a keeper ring. I didn't think this would happen either: I am the third member of my family to wear it: first my grandfather, then my father, now me. Or should I say, then me. The last. The ring had gone. I looked down the plughole and saw only darkness, imagined the heirloom plummeting down the narrow pipe – I'm on the third floor – into some tributary, water rushing through it towards a main artery in the vast subterranean network of London's sewers. The only hope of its rescue – but not by me – being that it might stall in one of the old Victorian pipes undergoing seemingly endless replacement, and be prized by its sweating finder, though most likely he'd have thicker fingers than mine. Otherwise, it was as good as vaporised.

What struck me was that I accepted the loss. I'd inherited the ring, worn it for a while, now it was gone. History. What happens.

At most, I felt a bit forlorn. This is not what I would have imagined feeling had the incident been hypothetical. I'd surely have conceived then that my mind would start racing, as fast as the ring, towards upset, distress. A flood of feeling. Who was this person, six decades alive, endeavouring to be commonly wise, a representative believer in self-examination, for myself and for the sake of others – indeed, a believer in *knowing myself*, lizard brain included, its existence the reason why we are so riveted by wild fellow creatures, birds or reptiles, whether threatened by or attracted to them – who was this cool, civilised stranger staring dumbly down a dark plughole where something significant had dropped?

I assume my father began to wear the ring, also on his left index finger, in 1953, the year his father died. I think I admired him. The men in my family have the hands of clerks, not labourers, slender index fingers to relay the gold band. But I always thought, with its buckle, it looked masculine, not an adornment – exhibiting strength, not foppery. What it first represented for my grandfather – assuming he was the first wearer – I don't know. He was a major in the British army on the administrative side, an accountant: not the only buckle he would wear. The one on his finger was part of a man's solid ring, of its time. Over the years countless molecules of gold have been rubbed off, and even when I was a boy the delineations of the buckle were smoothed. Soft gold. I wanted to hold it. On my father's finger it represented continuity, even authority, when there was family turbulence.

Now I had lost it, not far from where I spent my childhood. When very young I could not have conceived that I'd never want to wear it; that after my father died, in 1996, I'd reject its weight on my finger, having tried the ring on, as a thing I'd have to shake off. The weight of decades, for the widower and his son, of mutual impatience and blame, erosion of respect, words not said, kindnesses not built upon – mutually tough dependence, like the tongue of a belt in its buckle. Or, perhaps, mutual *need* of each other, blood-tied in a psychological grapple, no time limit, age eventually on my side. How could such a survivor suddenly wear the very thing that would signal a victory?

Eventually, I did wear it. It happened this way, unexpectedly. Do we best discover knowledge of ourselves when caught unawares? I'd returned the keeper ring to the small blue pull-top bag supplied by the funeral director, stored it in a drawer, and mostly forgot about it. Later, because I was going away for a long time, the ring and countless other items were stored in the roof of my house, prior to it being leased. When I returned, five or six years after the funeral, down came the stuff again – and I spotted the little cloth bag. I opened it, inspected the ring, tried it on, idly, index finger, left hand. It felt right. I left it there. Why? What had happened? I slowly realised that I'd changed but hadn't kept up with the pace. The change was subterranean, faster flowing than I could have conceived. Proof the self can be ever transforming – shadows capable of changing to shine. It struck me: I had become reconciled to my father without really knowing it. Now it was my index finger that burnished the inside of the ring.

Those years when the ring had been stored in the cloth bag, a forgotten thing, I'd been leading a partly secret life: conversing with myself about my father, indeed, sometimes internally talking to him. Long ago I'd realised that I was never going to treat my own children in the way my father had treated me. Cut out the fear, nurture the seeds of encouragement. Let affection bloom. Now I'd begun to see him, from a distance in time, in his own right, free of what I'd encouraged in him – so different to what my daughters have encouraged in me, and who loved him, that isolated, stoical man who never complained about his lot. Who could drown overcooked meat and two veg in a lake of gravy and be convinced that no finer meal could be ordered in any restaurant; who on a par three sank two holes-in-one in a single week but spent much of his time in the rough; who considered the hand-sized huntsman spiders he shared his house with to be his 'friends'; who smoked a pipe; who lived, after I left home, ever alone; who, being a fit, determined, punctual man, never took a day off work during his forty-four years as an actuary, except for my mother's funeral, in 1962; who had been a prodigy in mathematics; who, a lone campaigner for correctness, made lists of words whose pronunciation Australians, in his view, mangled; who wrote published letters to Melbourne's *Age*; whose eyebrows were long and wild; who once drew a wounded bull on a Cabcharge receipt and said to my daughters,

That's how they charge; who was a whiz at cryptic crosswords; who loved whisky; who *lived*, and wore, on his left index finger, a gold keeper ring.

It was gone. I thought the upset must surely come later. The loss. I looked down the plughole again, then realised that in my pocket was a keyring torch. I was glad nobody chanced to spot me so carefully examining the facilities which, if the owners are honest with themselves, require some capital outlay. To my astonishment, I spotted the glinting rim of the ring – saved from a freefall by an obstruction, a nail or something. I was no longer fatalistic or forlorn but, seized by the need for rapid action, ran to get that most protean artefact, a coathanger, unwound the neck, stretched the length of the wire straight, made a crude hook at one end and, nervously, lowered it. I'd been fooling myself when I accepted the loss: shocked. Now I was attempting surgical precision, a make-or-break raising manoeuvre, wire in one hand, tiny torch in the other. The ring shifted promisingly, then slipped past the obstruction. But not, amazingly, out of sight. It hadn't occurred to me that the downpipe would be U-shaped – what ignorance we can live with! Now, should any witness have been about, I was a novice plumber, crouching, engaged in frantic dismantling, heavy breathing. The ring! Soon I had it in my hand, and a lot of water on the tiled floor – had what the ring represents, and a reassertion of the importance of it. In the future I hope one of my grandsons will choose to wear the gold keeper and, hey, even flash it.

Griffith Review

Nine-eleven-itis

Shakira Hussein

I tried not to jump to conclusions. I remembered Oklahoma –
those few hours (or was it days?) during which people thought
that the blasted government building, its child-care centre lit-
tered with tiny corpses, was a Muslim crime scene. So I said, 'Bin
Laden couldn't do it.' Afterwards, I wondered whether my reaction, hearing about the planes crashing into the World Trade
Center, was 'denialism.' I had not meant that bin Laden wouldn't
do it, but that he had targeted the complex once before, and
failed. He would have done it, but he couldn't. Maybe the hijack-
ers crashing planes into New York and Washington were well-
organised white supremacists.

Somehow, I didn't think so.

I phoned friends and colleagues, woke them up and said,
'Turn on the television.' ('Which channel?' 'All of them!') We
calculated the date in America, wondering whether it was significant. 11 September, 11/9. My colleague translated it into
American – 9/11, the emergency number.

And so we crossed the border into the post-9/11 era, although
it took a while for the phrase to come into circulation, and
longer still to name the apprehensive, hyper-vigilant state of
mind that has characterised the past decade: nine-eleven-itis.

*

Sometime during a flight to Lahore at the end of September 2001, I went from being half-Pakistani to being half-white. I felt the transition as I slid between selves, a shift in gear marked by the change in the pronunciation of my name. English-speakers tend to place the emphasis on the second syllable; Pakistanis stress the first, just slightly. Sha-kee-ra; Shah-kira. With a half-caste's flexibility, I use both versions myself.

We are not supposed to feel comfortable with such slippery identities, but I have never minded. I like the duality, the not-quite-fitting-in, no matter where I am. It helps me to see things from a different perspective, and makes me careful. It excludes me from collective plurals, and from certainty. My skin changes shade according to the onlooker. Anglo-Australian friends and family give me T-shirts and dresses in pastel shades of pale pink or apricot to suit my dark complexion; Pakistanis give me *shalwar kameez* in a burnt orange that looks good with fair skin. I like the range of my wardrobe and I like my skin, with its mongrel capacity to lighten or darken according to the company I keep.

But September 2001 was a bad time to be a hybrid. Bodies were still being dug from the ruins of the World Trade Center and Pakistan was bracing itself for what George W. Bush called a 'crusade.' People yearned for absolutes. They were suspicious of complexity and shape-shifting crossbreeds. It seemed as though everyone was quoting Samuel Huntington and his *Clash of Civilizations,* a work that angered and frightened me. I knew that I did not want to live in a Huntingtonesque dystopia, forced to choose between my twinned selves. I like to live on the rich grounds of overlap and cross-fertilisation – the mongrel's true homeland. But I was afraid that this would soon become no one's land.

There were more concrete fears, too: destruction from the coming war, authoritarian politics that find justification amid the ruins and the grief. In the days before I left Australia for Pakistan, my mind was a jumble of images. The gleaming buildings pierced by the aircraft, an image on permanent loop in the collective consciousness, but also a delicate-boned Afghan girl crying for her mother still trapped in Afghanistan, waiting for another round of bombing.

So much already lost, so much more still to lose.

*

Javed picked me up from the airport in Lahore. It was an awkward situation. During my previous visit, a year earlier, he had told his mother that he intended to marry a half-white single mother from Australia, leaving out the bit where I'd said no. His mother was even less enthused by the idea than I was. She told him that such a match would disgrace his family for generations. I told him that I would never marry a man who couldn't make a cup of tea for himself. Javed didn't give up immediately. He told his mother that while I was a half-white non-virgin, I was nonetheless a descendant of the Prophet. And when I got back to Australia, there was an email waiting on my computer, announcing that he had learned how to make a cup of tea.

But his mother won that battle for both of us. While Javed was practising his tea-making skills, she was out looking for suitable brides. A few months after my visit, he was abruptly informed that he was to be married in three days' time – and not to me. He begged to be released from the match, or at least to be able to meet the girl in advance, just to glimpse her face. His mother was unyielding. To cancel the wedding at such short notice would shame both the families, and especially the bride. And you couldn't go around asking respectable people to show you their daughters' faces.

Javed was a journalist on one of Pakistan's major English-language dailies, but his salary couldn't provide him with the lifestyle he felt was appropriate to his social position. So, grizzling like a spoiled toddler, he allowed himself to be scolded into matrimony.

Since then, Javed and I had agreed to keep our relationship friendly but professional. This agreement was not rock-solid – my email announcing my next visit had been headed 'writing as a colleague only,' while his reply was titled 'U R still my little princess.' I'd bought him a wedding present at Sydney Airport, an alarm clock clutched in the arms of an angry plastic koala. I didn't think it was open to sentimental interpretation, and anyway, it was on sale.

It might have been more prudent not to contact Javed, but I'd been told that incoming passengers were having a difficult time with immigration, and like most middle-class Pakistanis Javed was adept at the threats, bribes and rank-pulling required when dealing with officials. With him to smooth the way, I was whisked straight through, a porter at my side to cart my luggage to Javed's battered little car.

I handed Javed the gift-wrapped koala clock.

'Why have you brought me a present?' he demanded, half-angrily, and tossed it into the back seat.

'It's a wedding present.'

'You give me a present, but nothing more. To tell you the truth, madam, I had a very torrid time after you left last year. Ten whole days I was in agony.'

'Ten days? You must really have cared about me.'

'Two weeks, even.'

'I'm sure Samina will make you a much better wife than I ever could. How is she?'

'Samina is well, I suppose. I have not seen her for a long time. She is still living with her family. We will not be living together until next year. I am not looking forward to it. She is a good girl, but to tell you the truth I have no feeling for her.'

'That's not her fault. You shouldn't have married her if you weren't going to care about her.'

'I told you, madam. I was in shock, absolutely. What choice did I have?'

'You could have left home. You have a job, after all.'

'I can't live on that money. I tell you, my wage pays only for my cigarettes.'

Already our relationship had fallen into its usual pattern – Javed complaining, me scolding. We might as well have been married.

'I have booked you into a very good hotel. The Amir. They have agreed to an excellent rate, half their usual price. It is in a good area, not like that stupid place you stayed in last year.'

This, too, was an old quarrel. I liked one of the cheap hotels along the cinema strip on Abbott Road. I liked the strings of coloured lights above the cinemas, the gigantic lurid film hoardings showing gore-splattered men silhouetted against the lavish bosoms of maidens in distress. I liked the stalls where street food and banter were available at all hours. I had never been game to taste the goat's testicles, which were set out in neat rows, pale and plump and glistening, waiting to be fried. But I did buy samosas, freshly baked naan and slices of crisp, sweet watermelon sprinkled with chilli. And a shop around the corner sold my favourite pistachio milk drink, a treat worth the airfare from Australia.

But decent girls weren't supposed to stay in hotels alone. Javed had worn out that argument last year; this year he had a new line.

'You can't stay there. The police are checking all those cheap hotels for foreigners.'

'I can't imagine why. If it's journalists they're looking for, they'll be staying in expensive hotels.'

'I am telling you, madam. Things are different here now. You must be more careful.'

I gave in. The Amir had a fancy lobby and lots of uniformed bellboys, but the room was no different to those in the cheap joint, and it smelled of insecticide. I dumped my suitcase and changed, then went with Javed to his newspaper office. It was after midnight, but Lahore is a nocturnal city. I was tired, yet I was also keen to talk to people, to hear what they were thinking.

We had all stepped through the looking glass on September 11. In Pakistan, just as in Australia, people kept saying things that sounded bizarre, out of synch. Back in the car, Javed told me, 'Of course I support Osama bin Laden. Everyone here does.'

I mistook the lurch of surrealism for jetlag. 'Scuse me?'

'Yes, why not? A strong leader, standing up to America and all.'

It wasn't what I expected from Javed, the lazy, dandified princeling who had danced the night away at the Pearl Continental's ABBA tribute a year before. 'I thought you hated the Taliban.'

'I do hate the Taliban.'

'So how does that work? Supporting bin Laden, but not the Taliban?'

'The Taliban are Afghan.'

Most of Javed's colleagues were still in the office, but few of them were actually working. I had talked to Australian journalists since September 11 who were powered by sheer adrenaline.

War fever had migrated from the ruined towers in New York, through the internet and over satellites, to grip editors in Sydney and Melbourne. It acted like speed, giving their eyes a manic gleam and sharpening the air around them.

If the Australian journos were speed freaks, their Pakistani colleagues were morbid drunks, nursing their gloom like flat beer and swapping dark predictions. Their mood matched the office, dingy with stale cigarette and food odours, moth-eaten furniture and ancient computers without internet connections. The journalists – all male – sat drinking tea, gossiping and listening to the cricket. I was updated on the office politics: a new editor, the odd promotion or transfer. Someone asked how I had managed living in the West since September 11. They were all familiar with the stories of Muslims (and those unfortunate enough to be mistaken for Muslims) who had been beaten and abused for having the same religion as Osama bin Laden.

'We hear about these things here, you know. There is a lot of strong feeling about it. There was a mosque burned down in Australia.'

'Yes, that was in Brisbane, where my grandmother lives. Some Muslim schoolchildren had rubbish thrown at them, too. And women in *hijab* have been abused by people on the street, but I haven't had any problems, personally.'

'Well, I suppose you just wear your jeans and all, and nobody can tell what you are.'

'I haven't been wearing jeans. I've been making a point of wearing *shalwar kameez*. I don't want people to think I'm ashamed of my background.'

'*Shalwar kameez?* In these times? Are you crazy?'

The others agreed. 'My brother is studying in London. He told us he doesn't travel on the Underground anymore. He doesn't feel safe there. People said racist things to him.'

'And in America, there have been so many Pakistanis arrested since September 11, just students and visitors, not terrorists.'

'It's getting too dangerous for Muslims to live in the West. I think you should come and live here. You could find a job teaching in a girl's school. Not some rubbish government place. A posh school. You would be safe, living here.'

Safety now lay in the familiar, in the homeland. My friends in Australia had not wanted me to go to Pakistan, either. Terror: it ran through the fissures and ravines of identity, leaving people clinging to their own familiar rocks.

And I was a half-and-half in Pakistan, just as I had been in Australia. I was also an unaccompanied woman who wanted not only to revisit the familiar landscape of women's space ('aunties and activism,' I privately called it) but also to come to grips with the hyper-masculine mood of the new political era. The journalists considered my safety.

'She doesn't really look foreign.'

'Those faces she pulls are very Panjabi.'

'And always with the *dupatta*. No one wears a better *dupatta* than Shakira.'

I asked whether the Pakistani press had come under increased government pressure since September 11. Although a military government, the Musharraf regime had allowed considerably more press freedom than its civilian predecessor.

'When this government came to power, it made the boundaries clear to us – what we could and couldn't say. We keep to those boundaries, and we have no problem with them.'

'So what are the boundaries?'

One of the younger staff laughed. 'You don't criticise the ISI!' Inter-Services Intelligence: ISI. The initials conjure a blend of mystique and menace.

'There are times when you don't even mention ISI!'

'ISI knows everything. Everything. They make the CIA, MI5 and all look like babies. If – if – bin Laden planned this, ISI knows. But I would never say that to just anyone. I would never write it.'

Javed took me through to meet the new editor. It was an encounter requiring his most deferential manner. 'Sir,' he purred, 'an Australian journalist who wishes to talk with you.'

Following his lead, I twitched my *dupatta* into place, lowered my eyes and murmured a demure '*Assalamu alaikum.*'

The editor gave a bewildered blink. 'This is an Australian journalist? She's more Pakistani than a Pakistani! Sit down, sit down. Javed, get the boy to bring more tea.'

He was an amiable man, his English smooth with the

'excellent accent' so prized in the Subcontinent, his belly nestled on his lap like a pet. The television in the corner was tuned not to the constant CNN updates on 'the crisis,' but to the cricket being played overseas. Between overs, he gave his reading of the political climate.

'It is impossible, really, to say what will happen. The situation changes so fast and there are so many rumours. But I do think that the foreign press is underestimating the anti-American feeling here. Musharraf can say all he likes that the people are behind him. But you know what we Pakistanis can be like. If the Islamists can convince us that Islam is in danger, the nation is in danger – oh my God. We go blind. We go mad. We won't listen to anyone. Ah, look at that. The South African side is in excellent form.'

It was like finding the eye of the storm. I let myself be soothed by the scalding sweet tea, by the mellow ripple of the cricket commentary and the editor's easy, sonorous conversation. Exhaustion began to flood through me. I returned to the hotel and sank into bed and sleep. The flit of insect legs across my face lit one last spark of irritation at Javed. The other hotel had been bug-free.

*

I had not anticipated finding pleasure on this journey. I had been too driven by the compulsion simply to be there, to observe and to write. I had forgotten how much I liked Lahore. Looking at the city from the back of a rickshaw the next morning, I remembered. It was a joy to see the Lahore streetscape, the relics of the British and Mughal empires. We passed the cannon that Kipling had made famous as 'Kim's gun' (*where he sat, in defiance of municipal orders, astride the gun Zam Zammah*), and a little further down the Mall the museum where Kipling's father had been curator (*Wonder House, as the natives call the Lahore Museum*). The lawnmower splutter of the rickshaw's engine was like a symphony to my rising spirits. I had the driver stop in a side street lined with food stands so I could cram my body with flavour. Mince and roti, freshly fried *gulab jamuns* in rose syrup and the special Lahori fruit salad, heavy with pomegranate seeds and walnuts, glittering like treasure.

Pakistan was awash with testosterone and conspiracy theories. It was hard to find people who were prepared to believe that bin Laden or any other Muslims were responsible for the attacks on New York and Washington. It was the CIA. Colombian drug lords. Mossad – the story of the 4000 Jews who supposedly knew better than to turn up for work at the WTC buildings on the fateful day was widely repeated. Or – my personal favourite – it was George Bush. 'The father. He wanted to test the mettle of his son.'

Many of those who were not thinking conspiracy were thinking blowback. 'Of course, I don't support terrorism. But really, the Americans were asking for it.'

I understood the seductive power of the conspiracy theories. I was prepared to believe that bin Laden was the prime suspect, but I had seized on the white-supremacist hypothesis as a more palatable explanation. And while I did not think that the Americans – and Australians, and Britons, and Arabs, and Israelis, and Pakistanis – who had died were 'asking for it,' I had begun to grow angry at the way the carnage in America over-shadowed routine, never-ending violence elsewhere.

Entering into a strategic pact with the Americans was always going to be a hard sell. The alliance came with financial sweet-eners, as General Musharraf reiterated at his press conferences – billions of dollars worth of development packages. 'Will all the money go to a few generals, like the last time?' one of the journalists asked.

Like the last time. The last time, when the Soviet Union had occupied Afghanistan, when the United States had propped up a previous Pakistani dictator as part of an Afghan strategy, when the Pakistani military and Islamist parties were used to channel aid to the mujahadeen across the border. The last time, when the Americans had left the battlefield after the Soviet with-drawal, allowing Afghanistan to sink into an abyss of civil war while Pakistan was encumbered with the infrastructure of 'Islamisation' that successive civilian and military governments failed to dismantle. As the editor had said the night before, 'People are worried that the Americans will just use Pakistan and discard us, as they did after the Soviet occupation of Afghanistan.' He had refrained from using the simile commonly used to describe Pakistan's fate – 'discarded like a used condom' – but the sense of having been defiled remained.

Now the feckless seducer had returned for another cycle of intimacy and exploitation, bearing aid packages rather than flowers and chocolates. Pakistanis were understandably cynical.

*

Over in Peshawar, Osama bin Laden's image was everywhere – painted on the backs of rickshaws, photoshopped against suitable landscapes and props in the posters that were spread out along the pavements of the bazaar, and used as banners in demonstrations. Osama as a desert warrior galloping across the desert, submachine gun over his shoulder. Osama as a kind, grandfatherly figure overseeing a young boy as he read the Qur'an. Osama wearing a white robe and a beatific expression as a plane slammed into the side of a gleaming silver building in the background.

The youths at the recruiting booth proudly displayed a book filled with the names of those who had signed up to join the battle. They looked so young – children. I asked whether there were any age restrictions on recruits. They said that they didn't take anyone over the age of fifty. They dismissed my suggestion that some might be too young. 'If they want to go, why not? It's a chance for them to fight for Islam.'

At seventeen, Anwar was already a seasoned fighter. His brother had already become a *shaheed* – a martyr – fighting Indian troops in Kashmir. At fifteen, Anwar too had joined the battle and crossed the border into Kashmir to fight with the Hizbul Mujahadeen. When I met him at an Islamist demonstration, he was preparing to leave for Afghanistan. He was a good-looking boy, with gold-rimmed glasses below his Arabic-sloganed headband and strong muscles apparent beneath his appropriately modest combat fatigues. Despite the muscles and clothes, he seemed more like a student. He showed no discomfort talking with a woman and shooed away a group of youths who'd been harassing me.

It was Friday and the crowd swelled as the worshippers emerged from the mosques after midday prayers, bearing

Jamaat-e-Islami (JI) flags, bin Laden posters, and banners in Urdu and English. BASTARD. UNGODLY. SATAN. HUMBUG. AMERICA IS TRYING TO ERESS PUSHTUN PIPPLES. ('I do feel like helping them out with their spelling,' a British journo commented later.) OSAMA IS THE HERO OF THE MUSLIMS; TONY BUSH WANTED ALIVE OR DEAD.

The crowd was warming up with chants of *Allahu Akbar, Osama bin Laden zindabad!* (Long live Osama bin Laden) and *Amrika murdabad!* (Death to America). Anwar started a new chant in my honour – *Australia murdabad!* – and smiled at me. 'Only joking.' He directed me up onto the stage, out of the crowd, where I would be safe. The bearded mullah alongside me did not look impressed. I was not happy either. Appearing on a public platform alongside leading Islamists as the crowd bellowed for jihad was a scenario that could easily be misunderstood. Misunderstood by ASIO, for example.

The boys in combat gear went into a frenzy when Qazi Hussain arrived, surrounding him protectively and clearing his path to the platform. He spoke in fiery language and at Castroesque length about God and His enemies and how the Afghan people would defeat the Americans just as they had defeated the Soviet Union, amen. JI never polled more than a tenth of the national vote, but watching the party's leader address the packed crowd, the sense of intoxication, the certainty that this was the future, was palpable. It felt like a scene from Samuel Huntington's worst nightmare.

*

Peshawar's good hotels were booked solid by international journalists, but the Rose Hotel was not a good hotel, and a bewildered-looking American was an attention-grabbing sight there. Kevin looked out of place at the check-in desk – he clearly wasn't a journalist, aid worker or thrill-seeker. He was a yoga teacher from New York who had been hired by Wall Street companies for their executives, including those based in the World Trade Center. Kevin had watched the towers crumble through the window of his apartment. 'I didn't want to see, but I couldn't look away.'

'Did you lose someone?' My question felt tactless as it came out of my mouth, and Kevin's silence and welling tears were answer enough.

He couldn't bring himself to stay in New York after the attacks, and his apartment had been deemed unlivable during the initial clean-up. So he had come to Peshawar, as near as possible to Afghanistan. George W. Bush had answered the question 'Why do they hate us?' but Kevin found that answer – they hate our freedoms – unsatisfactory. He had come in search of his own explanation, without telling anyone where he was going.

Peshawar was packed with traumatised refugees who lacked basic essentials. Kevin had a hotel room, an American passport, a ticket out. In Peshawar, these were privileges. And yet I couldn't dismiss Kevin's need as irrelevant simply because it was less acute. His desire to understand and be understood was honourable, but he was too fragile to be turned loose in the wilds of Peshawar. The sight of a Pakistani-looking woman in the company of a Western male tends to attract hostile scrutiny at the best of times, and these were not the best of times. So I told Kevin to keep me in view, but at a distance, as we made our way through the streets to meet people who I hoped would give a sympathetic reception to an emissary from New York.

After years of treating Afghan refugees, Dr Rahim was used to talking with traumatised patients. 'They fall into two categories. The middle-class patients suffer from psychiatric illnesses – depression, suicidal tendencies. Then there are the poor people, the majority. People whose level of existence is hardly human. They are so occupied with sheer survival that they don't suffer from mental illness.'

Dr Rahim accepted our invitation to dinner, listened to Kevin's account of his journey and talked about his most recent patients – the casualties of Operation Enduring Freedom. He did not see the latest conflict as different from that which had preceded it. 'The refugees are still coming, aren't they? We are on the main road to Jalalabad here – it is only two and half hours away. So long as there is war, they will come here. We are prepared for them.'

Kevin's bridge-building efforts were mostly sympathetically received. He told a fire crew he saw on the street about the heroism of their New York colleagues; he listened as refugees told him of lost families and homes. Occasionally his attempts to draw parallels between his own life and theirs were politely corrected.

'My neighbourhood looks like Kabul now.'

'No – no. New York is not like Kabul. What happened was terrible, but it was only one day. In Kabul this has happened over and over again. For years.'

*

It was time to return to Australia, to be reunited with my daughter, to work out how to live a hybrid life across barricades that I believed to be imaginary, but that others maintained were absolute and immutable. I was still unsure whether we mongrels were about to be crushed between colliding civilisations, or ripped in two as they drifted further apart.

People continued to come up with suggestions about how I might be able to return to Pakistan with my daughter and establish a life there, despite the difficulties for unattached women. Move to Abbottabad, a Pashtun journalist in Peshawar suggested. It was his childhood home, a popular holiday destination, with excellent schools, a beautiful location, far easier to navigate than the major cities. And a military town, so very safe. In a world that was descending into chaos, Abbottabad would provide shelter from the storm. He hoped to bring his wife and daughter to visit us there one day.

My time in Pakistan was a way of grappling with nine-eleven-itis, but it was not a cure. The war in Afghanistan, then Iraq, the imprisonment of 'mainly Muslim asylum seekers' in detention centres, headlines about Muslim gang-rapists, the Cronulla riots: the weight sank deep into my body. I ran through a list of synonyms for 'tired,' searching for the one that described how I felt. Exhausted. Weary. Drained. Tired to the bone. Crushed. All applied, yet none seemed adequate. 'Not normal tiredness,' I dubbed it; these were not normal times. This did not feel like tiredness – more like failure.

The sense of defeat pressed more and more heavily until the day when I reached for a pen to mark the attendance sheet for the class I was tutoring and could manage only a clumsy fumble. I did a quick audit. There was no pain or visible injury, and yet somehow the transmission signals between my brain and hand had broken down. My leg was not connecting properly either – but I could still speak and read. Nothing to prevent me from chairing a class on Confucius, so we talked about collectivist values for an hour before I was swept into the maelstrom of hospital waiting rooms, hammer-taps against kneecaps, blood tests, CAT scans, and then the appointment with the neurologist who told me that my problem was psychiatric.

'A psychiatric condition that stops you from *walking*?' my friends asked incredulously. But I remembered Dr Rahim's words: 'The middle-class patients suffer from psychiatric illnesses – depression, suicidal tendencies.' I was safely in Canberra – if anyone could afford the luxury of a psychiatric illness, I could.

By the time another neurologist referred me for an MRI scan, I had long since self-diagnosed. I had allowed my post-9/11 anxiety to cross the barrier between mind and brain, to cripple me. What could be more attention seeking, more pointless, more self-indulgent, than to appropriate the symptoms of other people's trauma to manifest my own stress? And how humiliatingly visible – an unsteady gait for which the explanation was uttered only in the most secret corner of my heart: I think I've just been letting this whole 9/11 business get to me.

I struggled to express this to the neurologist when I returned for my MRI results, and concluded: 'I'm working out some complicated issues.'

The neurologist paused before responding. 'The scan was abnormal.'

Oh. Not nine-eleven-itis. Multiple sclerosis.

Although no medical doctor would tell me this, mine was a case of 'co-morbidity,' assailed by both nine-eleven-itis and multiple sclerosis. The multiple sclerosis is remitting-relapsing, flaring once a year or so to blur my vision, drive red-hot nails into my face or disconnect limbs from my central nervous system, before subsiding.

There has been no remission from nine-eleven-itis for any of us. I write this essay during a flare of both my diseases, and amid hopeful talk of treatment breakthroughs. In the days after bin Laden was killed in Abbottabad, the safe military town that I had considered as a bolthole, the numbness that had been creeping into my left side jammed my fingers as I frantically attempted to write, write, write to hold back the clash of civilisations. My much-scanned brain went into overdrive as it tried to process the reports of the al-Qaeda leader's final years, the allegations of ISI involvement ('ISI knows everything'), the surreal ritual of his consignment to the ocean.

The consensus that seems to be emerging is that while it is too soon to declare victory, the post-9/11 era has drawn to a close, a decade after it began.

The neurologist is upbeat when I return for my review one month into the new treatment. The latest drugs are very effective. The long-term effect is not yet clear, and since the medication may suppress my immune system, I should have regular pap smears and breast checks. But if all goes well, I should have fewer flares, and I should be able to hold off the 'serious disability' she has warned me is otherwise likely. *Inshallah*, I add silently to myself.

As for nine-eleven-itis, I suspect that this improvement in symptoms may turn out to be a placebo effect.

Griffith Review

The Work of Catfish

Lian Hearn

The dark wave rises, and keeps on rising like the sea in a nightmare. Ships cascade over a wall built to protect the port town from typhoons and tsunami, and cars are swept away like plastic bottles. A flock of seagulls soars upwards. Out at sea, fishing boats ride over the huge swell just as the fishing fleet from Sanriku did in 1896, when another huge tsunami destroyed the east coast of Japan's Tōhoku region. In that earthquake and tsunami about 22,000 people died. In 1933 another tsunami struck; photos from both events bear witness to the total destruction.

People here get their living from the cold, rich waters of the northern Pacific Ocean. They cannot move away; they have always rebuilt before, but this time the cost and the sacrifice seem almost too hard to bear.

I was in Tōhoku last year visiting friends in Iwate and Fukushima prefectures. It was my first visit to that part of Japan. I'd always wanted to go to Sendai: I like its name (*sen* means 'hermit' or 'wizard' and is used in many words that suggest enchantment: *senkyō* – 'fairyland,' and *suisen* – 'narcissus') and its association with the great Sengoku *daimyō* (a feudal lord), Date Masamune, known as the 'one-eyed dragon.' Sendai is a modern city now but Masamune's presence can still be felt, especially in the Zuigan-ji, rebuilt as a Zen Buddhist temple for his family in 1609.

Zuigan-ji was mostly closed – it is being restored. Work started in September 2009 and will be finished in March 2018. At the moment it is sheltering the homeless, as temples have through the ages.

I took another small personal pilgrimage to Matsushima and Hiraizumi, in Miyagi Prefecture, in the footsteps of seventeenth-century haiku poet Matsuo Bashō. Traditionally Japanese travellers did not so much explore the unknown as visit and revisit sites made famous by poetry, legend and history. Matsushima, even in Bashō's day, had been described as 'the most beautiful place in all of Japan, the green of the pines is dark and dense, the branches and leaves bent by the salty sea breeze ... did the god of the mountain create this in the age of gods?' At first it seemed Matsushima could not have survived the tsunami of 11 March 2011, but it was protected by its islands.

Long before Masamune, the Fujiwara lord Kiyohira founded the temple of Chūson-ji at Hiraizumi, as part of a pledge before Buddha to honour the spirits of the dead, whether 'friend or foe, human or animal.' On 18 March 2011 Chūson-ji's bell tolled for an hour and a half for the victims of the earthquake and the tsunami. It was the week of the spring equinox (*higan*) and all over Japan people gathered to pray for the souls of the dead and to raise money for the living.

Only the Golden Hall remains of Kiyohira's building. With Chūson-ji's collection of sutras inscribed in gold and silver lettering on deep blue paper and statues of Buddha and Kannon, it is one of the most beautiful expressions of human spirituality I have ever seen. Amida, Buddha of Infinite Light, sits serenely in a glowing representation of his Pure Land (Western Paradise), as though time has stood still since Kiyohira's day. It is an illusion. The Golden Hall has fallen into disrepair and been restored over the centuries, most recently in the 1960s.

The Pure Land is also represented at nearby Mōtsū-ji. Once Mōtsū-ji had forty pagodas and 500 monasteries but they burned to the ground in 1226 and were never replaced. Only the garden remains. Here, reflecting on the death of one of Japan's best-loved heroes, Minamoto Yoshitsune, at Takadachi, Bashō wrote:

The Work of Catfish

Natsugasa ya
Tsuwamonodomo ga
Yume no ato

(Summer grasses,
The traces of dreams
Of ancient warriors)

Like Bashō I climbed to the remains of Takadachi and gazed down on the Kitakami River. Rain dripped from the trees and dappled the surface of the water. The cold wind from the north had a hint of snow, of winter.

It used to be believed that earthquakes were caused by a giant catfish, Namazu, thrashing underground. In one of the oldest shrines in eastern Japan, Kashima Jingu, lies a huge stone beneath which the troublesome catfish is said to be confined. Catfish woodblock prints were popular in the Edo period (1603–1867), originating as talismans against disaster, and then turning satirical and cynical. People connected with the building trade – carpenters, roofers, tatami mat makers – were pictured as cronies of Namazu, and merchants as his reluctant contributors: rebuilding after earthquakes forced them to unlock their wealth.

After a series of severe earthquakes in the Ansei period (1854–60), the catfish evolved again into a symbol of protest. Earthquakes were considered a sign that poor government was failing to maintain the natural balance between heaven and earth, and the inept Tokugawa shogunate (feudal regime) was an obvious culprit. Along with terror and destruction, Namazu also released powerful energy that cleared away obstructions and made space for something new.

Kashima, Deer Island, is an industrial town in Ibaraki Prefecture, home to the most successful soccer team in Japan's J. League, the Kashima Antlers. The land for miles around has been reclaimed, the courses of the rivers altered. In the earthquake of 11 March the reclaimed land went into liquefaction, roads split apart and all the power poles and pylons fell down. Power was cut to thousands of homes and there is still no running water. Helpful instructions have been issued: 'Line the toilet with a plastic bag, with newspaper at the bottom. Tie tightly after use and store on the veranda.' My friends get their water from a relative who has a well. Back to Edo days again.

'Your room leaned over,' they wrote, 'and we could not open the door, but it's fine now, so please come and stay again soon.'

It is impossible to spend any time in Japan without encountering earthquakes or typhoons. People are generally well prepared and unworried. Last October there was a small tremor when I was in Fukushima. The ceiling lamp began to sway, the pictures shook on the walls, everything rattled. It didn't last long – just long enough to wonder if this was going to be *the big one* that everyone agreed was well overdue.

The earthquake of 11 March was *the big one*, but not where it was expected, in Kant like the great earthquake of 1923 that killed between 100,000 and 140,000 people. It took everyone by surprise. It was unlike any other earthquake we had ever experienced before, said my friends in Itako.

And it was not the earthquake that destroyed so many coastal towns and took thousands of lives. It was the tsunami.

The day after, when the first images began to come through, I kept going over past memories, as if by the power of thought I could retain them all unspoiled like the Pure Land. I was worried about my friends, all beyond contact by phone or email, but I did not want to exaggerate my grief or make personal such a huge national tragedy. I wanted to cry but I wondered if I had the right. In the end I cried anyway, spent days in mourning. I sensed a similar outpouring of grief round the world, from a mixed cohort of all ages and nationalities who have come by many different routes – samurai films, haiku, Zen, art and sculpture, *ukiyo-e*, *netsuke*, anime, manga, J-pop, NHK taiga dramas, Shōgun, martial arts, Mishima, Haruki Murakami – under the spell of Japan.

Japan is a country of extremes, its character forged by its unstable geography and climate. The arts, both traditional and modern, are fuelled by images of disaster, the creative energy of regrowth and the stillness that comes in the intervals between. These extremes have produced, through the ages, a singular courage in the face of death. To live with this disregard for death, not fearing it, not seeing it as an unfair personal tragedy, makes room for humility and self-sacrifice and banishes self-pity. It puts human life into a realistic relation with nature, accepting the unpredictable power of wind, water, fire, of earth itself. In this acceptance lie the seeds of hope. Words of deepest despair – *we cannot live here again* – are followed almost immediately by *but we will rebuild our town; I cannot live without my loved ones* by *I must live to pray for them and honour them.*

A friend sent me a link to a news story from Kamaishi: deer, not seen since the disaster, have returned to Yakushi Kōen – the park of the Healing Buddha.

Looking at the picture of the deer above the ruined town puts me into a reverie where I see Japan's history unfold as if in time lapse. Kashima is an island inhabited only by deer, surrounded by unimpeded rivers. Towns grow, the waters are dammed, the rivers flood, channels are excavated. The land shakes, tsunami sweep in, temples catch fire and burn, whole towns are destroyed. Minamoto Yoshitsune is betrayed and killed. The Fujiwara and a hundred other warrior houses pass away. Mōtsū-ji disappears, Zuigan-ji rises again. Homes are rebuilt, land reclaimed, sea walls constructed. Petals open and fall; trees are green, red, leafless, then green again. Typhoons, volcanoes, earthquakes, war and again war, firestorms, bombs, radiation. Destruction. Healing. Recovery.

The seagulls rise over the black wall of water. My friend plants narcissus in a window box. The deer return to the garden.

The Monthly

High Priest: David Walsh and Tasmania's Museum of Old and New Art

Amanda Lohrey

The Moorilla estate is set on a peninsula of sandstone cliffs that juts out into the Derwent estuary on Hobart's northern fringe. Framed to the south-west by the looming grandeur of Mount Wellington and to the east by Mount Direction, the slopes of the peninsula are planted with grapevines, and a cluster of modern buildings perch atop the rise. It is here that the visionary project the Museum of Old and New Art (MONA) is due to open on 21 January 2011, an $80 million wonder that will house a private art collection valued at over $100 million dollars. Already it has been hailed as the 'Bilbao of the south' and the 'Getty of the Antipodes,' expecting an estimated 350,000 visitors per annum, contributing a major boost to the Tasmanian economy.

The owner and presiding spirit of MONA is 49-year-old David Walsh, a professional gambler and art patron. I have arranged to meet Walsh in Moorilla's restaurant, The Source, named after a John Olsen painting suspended from its ceiling, and on a wintry July afternoon I wait there in the company of his research curator, Delia Nicholls. It has been reported that Walsh dislikes being interviewed and can be difficult to engage, and while I dwell on the prospect of a fraught afternoon the man is suddenly beside me. He is tall and slim with grey-white hair that hangs almost to his shoulders; he is dressed in jeans, sneakers and a street-chic grey wool jacket. He looks younger than I expected, almost boyish, but has a vague, distracted air. When I thank him for agreeing to the interview he stares out over the winter-bare vineyard and says, 'Oh, well, Delia tells me I have to do this.'

Walsh is a man about whom a good deal of urban myth has arisen and I've long been curious as to how a working-class boy from Hobart's struggle-town suburb of Glenorchy, raised by a single mother, came to be a warlord of the international art world. I've read a rare interview granted to the German art magazine *Kunstforum International* in which he describes himself as a 'misfit' child, 'internal to the point of autism,' a boy who lived inside his head and read his way through the classics of the Western canon while collecting coins and stamps. Academically gifted, he might well have gone on to a career in research but, in the second year of his science degree at the University of Tasmania, he was asked by friends to develop a model that would enable them to win at blackjack in the nearby Wrest Point Casino. When he discovered that the scope for winning at card games was limited he dropped out of his degree and, for most of the '80s and early '90s, spent 100 or more hours per week developing a mathematical model that would enable him and his partners to win at other forms of gambling, especially horseracing. This he now pursues on a large scale in a number of countries.

There is a network of people involved in Walsh's outfit, most notably his business partner of thirty years, Zeljko Ranogajec. Walsh met Ranogajec at university where the latter studied law and economics before he too dropped out to pursue a career in gambling. Walsh describes Ranogajec as a 'relentless motivator and a loyal friend' who, despite not sharing his interest in art, has provided financial support for his collecting mania 'whenever my cashflow dried to a trickle.' As Walsh inelegantly puts it: 'I am throwing the shit, he is happy to be the fan. And he doesn't even like the shit.'

In 1995 Walsh and his consortium bought the picturesque Moorilla estate for a modest $2.53 million. The estate and its winery had been established by the Alcorso family, immigrants from Mussolini's Italy in the late 1930s, who set up a successful textile business and then moved into wine-making. Claudio

Alcorso acquired a national reputation as a patron of the arts until family strife and insolvency forced Moorilla into receivership. Whereas Alcorso was an art patron in the patrician European style, Walsh – by this time a collector of antiquities – was more your local high-tech super-geek model.

While in South Africa in the 1980s on a blackjack expedition, he made his first significant art purchase, a Yoruba palace door from Northern Nigeria. As he tells it in the *Kunstforum*, he saw it in a gallery in Sandton with a price tag of $18,000. At that time it was illegal for a visitor to take more money out of South Africa than they had taken in, and since $18,000 was the approximate amount of excess money Walsh had on him, he bought the door. This was the beginning of a world-class collection encompassing Roman, Hellenic and Egyptian artefacts and, in need of somewhere to store them, he set about transforming the original villa on the Moorilla estate – designed by the Australian architect Roy Grounds – into a small antiquities museum. It was an enchanting little place of rare intimacy and charm; when I first visited it in the late '90s I was smitten. Little was known about its obscure owner and few visitors to the museum even knew his name.

All this has changed with the construction of MONA. It's an ambitious venture with estimated running costs of $7 million per annum and Walsh has decided it must pay its way. Reluctantly, he has begun to make himself more accessible and he offers now to take me on a tour of the museum construction site. I know that almost the entire gallery space of MONA is underground and as we walk to the site office to don hard hats and fluoro vests, I ask the obvious question: why down and not up? Most wealthy art patrons build great edifices that rise into the air like modern cathedrals, so why has he chosen to burrow into the earth?

'When you go to the British Museum,' he begins, 'you know what you're going to get. It's amazing, but it doesn't confound your expectations.' What Walsh wants is for you not to be able to see what you're getting. 'Great museums are like temples and would have you believe that knowledge is a matter of revelation and you are the empty vessel that has to be filled. You turn up and there it all is, laid out for you, the sum total of human wisdom, and you're there to be enlightened. You always walk upstairs and you always walk into some grand citadel. In my opinion this is not how we learn things.' He wants the layout of the museum to reflect the scientific paradigm: 'Gradualism would be a better metaphor, learning by increments through guesswork and experiment, but with constant attempts to falsify.' He says it's fairly well known that he is a 'rabid atheist,' and this has determined the philosophy of the layout. 'I'm trying to build a museum that you discover gradually. It's a secular temple, or you might call it an un-temple, which means it has to be concealed.'

He describes how the ground on top will be landscaped to look nondescript: 'I'd make it a car park if I could.' He contemplated turning it into a skateboard ramp but the council deemed it unsafe. As it is, he might hold concerts on the surface or a weekend market. He wants the museum to be fun: a 'subversive Disneyland.'

By this time we have arrived at the entrance to the museum, which is the old Roy Grounds villa and former antiquities museum, now partially gutted. As we descend a winding staircase some twenty metres into the earth, Walsh points to the foundations of the original house; he intends to keep them exposed because 'they are in themselves interesting.' It becomes apparent that everything is of interest to Walsh – that he is a man who takes nothing for granted and has thought about every detail on the site. He describes the excavation as inverse archaeology and tells me the builders and engineers had to remove 60,000 tonnes of earth and sandstone before the building could begin. To line the interior walls took three kilometres of rock sawing, 1.5 kilometres of drilling for rock bolts to maintain the rock face and 5500 cubic metres of concrete to fill the ensuing hole. That 'hole' is now 6000 square metres of exhibition space over three levels.

At the bottom of our descent is a vaulting space like a cathedral nave with walls of golden sandstone that look as if they've been hauled from some pharaoh's palace but have in fact been cut from the site. 'This will be the bar,' he tells me. 'It's the first thing you'll see. We'll have functions here, rock bands, DJs, all kinds of events.' Then he points to an area adjacent to the bar.

'Just along here will be a little cemetery where your ashes can be interred.' There will be a charge for depositing these, he explains, and they will be stored in huge urns etched in an eighteenth-century style and displayed in ornate cabinets with velvet curtains on either side and a steel fence in front, of the kind you sometimes see around gravestones. 'I like the idea of a resolved secular death where you can go and have a glass of chardonnay and commune with the dead person. I'd love to have had a crematorium but that proved difficult.'

Already I can envisage MONA as a popular site for secular funerals, perhaps with its own resident civil celebrant and performance artists, and I tell him he might be surprised by the demand. 'In that case,' he quips, 'I'll put the price up.'

We walk on through empty spaces, a network of nooks and crannies and long vistas from viewing platforms, and a giant industrial staircase that is the one feature visible from almost every vantage point. Walsh is explaining where the major artworks will be installed. Here will be a work by the Mexican artist Rafael Lozano-Hemmer, a network of electrodes and light bulbs that will measure your pulse rate; nearby, an installation by the German artist Julius Popp, a waterfall that monitors the internet so that words popular on Google News cascade in the water. The Pausiris gallery on the second level will resemble a swimming pool where you walk over stones in shallow water to see a sarcophagus. In one of the smaller galleries, loosely referred to as 'the catacombs,' will be the Cuban artist Wilfredo Prieto's *Untitled (White Library)* (2004–06), a library of 6000 white books and papers, all of them blank. The overall number and variety of works in Walsh's collection is staggering.

Walsh describes the spirit of the building as one of 'anticompartmentalisation' in which design mirrors philosophy. The three levels will consist of temporary walls to maximise the adaptability of spaces, all walls will be angular and there will be no tyranny of the rectangle. 'Everywhere is everywhere and there's no thematic structure, apart from the Sex and Death gallery, which will be the one curated space,' he explains. It will be a 'sparse hang,' full of surprising juxtapositions, so that, for example, an exquisitely detailed Egyptian mummy case may sit beside a model of the euthanasia machine designed by Dr Philip

Nitschke. *Everywhere is everywhere*: it reminds me of Salman Rushdie's description of postmodernity in his novel *Fury*. Under globalisation everyone's story will sit alongside everyone else's, and this is just how Walsh wants it. It drives the more rigid academic curators crazy, he says, but he wants you to contemplate conflict and contradiction: he wants you to think.

Several works in the MONA collection have already generated a fair amount of thinking. These include the Chris Ofili portrait *The Holy Virgin Mary* (1996), in which the British artist of Nigerian descent depicts a black Madonna with elephant dung over one breast and a background collage of female genitalia from magazine clippings (the work sits on the floor supported by two balls of elephant dung). It's the same work that caused a scandal in New York when exhibited at the Brooklyn Museum of Art in 1999 as part of the Charles Saatchi collection *Sensation*. Mayor Rudy Giuliani denounced it as blasphemous and initiated a court case against the museum, threatening to withhold its funding. *Sensation*, which was scheduled to exhibit at the National Gallery of Australia the same year, was rejected by former director Brian Kennedy at the last minute and there have been hints of federal intervention. In a characteristically finger-raising gesture against official piety, Walsh bought it, though he doesn't even bother to mention this on my tour. He's more concerned to explain a new version of the Belgian artist Wim Delvoye's provocative *Cloaca* machine – an elaborate model of the human digestive system that will hang from the ceiling and excrete mock turds – or the ingenious *Locus Focus*, commissioned from the Austrian artists' collective Gelitin. Concealed within the cubicles of the public lavatories, this work uses a binocular mirror system to give you a view of your own anus. 'I'm interested in the way we compartmentalise our lives by concealing from ourselves the processes that make us,' he says. 'We sanitise things so we can defer responsibility. So this is a rather unsubtle metaphor.'

I tell him I like this idea of the mirrors, that while it could be interpreted as deconstructive it also takes you back to the innocent curiosity of childhood where you lock the bathroom door and investigate your body with a hand-held mirror. 'I never did that,' he says.

While he denies having any collecting strategy, over the years Walsh's acquisitions have tended to cluster in three major categories. There are the antiquities – everything from Yap stone money to a 5000-year-old basalt altar from the Golan Heights – and there's a significant collection of Australian modernist painting, with artists such as Sidney Nolan, Arthur Boyd and Brett Whiteley. In 2006, as an anonymous phone bidder, Walsh bought John Brack's *The Bar* (1954) out from under the nose of the National Gallery of Victoria for $3.17 million and sold it back to them in 2008 for what he paid for it. Then, when the NGV set up a public appeal to help pay for the painting, he got caught up in the fervour and made a donation. 'My strategy is not very cohesive.'

The third category of works is by far the most controversial: his cutting-edge collection of conceptual art by leading international modernists such as Paul McCarthy, Erwin Wurm, Damien Hirst and Jenny Saville. The popular press has chosen to sensationalise acquisitions such as Stephen J. Shanabrook's *On the Road to Heaven the Highway to Hell* (2008), a chocolate sculpture of the mutilated body of a suicide bomber, or Walsh's decision to pay the French artist Christian Boltanski to video his every move for the rest of his life (shades of the Warhol movies of the '70s). But Walsh says he welcomes confrontation and would be quite happy for people to picket the museum. 'I like a bit of drama.'

Given these elements of the scatological and high-tech avant-garde, it may come as a surprise to some visitors to discover that the heart of MONA will be Sidney Nolan's *Snake* (1970–72), a gigantic rainbow serpent of 1620 individual panels of flowers, animals, birds and human heads that will extend forty-five metres along a huge curved wall. All of MONA has been built around this single work on the myth of creation. 'We started with this and worked out,' he says, and describes how it will be exhibited in concert with three other works on the nature of myth and how the mind processes it: a 6.5-metre-high painting by Anselm Kiefer on the nature of myth, a sculpture commissioned from the American artist Gregory Barsamian on 'the chaos of thought,' and an installation by Jannis Kounellis of seven sides of freshly slaughtered beef, slung on hooks above sacks of coal. 'I wanted to put an abattoir in the museum where the beef could be slaughtered but the idea had some logistical problems,' says Walsh, as if this were merely a mundane practical detail. What he loves about the myth gallery is that each work has 'a lot of intellectual complexity and is also a really beautiful thing in its own right,' although I'm having some doubts about those sides of beef. Will the four works come together as a meaningful whole? 'We've made a video-game model of the gallery,' he says, 'so we've got a pretty good idea.'

A winery, an abattoir, a cemetery, a bar, a market, a space for music, a library, a gallery on sex and death, a museum that radiates out from the serpent rainbow of creation – it brings to mind something I once read about the design of the Taj Mahal. The Taj may well have been part of a larger plan that sought to create in marble the Islamic model of paradise. And here is MONA, designed to be an exemplary experience of the phases of earthly being, a secular map of the underworld. By this time I'm beginning to feel that I'm in some magnificent labyrinth and I half expect to see the Minotaur hoofing it around a corner. What happens if visitors get disoriented?

'MONA is very difficult to navigate and that's the point,' says Walsh. 'I'm trying to say that what we know is extracted painfully and what we know, or what we think we know, is constantly changing. The layout of the museum is a metaphor for that.' But he doesn't want you to get lost, so every visitor is going to be issued with an ingenious device he's commissioned that knows where you are. This high-tech equivalent of Ariadne's thread will be multi-functional. It will not only guide you, it will tell Walsh and his team how long you spend in front of an exhibit, with a LOVE/HATE button you can press for feedback. It will also provide some information on the artworks, though not of an orthodox kind. 'I want no labelling or visual explanation on the wall. I don't want to create expectations or pre-judge your responses. The need to explain works with interpretive material vanished with the internet. Go home and look it up. I want to create a need to know. If people leave more curious than when they arrive then that would be a great outcome.'

This doesn't mean there won't be some intriguing material on the device: music, videos, gobbets of information but no monological or homogenised commentary. Some of the content will be creative in its own right and he cites the involvement of Damian Cowell, former member of the rock band TISM (This Is Serious, Mum): 'We showed him a bunch of art and he wrote songs about it specifically for the device.' But not all devices will have the same content. If a couple go around with different information on their devices it will be more likely to stimulate conversation, he says. It's an idea that arose out of a discussion he had with a museologist in Florence. 'You'll have something on your device that your friend won't have. You'll have something to contribute to the discussion so you won't feel foolish or out of your depth.'

When MONA is completed there will be one way in and the same way out, like a womb, but this afternoon we are exiting through an opening in the unfinished construction works – up and out into the air, where Walsh points to the river, ashimmer in Hobart's crystalline light. There won't be enough parking on-site, so he has contracted a company to run ferries from the city's docks up the picturesque Derwent. He shows me the jetty where visitors will disembark and ascend a steep concrete staircase to the museum entrance; he says it has been designed to resemble in feeling the disembarkation from a dangerous sea voyage to a Greek island. 'The first thing you did was walk up the hill to give thanks in the temple for safe arrival,' he explains, and this reminds me that his architect is the Greek-Australian Nonda Katsalidis. Walsh met Katsalidis when buying his Melbourne apartment from the architect-developer, and MONA is the eleventh building Katsalidis has since designed for him. 'The sort of thing Frank Gehry builds are temples to himself,' says Walsh. 'The inside and outside have nothing to do with each other.' This leads to a discourse on form and function and his admiration for Katsalidis, whom he thinks relates the two 'better than anyone else in Australia.'

I ask how many people the site will employ and he says 'around fifty,' with thirty or so already fully involved. After the Yoruba door, he began collecting through dealers and auctions; he found that he got on well with some of the Sotheby's staff and offered them employment at the museum. One of them is the former managing director of Sotheby's, Mark Fraser, whom

Walsh describes as having had a lot to do with shaping MONA's present business model. But there is no resident curator. 'We've got curators on staff,' he says, 'but it's all of us really.' That 'us' includes an office in Melbourne with Jane Clark, who advises on the Australian modernists, Nicole Durling, who is also ex-Sotheby's, and Walsh's curator for contemporary Australian art, the French-Swiss curator Olivier Varenne, based in London, and the internationally regarded French consultant curator Jean-Hubert Martin. There are other curators who research and write, a librarian, an exhibition designer and design staff, a registrar and technical staff. Walsh's older sister, Lindy-Lou Bateman, studied painting and photography as a young woman and is involved with several aspects of the museum.

*

After the tour we return to The Source for coffee and settle at a table in the corner that looks out through plate-glass windows to the river. I tell Walsh that people often remark on his decision to live in Tasmania, not far from where he grew up, and to build the museum there. 'I kind of like it here,' he says, adding that he has joint custody of his six-year-old daughter, who lives in Hobart. In any case, he adds, globalisation creates a vertical market, so that people will travel to see what they're interested in 'and being in Hobart makes it more interesting.'

In New York it might be just another museum and gallery? 'In New York it would probably emerge as having some validity but it would become less a temple, less a destination. The philosophy of the thing that I'm screaming through a megaphone would be drowned out by the crowd noise.'

It's clear he wants to create a kind of secular pilgrimage and, insofar as the museum is exploratory and isn't trying to objectify taste, he hopes it may become a rallying point for secular human-ism. He also wants to expand the conversation he is continually having in his head. He likes people who are direct, who argue back and who challenge him, though they had better make a good case, something he doesn't always get from artists. While he credits Gregory Barsamian with helping him to understand 'why art is an efficient communicator,' many others, he says, have little idea why they do what they do. 'When interrogated their ideas can be vapid.' His own theories about art derive from evolutionary biology. 'The underlying motives of artists are either satiation or propitiation, access to sex or avoidance of death.' There's also a reproductive drive involved; artists are peacocks competing to exhibit the best display of feathers as a way of attracting mates. 'I built a museum because I'm a peacock shaking its feathers.' That said, he can imagine a 'valid' life without art and the mathematics of gambling still remains his first love.

One of the more remarkable things about Walsh is that he appears to have no sense of entitlement and occasionally refers to his wealth as unfair: 'I've done nothing for the money.' He believes that his path in life was a fluke, a product of circumstance, and when I try to press him on this I get nowhere. I know, for example, that he attended a parochial Catholic school; I ask him about the influence of his Catholic childhood and he is dismissive. As a child he had an aptitude for science and this brought about his loss of faith, not vice versa. When he gave his religious instruction teachers grief by demanding evidence for the existence of God he was often made to stand outside the classroom in the cold and he resented it. Yes, but might not this humiliation have driven him to construct his secular temple? Christian dogma is full of suspicion of the body, I say, hatred even, and isn't MONA a form of riposte? 'Hatred of the body has no wit,' is all he will say, before launching into a discourse on how the influence of childhood is overrated. There could be a million people with his bleak religious upbringing and exceptional mathematical skills where a different decision or accident brought a different outcome. He describes himself as 'basically lazy'; 'If Zeljko hadn't walked into the uni bar I doubt I would ever have made the money.' This is a very important point, he stresses, and tells me he subscribes to the theory of survivor bias. When I ask him to elaborate, he offers a gambling analogy. 'There are over 6 billion people on Earth. Let's say they each have $1000. Let's have half of them toss a coin with the other half. We then have 3 billion with $2000 and 3 billion with nothing. Repeat: 1.5 billion with $4000; 750 million with $8000; 375 million with $16,000; 187 million with $32,000 dollars;

93 million with $64,000; and so on. When we have one person left, after thirty-three consecutive winning tosses, he (of course) will have all the money, which was 6 trillion dollars. He will believe he is a very good coin tosser indeed, and a very shrewd operator. He will get an article written about him for the *Monthly*.' People who don't understand this, he says, believe in the power of positive thinking, something for which he has considerable scorn, and I realise that the coin-tossing analogy is not about gambling as such but his absolute faith in the science of probability. Unlike many who claim to operate on the basis of a scientific paradigm, Walsh is prepared to subject his ego to the logic of that paradigm: 'I know that my life is only peripherally related to my own intervention.'

Nevertheless, choices do get made, like building a museum around a single artwork. I ask him why he has such high regard for Sidney Nolan and he says he admires Nolan's relentlessness in the pursuit of understanding: 'He doesn't give up on a subject, he tears it apart and sees every bit of it.' It could be a description of Walsh himself. After all, this is a man who posed nude for Andres Serrano – despite having a poor body image and knowing he would most likely hate the outcome (he does) – because it might 'produce some thought or feeling that turns out to be important to me.'

Though Walsh describes himself as an atheist, I observe that he seems quite unlike the Richard Dawkins variety. Dawkins is a high priest of certainty if ever there was one, whereas Walsh strikes me as a man of restless intelligence who is suspicious of all dogma, of any thought or statement that sends the mind into lockdown. He agrees, and remarks that Dawkins has often pursued the wrong strategy in making his case, that he doesn't have enough to say about 'the grey areas.' We agree that *The God Delusion* is a crude polemic and he recommends I read Dawkins's earlier book *The Ancestor's Tale*, 'in which the complexity of the real world is allowed.' Part of that complexity, he says, is that 'ideas are very fluid things, they come and they go. I like a work of art today but I might not like it in six months, or even three. Every conclusion is tentative, and that's the key: that's what the museum says. Any time you ask someone something you get what sounds like a cohesive story but it's all bullshit, it could be different tomorrow.' For this reason the contents of MONA will change from year to year and possibly every few months. It may be that Walsh decides that some of his artworks are not in the end profound, are indeed stunts, in which case he will replace them. MONA will be nothing if not a work in progress.

I put it to him that there is a latent politics in his actions, that he seems to have an egalitarian streak. He wants to keep the museum free of admission charges, he is keen for visitors not to feel intimidated by art as some elitist calling and he wants 'the device' to make them feel as if they themselves have a contribution to make. He hates pretension, dislikes the deification of artists and believes in a secular globalised community as a level playing field that is tolerant and inclusive. He seems uncomfortable with this notion, perhaps because he senses I'm manoeuvring him into a position of virtue he thinks is dubious. This is when he's likely to make some throwaway cynical remark, to pull out the analogy of the peacock feathers or tell you that he's just another male show-off and in truth he has no fixed opinions.

*

It's just after five and the winter dusk is creeping in over the river. Walsh escorts me to the car park, saying he has one last thing to show me on the way. We walk past the winery and the row of luxury accommodation pavilions he has built, each overlooking the river and with its own in-house artworks. Earlier in the afternoon I had asked him about his interest in the *Wunderkammer*, the Enlightenment idea of a cabinet of curiosities in which the wonders of the world are arrayed in miniature. He thinks I might be interested to see his own 21st-century version of the concept; as we walk he directs me to an object at the end of the garden that looks like a smaller version of the monolith in Stanley Kubrick's 1968 space epic, *2001: A Space Odyssey*. It's a plain concrete and metal case, around three metres high and curved at the corners. At a certain point our bodies trigger sensors on the path and the metallic facing rises and disappears behind the monolith to reveal a glassed-in display cabinet. It stops me in my tracks. There are coins from the Doges of Venice, pre-Columbian and Egyptian figurines, a huge wheel of primitive stone money and, of course, a television set, flashing with an expressionist video installation, which ought to jar but instead injects a dynamic quality into the ethereal stillness of the antiquities. Unlike the rough miscellany of the traditional *Wunderkammer,* this is a work where the whole is greater than the sum of the parts. It has a magical quality, like some high-tech garden shrine or grotto. As I gape at it admiringly Walsh tells me he curated it himself, and I see that MONA is not all about scale, that he loves his mini-museum as much as he loves anything, and he likes the fact that I like it. I can tell this because he's smiling. I've just spent three hours with David Walsh and this is the first time he's smiled.

In an essay on Sidney Nolan, the art historian William Laffan writes: 'There is a dynamic flux within the art of Sidney Nolan. A fault line lies balanced precariously between the local, specific and quotidian and the universal, metaphorical and mythic.' It's a line, he observes, that is 'blurred constantly, and enigmatically, shifting' and I can think of no better description of MONA, or of its owner. Like his ingenious device, David Walsh is original, surprising, engaged, educative and above all mercurial. I understand now why so many myths have attached to his persona and I sense he likes it that way. It's not about the money, or art as a collection of trophies; it's not even about the peacock feathers. It's about a restless mind and its relentless drive to test the meaning of things, of whatever boundary or reality principle it encounters. MONA will be one long exploratory journey, and in a generous impulse David Walsh wants to take you along with him.

The Monthly

In the Wee Small Hours

Paul Kelly

From Mascot Airport in Sydney to the city usually takes half an hour by car. Sometimes more. Frank Sinatra did it in twelve minutes. According to Michael Chugg, aka Chuggy, the Australian promoter who toured Frank in the '90s, the singer was met as he came off the plane by two federal police and taken to a waiting limo, which then cruised through synchronised traffic lights all the way to his hotel without stopping. I've heard that visiting American presidents can have this kind of thing arranged. The Queen too. And the Pope. But an entertainer? Who describes himself as a 'saloon singer'?

I'm agog, backstage at a festival with Chuggy, talking about Frank. 'Well, you know what they say,' he says. 'It's Frank's world. We just live in it.'

Frank truly created a world. Down and out in the early '50s, after a dizzying rise and fall in the '40s, he teamed up with young arranger Nelson Riddle and Capitol Records to make, over the rest of the decade, a string of albums brilliant in conception and execution.

Long-playing records were just coming into their own as a way of selling music. The first albums were, as the word suggests, collections of singles. Frank and Nelson were the first to think of them differently. They sensed the possibility of making an album a considered and coherent statement, by conceiving a theme and then seeking the songs to fit. Frank didn't write songs himself but knew where to find them. He took old songs which, in the novelty-seeking musical climate of the time, were considered passé, and with the help of Nelson's fresh and bold arrangements made them new again. And in so doing established a large part of what is considered to be the canon of American popular music. The golden age, just when people thought it was gone, now had its king.

That's how golden ages work. They never actually exist at the time. They get invented later. Frank and Nelson were inventors, like Bill Monroe, founding a new kingdom on a mythical past. And through that vanished/present world walked a new man – tough, tender, bruised, knowing. A traveller reporting back from love's far shores of ecstasy and heartbreak. Swaggering on one record, staggering on the next.

*

The night of the day Frank died, 14 May 1998, I waited till the children were asleep, poured myself a whisky, shut the door to the back room, put *In the Wee Small Hours* on nice and loud on the stereo, lay down on the couch and turned out the lights.

The first 12-inch LP Frank and Nelson made – they'd made two 10-inch records of eight songs each the year before – *In the Wee Small Hours* was a chance to really dwell on a theme. They carefully chose sixteen songs. Half of them are under three minutes. None go over four. Every single song deals with the aftermath of a love affair. One sad song ends and another one begins. Then another and another. There's no letting the listener off the hook, no mid- or up-tempo songs to balance the mood or provide a contrast. 'We're serious here,' Frank and Nelson seem to be saying to us. 'Can you go the journey?'

Frank's swinging records – *Songs for Swinging Lovers, Come Fly with Me, Sinatra at The Sands*, and so on – are great to put on in company. People sing along, start talking differently, snap their fingers, feel like changing their clothes or mixing a martini. But you have to play *In the Wee Small Hours* alone, or with somebody in your arms. Put it on as background in a crowded room and it all sounds the same. Someone will inevitably say, 'Turn that sad sack off. He's bringing everybody down.'

It's a record that requires concentration in order to mine its deep lode of riches, and each time I come back to it over the years I'm struck by the concentration brought to bear on its making. You can feel the fierceness of its aesthetic, the uncompromising realisation of a vision. The record has a low, subdued pulse. Every song sounds slowed down. Frank and Nelson take standards and melt them in their glowing crucible to forge new shapes, taking the rhythm out of Duke Ellington's 'Mood Indigo' and ruthlessly chopping verses in other songs to raise the intensity. In 'What Is This Thing Called Love?,' written by Cole Porter, who was no slouch with a lyric, two-thirds of the words are tossed out. Who needs verses? Nelson's opening clarinet figure says it all, before Frank steps in to say it all again in one chorus. That's all they need. By reducing the song they enlarge it beyond measure.

Anyone who's serious about singing popular music gets around at some stage to studying Frank. Listen closely and you hear all the things people talk about – the timing, the detail in each word, the long breath, the tone like a horn, the little slurs up and down to the note, and so on. Other singers have all this too. Many got it from Frank, true, but others had it before him, Billie Holiday, for example, Louis Armstrong. What's so special about Frank? You can talk about the perfect balance he has between talking a song and singing it. 'The microphone is my instrument,' he said. But that came from Bing Crosby. Before Bing realised the possibilities of the microphone – how you could use it to create a mood of intimacy, a warm conversational tone – most popular singers were belters, like Al Jolson. Bing changed all that. And Frank studied Bing.

So what *is* so special about Frank? What's the X-thing? Sex? The bobby-soxers heard that, sure. Frank put the ba-da-bing into Bing and we've been hearing it ever since. But sex symbols come and go. Frank has remained. There must be something else.

I remember my shock the first time I saw a photo of Frank as a young man. My image of him up to that point was of someone eternally middle-aged – someone who made music for grown-ups. That whippet-thin, high-cheekboned, wavy-haired, handsome boy-next-door in the photo – that was Frank? The same person as the round-faced, sinister-looking balding man who made lame jokes and crooned with his drinking cronies in Las Vegas casinos? It seemed unbelievable to me. I was young myself when I received this shock, and over the years since then, like everybody, I've had plenty more of the natural shocks flesh is heir to.

The gap between youth and old age, that big sea we cross, is the story of our life, and all our other stories – of love, work, power, family, health – fit within it. We all make our adjustments to that slow-unfolding car crash as best we can. If you look at photos of a person over the course of their life you can see their different stages, sense the transitions. But when you examine photos of Frank Sinatra, one of the most photographed humans on the planet, there seems to be a gap in the record. One minute he's young, the next middle-aged. It's weird.

Did no one take photos of him during those few years in the late '40s when he bottomed out? Well, of course they must have, but in my imagination there's a short crucial period they missed. It could have been just a few weeks or months, maybe around the time of which Sammy Davis Jr said, 'Frank was walking down Broadway with no hat on and his collar up, and not a soul was paying attention to him. This was the man who, only a few years before, had tied up traffic all over Times Square. Now the same man was walking down the same street, and nobody gave a damn.'

Not long after that his own publicist said, 'Frank is through. A year from now you won't hear anything about him. He'll be dead professionally … The public … doesn't like him anymore.'

He was thirty-four years old.

*

The story's been told endlessly. Everybody loves a comeback yarn. Frank, dropped by Columbia Records, going through the wringer with Ava Gardner, deserted by his fans, the younger stars shooting past him, begs and pleads his way into an acting role in *From Here to Eternity*, meets Nelson Riddle and has the brainwave, survives a long count on the canvas and comes up swinging. And stays swinging into the '60s and '70s and beyond. Along the way he flounders here and there, snarls at rock'n'roll, gets stood up by the Kennedys because of his mob connections, gets fed up and retires for a minute, gets into punch-ups with reporters and cameramen, and travels with a large collection of toupees and assistants, including a dedicated toupee minder. He loses his hair but never loses the crown again.

Music writers like to say that *In the Wee Small Hours* derives its intensity from his break-up with Ava. Breaking up with Ava would be tough, no doubt. The publicity machine had him supposedly breaking down in the studio after he sang 'When Your Lover Has Gone.' All this may be true, but his singing goes deeper and further than that. It's more than despair at the end of an affair. Just as his appearance in photos suddenly changed, so too had his voice. Bono, who writes beautifully about Frank, describes his voice as 'a knotted fist.' Someone else said the violin had turned into a viola. Others speak of ageing wine. The voice is now more knowing. It knows loss. Not just the loss of the love of one woman but the loss of status, the loss of reputation, the loss of fame, and most important of all, the loss of the opportunity to make art. It's as if he stared at the possibility, however briefly, of his music being taken away from him and the shock turned him old overnight.

He came back from that dark night down at the crossroads like Robert Johnson, needy and dangerous, armed with a whole new power.

*

So you lie in the dark on the night of his death, listening to Frank singing 'Glad to Be Unhappy' and 'I'll Never Be the Same' and all the songs between, and you enter a wondrous church of conjuration. Frank is praying to his icons. He summons up his pictures of worship, and like the old-time fasting saints, surrenders to ecstatic visions. In 'Deep in a Dream' the walls of his room fall away and the smoke from his cigarette becomes a staircase for his lover to descend on. Even when his cigarette burns him he feels no physical pain, such is his trancelike state. 'Deep in a Dream' is followed by 'I See Your Face Before Me.' And further along, in another hallucinatory song, his beloved dances on the ceiling as he lies in bed.

You lie in the dark as Frank sings of loss and try to pay attention to all the little exquisite details – the way the rhythm section drops out temporarily in the title song, leaving us with floating strings before the voice comes back in: Frank's playing with the melody in 'Mood Indigo,' his eleven 'no's when he restates the opening lines, the burbling, muted trumpet breaking loose from the horn section before rejoining – but after a while you find yourself drifting off and thinking about your own life and all its losses, how life over time is simply a series of losses: loss of parents, of friends, of love, of possibilities; loss of innocence and your children's innocence.

The knowledge that you'll never be able to sing like Frank is another kind of loss. You'll never even get close, and Frank will never sing 'Winter Coat,' the song you wrote to conjure him. It was always a long shot, getting longer by the day, but now that tiny daydream is forever snuffed.

Loss's sphere grows wider now, and included in it is all possibility. You reflect on all you've missed – how much of your life you've forgotten, how much has streamed by you, how paltry the haul in your little net. There are the books you haven't read, the ones you've read but don't recall, the history you don't know, the languages you haven't learnt, the music you haven't heard, the songs you haven't written, the things you wish you'd asked your parents, the hugeness of the world, the tiny fraction of it you've gleaned, its sadness and suffering and deterioration, the friendships you didn't have with people you admired, that beautiful stranger you saw in the street the other day who you'll never know.

Still you lie in the dark. Frank has sung every permutation of unrequited love. He's covered the classic kiss-off – 'Can't We Be Friends?' He's said he'll wait around till she breaks up with the new guy. He's looked ahead and seen himself growing old alone. He's sung about the pleasures of melancholy. The entire record, in fact, luxuriates in its sadness. It dawns on you that there's one permutation he's avoided. Not one song expresses anger. Deep hurt, yes, but not the rage that hurt can engender. There's resignation, yearning, and a glimmer of hope. Every song is bathed in love.

'This love of mine goes on and on' is the very last line you hear as the album ends. The torch will never go out. You get up off the couch, refreshed by tears, thankful for Frank, and drain the last dreg of whisky, forty-eight minutes older and glad somehow to be sad.

How to Make Gravy

Real Food

Peter Robb

Food people are news, and Tony Bilson was talked about last April when he introduced, at Bilson's in Sydney's Radisson Plaza Hotel, a new degustation menu of fifteen courses for $280. This is probably the most expensive *prix fixe* in town. Nobody spending that much on their food would be likely to skimp on the wines, which implies a meal costing $500 per head. Or a thousand, easily. The menu was news not for the price – this is Sydney – but for one dish, a raw egg yolk 'encrusted' with gold and served on sprinkles of something called 'chicken sand,' rye and parmesan.

Tony Bilson has done incomparable good for eating in Sydney over a long time. The gold-coated egg yolk was a Melbourne boy's astute pitch at Sydney's easily bored diners – he talked of 'keeping them interested.' Yet you wondered whether Bilson, who has been thrashing around a bit lately, losing hats and speaking out sharply, didn't feel a twinge of regret. Was that all it came to, forty years on from Tony's Bon Gout? After decades of labour in Sydney and environs? A raw egg yolk coated in gold dust?

Tony and Gay Bilson became famous for their food in the 1970s, though I couldn't dream of eating at a Bilson place then, and haven't yet. About the time they were opening Berowra Waters Inn on the Hawkesbury, north of Sydney – the most famous restaurant in Australia's memory – I took off for Naples, where however bad things got, and they quite often did, I could always afford to eat out like the locals. Often pretty well.

*

One of those long ago days a friend in Naples suggested I write a book about the poor food of the city. Meaning not bad food but the contrary. *Cucina povera* was the food and the cooking of the poor people in Naples, who were most of the population. Nobody has ever done more with less in the kitchen than the Neapolitans.

The lady who proposed this did not herself belong to this group. She lived in an enormous palace that rose massively from the water's edge at Posillipo. It had been built, she told me, for an Armenian prince in the nineteenth century, but for a long time it had been shared – a level each – by her husband and his brother and their respective large families.

There was plenty of room for everyone, even in the shared courtyard garden and the boathouse on the lowest level with its slipway into the sea. Something in the palace's craft and style recalled the residential buildings of Gaudí in Barcelona. You could see it, with its deep puce walls and granite trim, from well out to sea when arriving or departing on the Palermo night ferry, or sailing to Capri on her brother's yacht.

The lady had people to cook for her, and people who attended to other tasks that running her vast establishment involved, but she was an attentive mistress of her household. On the basis of a few unscheduled meals in the palace at Posillipo and some summer weeks at the villa in Sardinia, I'd place her family as the luckiest eaters, day by day, I've ever known.

And what they ate, a lot of the time, were the same things the poor ate. It was done with the finest ingredients and occasional extras but was not essentially different. This was the point of the distinguished lady's interest in what I knew about what people ate in the homes and trattorie of Naples. She knew it too, and she knew that the knowledge was special; she thought it deserved to be known outside its native ground.

I later met, far from Naples, a wealthy and urbane art merchant who lived in a castle in the Italian north – and had once been thrown fully dressed into Sylvester Stallone's swimming pool. When I mentioned the ignored glories of Neapolitan cooking his diffuse amiability became focused passion. He was a secret Neapolitan. In Naples, he said, you can walk into the simplest trattoria – he was thinking of a hole in the wall *Vini e Cucina* – and eat the same things you get in the fancy places and just as well cooked.

*

There are reasons Neapolitan and southern Italian food is ignored by serious people. A century ago, when the people of the south – millions of them – fled to the Americas, they took their basic foods with them to the raw societies of the new world. Pasta and pizza adapted downwards as the fast foods of the new industrial societies. The omnipresence of industrially produced tomato sauces in North America's favourite Italian dishes was another backhanded gift from Naples.

The Campania region around the city produces better tomatoes and more varieties of them than anywhere else. They come sequentially through the seasons. I counted seven or eight kinds once, from green salad tomatoes in early spring to the tresses of little mountain tomatoes that you hung on the wall and cooked through winter.

History can be written over. The ugly past of Neapolitan food in North America needn't matter today. But *cucina povera* still uses the cheapest ingredients you can find. Much of the food starts its life as wheat. Bread in Naples – a Campanian country *pagnotta* from a woodburning stone oven, with a blistered crust like hardened lava and combed with great holes inside like the ground under Naples – is the best in the world if you have teeth to break the crust and jaws to chew, and a great cleaver to hack it into pieces. With a drizzle of olive oil and a ripe San Marzano tomato pressed into it, the bread is a meal.

Durum wheat became dry pasta in endless shapes and sizes; soft grain flour also became fresh pasta when mixed with eggs, and pizza dough leavened like the bread. In Milan, in the boom years of the early '80s, pasta was tossed with smoked salmon and vodka and other arriviste novelties. In Naples after the earthquake, torn apart by hard drugs and gang murders, the core choice remained pasta with white beans, pasta with chickpeas, pasta with potatoes, pasta with lentils. Made with assorted fragments of broken pasta from the bottom of the bag, these were exquisite.

The daily staple of white bean pasta became a luxury dish when a few fresh mussels were added. There was spaghetti with tomatoes, with baby clams, with baby clams and tomatoes. The clams were already a luxury component, and in harder times before the war cloves of garlic were trimmed to look like small clams without their shells.

A decent fish was treated with the respect it deserved of total minimalism. It was grilled or steamed in the simplest way and delicately picked apart. Sometimes done in *acqua pazza* – cooked very fast in a pan with seawater, olive oil and fresh tomato that had reduced to a dense liquor by the time the fish was done. Baby squid and little prawns and tiny pink rockfish were cheap and fried up together.

Octopus made a salad – another friend told me she added a wine cork to the boiling water to help the never-quite-achieved tenderising – and slow-cooked baby octopus a stupendously subtle and endlessly giving stew. My favourite fish were the most despised, the beautiful fresh silver anchovies, with their dense, oily, pungent flesh. Nothing was better than a plate of them, dusted with flour, briefly plunged in hot oil, and served with half a lemon and some of that bread. Salted *baccalà* and sundried *stoccafisso* from the North Sea were medieval survivors that came into their own in winter.

The vegetable glory of Naples, antedating the arrival of dry pasta from Sicily – the food storage system of the Arab navigators changed the world's eating – and the arrival of tomatoes and eggplants from the Americas, was the green leaf plants grown in its volcanic soil. I bought mine from Antonio in the street market at Borgo Sant'Antonio Abate. He grew his own, harvested them at dawn and drove them into his place on the street each morning, along with the chooks' new eggs, on the back of his three-wheeled transporter.

Folded into a book, I still have Don Mario Silvestri's handwritten instructions for making a proper *minestra maritata*. The soup marries masses of these greens with a modest quantity of meat in a good stock, and made the Neapolitans famous in Europe as 'the leaf eaters' of Italy. Mario's notes specify seven different green leaf vegetables – among the many – all prepared and cooked separately before being added to the stock in the right proportions.

All of these breads and pastas and pizzas, all of these vegetables, all of the fresh cheeses that were another marvel of food in Naples – the daily mozzarella, the *fior di latte*, the smoked provola – and all the combinations of the three into the city's favourite dishes, and the wine and the oil, were immensely labour-intensive, in the peasant labour of their production and in the female domestic labour of their preparation. They still are, though the labour is mostly immigrant.

I never wrote my book on the *cucina povera* of Naples. Who would ever have used it? People who use recipe books now, like people who go to restaurants, are not making desperate economies. Their aim is not to make delicious food out of things that cost next to nothing. They aren't ready to spend hours and hours and hours peeling, kneading, grinding, pounding, sieving, watching, soaking, shelling, stirring, turning, rinsing, testing, separating, combining, marinating, skimming, moistening, ladling the things they will eventually eat. And if they were – the urge to cook a splendid dinner can invest unlikely people – the makings would have to be special and costly. The language of *cucina povera* is a dying tongue even in Naples.

*

Italian food travels well. Especially to Australia. The Italians who came here in the decades immediately after World War II made a gentler landfall than their grand or great-grand relatives had in the Americas. They found neither the chaotic violence of Brazil and Argentina nor the brutal industrialisation of the United States, nor the freezing puritanism of Canada. In Australia they found a modest provincial Anglo settlement not unaware of its own limitations and touchingly eager, as the money started coming in, to get to know the new, the exotic, the glamorous.

The Italians also found, on the continent's south-eastern sea-board, a climate much like the one they'd left, a sea richer than the Mediterranean in edible life, and a soil infinitely receptive to plantings of zucchini, melanzane, peperoni, carciofi, fave, basilico, oregano, bietola, rape, broccolini, radicchio, *purchiac-chelle*, olive, mandorle, noci, melograni. And all the new strains of tomato and endless grapevines. The people of the Mezzogiorno – serious, modest and skilled market gardeners, winemakers, fruit growers, fishers, butchers, greengrocers, poulterers, bak-ers, pastry cooks, confectioners, ice-cream makers, cooks and waiters almost to the last man and woman, complemented by a clutch of self-dramatising rogues, conmen, amiable losers and brilliant improvisers – never looked back.

Who from Melbourne in the '60s will forget that theatre of abundance round the corner from Pellegrini's coffee bar, in the lane off Bourke Street – a little Cockayne where you pointed at what you wanted among the things you'd never seen or tasted before? The gelati and cassate that followed? The coffee? Who will forget the coming to life of Carlton's Lygon Street, the strip of coffee shops and restaurants for students and migrants that grew gaudy as the decade ended? Unassuming little places like the Perla Nera vanished without trace.

Uniquely among the immigrant peoples after the war, the Italians knew how to seize what their new land offered to refine and develop their arts of food. What's left now of the *cucina pov-era* they brought from the Italian south? After half a century, what remains of that core understanding that a restaurant's business is to satisfy hunger and modestly gratify the senses? What does 'Italian' mean, in a time when nearly everyone has more money than they know what to do with, and no idea how food is produced, how it's cooked, or what it costs?

I went to the Enoteca Sileno in Carlton, where everything was costly but so well chosen and so well prepared, so amiably and unobtrusively presented, that it was beyond reproach. Not many could make the Enoteca their daily resort, but anyone would. In Sydney, Lucio's in Paddington is on a different and Ligurian matrix but fresh, punctilious, complete, inventive as it needs to be and never more. Neither the Enoteca nor Lucio's has an Italian cook: Italy in Australia has created its own culture and educated a generation. At Lucio's you can have a fish baked sealed in a crust of salt: as I learnt in Palermo once, the best way of all to cook a whole fish.

*

Neapolitans themselves travel badly. The infinite complexities of their city disqualify them from the simplicities of success elsewhere. They make the world's worst emigrants. Lots return to Naples, some sooner, some later, preferring failure at home. Di Stasio in St Kilda had a good Neapolitan name and a proprietor born in Melbourne. I'd enjoyed a Sunday lunch there once in the alcove by the bar. Dinner now was desolating. The main room's tobacco tinted, unpainted hard plaster looked like a Kings Cross crime scene from the '40s. Shadowy clients begged for recognition and pretended they still liked it. The pasta was OK. It was radio days. Everything dies.

I'd sometimes dined with my father in the austere old Florentino in Bourke Street, patriarchal Ernesto standing by the enormous antique coffee machine in the corner, Bill the doorman still downstairs from the last war. And in London at stately Gennaro's in Soho, a restaurant adored by the younger Virginia Woolf. I'd caused unhappy family scenes in the Dorchester Grill. Gennaro's is long gone, the Florentino carpeted and monogrammed out of existence, the Dorchester Arab glamour. The Di Stasio details reduce to a chunky glass calyx of hard plain ice-cream topped by a maraschino cherry. I clung to the pinot bottle for its ancient rectitude. Sometimes the past should be oblivion.

Back in Sydney, home of instant gratification – nothing could take less time than sprinkling gold dust over a raw egg yolk, or swallowing it – I looked at Tony Bilson's online menu and found that his yolk had proletarianised. In April it was gold encrusted. By mid-May it was arriving with cauliflower, sprouts and Vegemite. Three of my least favourite early food memories on the same *nouveau* plate. It was nothing to do with hard times. The set menu still cost $280 without wine.

When the stars make you drool just like a pasta fasul', that's amore.

The Monthly

How Broadway Conquered the World

Clive James

Though his book is unusually good, Larry Stempel is not the first to sum up the history of the Broadway musical theatre. The literature, as they say, is vast. They say that about subjects where literature is not the first thing you want. You want it only later on, after you have already fallen for the subject because of its inherent enjoyability, and not because of what can be brought to it by way of explanation. In that respect, Broadway itself was vast almost from the start, when a musicalised version of *Uncle Tom's Cabin*, first staged in 1853, included Stephen Foster's catchy lament 'Old Folks at Home,' of which even the lyrics were in blackface. 'All de *world* am sad and dreary ...'

The way the word *world* sat on the note clinched the deal. Anybody's grandmother could have a crack at singing it, even though she herself was as Old Folks as you could get. Something similar was true for any other show that clicked. People would come to it so that they could go home singing. People who didn't go to the opera loved going to the musicals. Eventually people who did go to the opera went to the musicals as well. More eventually still, the musicals turned into operas – *Carousel* and its many successors are essentially operas, but with easier arias, and plots that add up – as America's most energetic indigenous art form went on conquering the world. Most eventually of all, the British musicals conquered Broadway, but they got the idea from the place they conquered. The same would be true if a show starring Kim Jong-il – also responsible for music, book and lyrics – started its New York run next week.

It's a big cultural story, and Stempel does well to fit it neatly into one volume, with an inoffensive neutral style – except for the word *diegetic*, which we will keep caged until later – and a wealth of information. (Did you know that the first lyricist for *Man of La Mancha* was W.H. Auden? He was paid off and replaced: a telling illustration of the Broadway principle that commerce comes first, even in an off-Broadway production.) Apart from the word *diegetic* – my God, it broke loose, throw a net over it – Stempel's book is a large but light-footed embodiment of the truth that nothing keeps you sane like being mad about your subject. Enjoyment keeps theory at bay. If you can do a fair bathroom impersonation of Ezio Pinza singing 'Some Enchanted Evening' from *South Pacific* ('You may see a stranger-*or*'), you are less likely to talk high-flown nonsense about an influence that got into you by a low route, under the radar of the higher brain centres. 'I'm gonna wash that man right outta my hair ...' Ensign Nellie Forbush (Mary Martin onstage in New York, Mitzi Gaynor in the movie) sings that line three times in the one stanza, as if it were an interesting line in the first place. It isn't, but just try forgetting it. Some alchemy of words and music, some enchanted something or other, benumbs the critical powers.

It's hard to know which is the bigger waste of time, insisting that the Broadway musical is an art form or insisting that it isn't: but we can be sure that the question would never have arisen if the shows that became famous all over the world hadn't been full of singable moments in the first place. And the singable moment, the moment you can't get out of your head, got in there before it could be asked for its credentials. It could cross the globe without a passport.

When I was growing up, in Sydney in the 1940s and '50s, the local production of the latest hit American musical was always the biggest show in town. The principal roles were taken by the most famous local performers, who worked hard on their American accents, not always to convincing effect. Performers who would become famous later on got their start in the chorus. (In the London production of *South Pacific*, one of the sailors

was the young Sean Connery. 'There ish nothin' like a dame ...')
Even if you didn't see the show, the numbers were in the hit
parade, and later on, they were on the cast albums. *South Pacific*
I actually saw onstage when I was still in short trousers. My
mother took me because everybody went: it was the thing to do.
Though it might seem, at this distance, a pretty extraordinary
thing to do – the Americans were behaving not only as if they
had won the war against the Japanese all on their own, but as if
they intended to win the peace as well – nobody questioned it
then, partly because, as the Hollywood movies had already
proved, American cultural imperialism was not only too big to
fight, it was too seductive to ignore.

I had no idea what the chorus of male sailors were on about
when they kept singing 'There is nothin' like a dame' – what did
they have in mind? – but I still thought 'Some Enchanted
Evening' was fabulous. I had already memorised some of the lyrics before I left the theatre, and subsequently I learned the rest
from listening to the radio. On the radio, they were playing the
song as sung in the original Broadway production by Ezio Pinza,
he who had created the role of Emile de Becque. A favourite at
the Metropolitan Opera, Pinza was a bass in the fine tradition
of Chaliapin and Kipnis, the tone warm and the timbre profound. For someone my age whose voice had not yet broken, imi-
tating Pinza was not easy, but I managed it by tucking my chin
well into my chest. 'Once you have *found* her, never let her *go* ...'
My bass notes shook the bathroom.

When the movie came out, Pinza wasn't in it, his death having preempted the break that would have turned him from an
artist into an icon. Because the studio bosses couldn't cast Pinza,
they decided not to cast Mary Martin either. (These details are
not in Stempel's book, for a reason we will get to.) Those in
charge of the movie, who included Rodgers and Hammerstein,
were unanimous in wanting Rossano Brazzi for the role. As
European and distinguished as a Romanesque cathedral with
only superficial bomb damage, Brazzi was perfect in every way
but one. He was lying when he said he could sing. When Rodgers
and Hammerstein found out that he couldn't carry a tune any
further than a few inches, they insisted that his voice be dubbed,
even though Brazzi himself was adamant that he could do the

job. Dense as well as proud, he never got over not being allowed to, and for much of the filming, as the recorded sound was played in so that he could make with the mouth, he behaved like a beast with its amour-propre on the line. They could have got me for half the money.

Brazzi could afford to be petulant because his arse, or at any rate his throat, was being covered by Giorgio Tozzi, whose voice equaled Pinza's in the professional accomplishment that is known on Broadway as 'legit' – that is, trained. Broadway has always been able to use trained voices as long as they don't *sound* trained. The underlying assumption is that the audience for a musical doesn't want to hear what it can't possibly do: it wants to hear what it might have done if life had worked out differently, and still might do after a few drinks.

Later – much later – I learned that Rodgers and Hammerstein, while the war was still on, had worked a revolution in the musical when they concocted *Oklahoma!*, the first show to be fully 'integrated,' with every number growing organically out of the book and back into it, instead of just decorating a flimsy plot line as of old. Stempel gives a good account of the historic moment when Rodgers and Hart gave way to Rodgers and Hammerstein, although he might have said a little more about what was undoubtedly lost when the cleverness of the old numbers gave way to the organic relevance of the new ones. Even then, before I had started listening to Hart's lyrics, I could tell that Hammerstein's were straining to sound so relaxed. (And anyway, Hammerstein himself seemed oddly unready to quite give up the old tricksiness: has anybody ever asked what Nellie Forbush, theoretically a down-home girl in love with a wonderful guy, is up to when she sings a word like *bromidic*? Stempel doesn't.)

But that transition from the simple form that had the complex songs to the complex form that had the simple ones was part of the history of the genre: the succession of events that Stempel so meticulously covers in his text. Once, the show had existed so that a song could stand out from it: pre-war, Cole Porter wrote songs for shows with not much more structure than had once been boasted by the *Ziegfeld Follies*. Later, the songs existed for the show: either they were part of the structure, or they got cut before the show reached town. Such was the dynamic of artistic development, which always looks inevitable in retrospect. But at the time I am talking about – a time when almost everything from *Oklahoma!* through to *West Side Story* was either already onstage or in the works – very few people even in New York, and almost none at all elsewhere in the world, had any idea of an art form developing. They were just being hit by an experience: or rather, one experience after another, as the musical shows and movies unfolded a wonderful and unexpected wealth. Thus it was that I moved on from being Ezio Pinza to being Marlon Brando in *Guys and Dolls*.

Frank Sinatra was in the same movie, but I didn't want to be him. After seeing *The Tender Trap* several nights in succession, I had put a lot of effort into adopting his identity (I owned one of the first Sinatra-red shirts to reach Australia, probably in the cargo hold of a Pan Am Stratocruiser), but my impersonation was hampered by the fact that Sinatra could sing. Brando's Sky Masterson was more in my range, especially after my voice broke. I had a sinus condition anyway, so it wasn't hard to get the intonation. All you had to do was pull in your nose as if you had just run into a closed door. If I had lived in New York I might have been watching Robert Alda on Broadway, but I was in Sydney, and I was watching the same guy who had been strictly incomprehensible in *The Wild One* being almost lyrical when he sang 'Luck Be a Lady.'

Lyrical, perhaps, but not really musical. Brando could barely carry a tune, and I could tell he couldn't. But it didn't matter. The numbers came across. That was what the stars were doing up there. They were delivering songs to a not very music-minded mass audience, which would listen a bit harder because the face was famous. The face was delivering Broadway. *Singin' in the Rain* was never a Broadway show, but after I saw Gene Kelly starring in the movie, he, for me, was Broadway. (In fact he had been the original star of *Pal Joey* on Broadway in 1940.) Though it went straight to the screen without even touching the stage, *Singin' in the Rain* was made possible by a hundred years of know-how from Broadway and Tin Pan Alley. In long pants now and all set to burn the boards, how I loved the songs, how I adored Debbie Reynolds, how I laughed at Jean Hagen, and what a mistake I made when I copied Donald O'Connor's trick of running up the wall and turning a back somersault. In the few seconds of consciousness remaining, I began to realise just how good O'Connor was.

There were other movies of the post-war period that showed a similar ability to draw on the Broadway tradition while having been concocted almost entirely in Hollywood. *The Band Wagon* kept only the title and a few songs of a pre-war Broadway show. Yet the movie's magnificent final dance number, 'The Girl Hunt,' would never have looked like that if its choreographer, Michael Kidd, had not developed his craft on Broadway. *Seven Brides for Seven Brothers* was another movie masterpiece that was never a Broadway show: it just looked as if it could have been. The stage form was driving the cinematic form, like a tail wagging a dog.

Other Hollywood musical movies adapted Broadway vehicles, but dug them up from the far past, like war chariots from the desert sands. *The Student Prince*, scored by Sigmund Romberg, had been a hit Broadway show in the 1920s, had been revived successfully in each of the next two decades, and now was back yet again because of Hollywood's unquenchable fondness for Ruritania, the abstract European kingdom for which so many Jewish Hollywood executives longed in their exiled hearts. Mario Lanza, with much fanfare, had been cast in the lead. Lanza got into a dispute with the studio and was fired from the movie in the brief time between recording the songs for playback and the moment when he would actually be filmed pretending to sing them. To fill the space onscreen, Edmund Purdom was whistled in. He couldn't sing, but he was there to move his mouth while the voice of Lanza came pouring from the sound track. In that sense, all the stars in the film musicals were dubbed, but the average moviegoer was presumed to like it better when they were dubbed with their own voices, as if contact were somehow being maintained with live theatre.

Though my version of 'Serenade,' ringing from our bathroom at all hours of the day, lowered property values at our end of the street, I never wanted to be Edmund Purdom. I did, however, want to be Mario Lanza, whose voice I thought glorious. As it happened, I was right about that, and today there are experts on opera (tenors such as Rolando Villazón among them) who are ready to say that Lanza's voice was one of the greatest of the century; but at the time he was a figure of fun, because he could not control his weight. This is not the place to talk about Lanza, just as Stempel's book is not the place to read about him: the book has very little about musicals onscreen. As a one-volume work, it was bound to have some limitations, but this is a serious limitation, because the movies were the medium by which Broadway got to all those millions of us who weren't going to get to it. All too obviously, going to the actual show, or anyway to its revival, is Stempel's ideal. He is a buff. But the musicals, in my view, worked their most remarkable effect on those of us who weren't buffs at all. We were just ordinary people, most of us a long way away from the action, and yet somehow this thing reached us, like an airborne virus, or a swarm of bees with inter-continental fuel capacity.

Sometimes the cast album was enough to do the trick. I never saw *The Music Man*, either onstage or onscreen, but in Sydney one of my friends owned the cast album. In this and in all the other Broadway shows none of the musical effects would have meant much without the lyrics. When I started listening to grand opera, I soon realised that its musical resources hugely exceeded most of what was available in the Broadway musical, but I also realized that any opera spends most of its time proving, through the music, that the text is a pretext.

In the musical, the words make the music happen. Among those who wrote or even just talked about musicals, it was generally assumed that in the old pre-*Oklahoma!* tradition, the words had been self-consciously marvellous. After all, everyone could sing a few things by Irving Berlin and Cole Porter and Rodgers and Hart. But the shows were long gone – this was in the days before anyone thought of running old-Broadway revivals anywhere, let alone on Broadway – and it was hard to check up, except through what the more respectable popular singers chose to sing. Then Ella Fitzgerald chose to sing everything, and the whole picture emerged seemingly overnight. In the 1950s and early '60s, Ella's Song Book albums were so absorbing that you were still on the previous one when the next one arrived. The wealth of great material made it all too easy to conclude that something had been lost when the integrated musical took over.

But it wasn't necessarily the right conclusion, or not immediately, anyway. Even Hammerstein, whose lyrics I took to be the sticky outpourings of a sentimentalist even when I couldn't get them out of my hair, hadn't lost touch with the old heritage: because he knew it so well, he knew exactly how to avoid its flashy elements while retaining its easily pronounced articulation, although often he overdid the simplicity and lapsed into the banal. At his best, he could mimic speech. In *Carousel*, the long song 'Soliloquy,' a virtuoso musical construction by Rodgers, has bravura lyrics by Hammerstein. The lyricist's determined avoidance of cleverness suited the character, who isn't clever either: he's just Billy Bigelow, the carousel's barker. In the song, he reveals his ambitions as a father, which are very ordinary, and ordinariness, despite the opulent invocation of the supernatural, would have threatened to overwhelm the whole show, if Rodgers and Hammerstein hadn't combined so successfully to turn out the sonic equivalent of a Norman Rockwell cover for the *Saturday Evening Post*. (Both of them thought it was the best show from their collaboration.)

Perhaps Rodgers's single most glorious outlay of melody, 'Soliloquy' was too long for the hit parade, but Frank Sinatra went ahead anyway, and cut a disc that had half the song on each side. Stempel might have written more about 'Soliloquy,' and of how seemingly colourless words can take colour from musical notes, but it has to be admitted that the analysis of lyrics is not his greatest strength. (The best writing about 'Soliloquy' I have so far seen comes from Mark Steyn, who echoes and often exceeds the capacity of Alec Wilder in his knack for bringing out the complexities of a song's construction.) It takes an ear, and finally anyone who can use a word like *diegetic* without laughing at himself has to be suspected of deafness. To put the word out of its misery before we bury it, a song is 'diegetic' if the character knows he or she is singing it. When Maria sings 'Do-Re-Mi' to the unfortunate von Trapp children in *The Sound of Music*, she's singing something diegetic. On the other hand, Billy isn't singing something diegetic when he sings 'Soliloquy' in *Carousel*. Better, perhaps, just to accept that he is singing something amazing. Certainly Sinatra thought so, to name only one person among millions who would have thought that a diegetic condition might be cured with Pepto-Bismol.

On the whole, the integrated musical after *Oklahoma!* was not as prodigious a generator of hit songs as the old-style formats had been, because hit songs had been their main reason for being, whereas the integrated musical was providing a different, supposedly more elevated, theatrical experience. But not even the most advanced of the new musicals could recoup its investment if it didn't give the audience something to go home singing. Cole Porter turned the new rules into an opportunity. A song like 'You're the Top,' from *Anything Goes*, had taken off from the show and established a life of its own, to the extent that many of us can sing whole chunks of it without being able to name the show it comes from. On the other hand, all the numbers in the wonderful *Kiss Me, Kate* are anchored in the book by Sam and Bella Spewack, who had taken over *The Taming of the Shrew* and incorporated it into a nest of plots whose intricacy is endless: Tom Stoppard's *Travesties* before the fact. Every song Porter did for the show fits its labyrinthine structure. But still the numbers fly: 'Brush Up Your Shakespeare' is something you can't stop yourself singing along with. The only danger with the new form was that if the numbers didn't have to be separable hits, then they wouldn't be.

With the advent of *West Side Story*, the danger was still hard to identify, because it was disguised as a glittering cluster of some of the catchiest numbers Broadway had ever produced. Leonard Bernstein, the composer, knew everything about how to make a melody memorable. He could put the word *America* on four notes so that it became a mini-anthem, a kind of musical flag, and then vary the notes so that the flags turned into a carnival. And the words were put together by a frighteningly young man who had not only learned from Hammerstein about how to grow a song out of the plot, he had learned from the previous tradition about how to be clever. He was a precocious master of the complete heritage, but the heritage was still bolted firmly to a precept that until then had been so unquestionable it didn't even need to be formulated, except as a wisecrack. Somebody had once said that nobody ever went home whistling the set. It was a neat way of saying that the song comes first. There has to be something to sing, and the chief danger presented by the new musical – the danger that there wouldn't be – was already there in *West Side Story*. The danger's name was Stephen Sondheim.

Sondheim was, still is, a genius. The term *genius* has always been tossed around freely in the Broadway context, for the good reason that the main street of musical show business has always teemed with greatly talented people motivated by the two great spurs to creativity, the urge to express oneself fully and the urge to make a million dollars. But Rouben Mamoulian, to take only one example, undoubtedly was a genius: for the man who put *Oklahoma!* together onstage, there would have been no other suitable description, even if he had done nothing else except direct the Hollywood movie *Love Me Tonight*. Similarly, there could be no doubt about Sondheim's right to the title: the lyrics to *West Side Story* were sensational. Snapping my fingers as I moved forward in a threatening crouch, I spent a lot of time being a Jet, and it occurred to me even then that the Cold War was already over: the Soviet Union was never going to pick at its own wounds like this. Sondheim soon proved that he could write music too. To adapt the phrase he put in the mouth of Miles Gloriosus in *A Funny Thing Happened on the Way to the Forum*, Sondheim was a parade. But so much talent, in the popular arts, can easily find itself with only one boundary left to burst: it wants to move up, to be Art. And the danger represented by Sondheim lay in his having the wherewithal to bring this about.

The latter part of the book is haunted by Sondheim, about whom Stempel finds it hard to come clean. What does this guy want? What if everybody catches this Art thing, and we all go broke? Back before World War II, Kurt Weill, in exile from Germany, where he had composed the music for *The Threepenny Opera*, had been proud and happy to work on Broadway. Many times he announced that it was better for people like him to take their chances in the commercial world of Broadway than to be subsidised: you can imagine him saying the same sort of thing in a Fox News interview today. Weill, however, still couldn't help wondering what might be created in that increasingly tempting space between Broadway and Art. It's a perennial longing, it comes with the territory, and often the results are to be admired.

After all, a lot of Broadway shows are pretty stupid underneath the razzmatazz: they could do with being superseded. But there is always the risk that an essential requirement might go missing, and the lack be felt not only in the wallet, but in the blood and bone of the form. Is there something for the audience to sing?

Stempel marches dutifully through all the shows that made sure there was, no matter how tightly integrated they might happen to have been. From *Cabaret*, everyone can sing the title song. There are probably nonagenarian ex-Nazis who can sing it. Whether on or off Broadway, most of the shows in the latter part of the twentieth century went on dishing out the take-out melodies. But sitting above it all was Sondheim, doing stuff so elevated, it was almost impossible to grab a piece of. The upshot is a strong reputation and weak box office, a fact Stempel faces squarely. He might have illustrated the point more tellingly, however. He could have talked about the urban legend – if it isn't true, it ought to be – that the compulsively hummable 'Send In the Clowns' was written at the last minute as a sop to backers. By Sondheim's later account, he had artistic reasons for leaving it so late, but the story about the panicking moneymen steers you in the right direction: Sondheim's later work is short of things that you can't help singing. And he must mean it to be. After all, he wrote and placed those beautiful phrases about the clowns. You should hear my version. 'Isn't it *rich* ...' The know-how of my early Pinza period comes in handy.

Whether there will be many more home-grown hit shows to rival *The Producers* at the Broadway box office – a good show about a bad show, it made you hope that self-reflexivity is not always a sign of terminal decadence – probably depends on the British going home and leaving the theatres free. The British come in waves, and one of the waves is Andrew Lloyd Webber. He is often mocked for writing a species of sub-opera, but he is really writing a species of super-musical. From the London productions, from the movies, from the cast albums, from all the sources through which the Broadway musical reached my generation, it also reached his, and he knew just how to take inspiration from it. His melodies are sometimes accused of being derivative – in *Jesus Christ Superstar*, the notes behind the name-check of the title song exactly match a phrase from one of Richard Strauss's *Four Last Songs* – but usually they aren't: they are just so catchy you can't believe you are hearing them for the first time. And to have Tim Rice as his first lyricist was a break, because Rice understood that successful pop songs consist entirely of hooks.

Rice gave Lloyd Webber the verbal phrases with which to practise his knack for laying words on the line. He can do it dauntingly well. In the hit song 'Don't Cry for Me Argentina' from *Evita*, the phrase 'So I chose freedom' is coupled as delectably to the notes as is the phrase '*Te revoir, ô Carmen*' in Don José's 'Flower Song.' The difference – the crucial difference – is that Webber's aria might just conceivably be sung by you, whereas you had better leave Bizet's to Rolando Villazón and the other boys, unless you want to sprain your spleen on the interval at the end of the seventh line. Finally it's the difference between the musical theatre and the grand opera. But who, except the tone-deaf, cares about that difference? Why not love both? You only have to love music, and Stempel has written a book to convince us that the history of Broadway has multiplied our reasons to do that.

The Atlantic

Sweating

Delia Falconer

It is a month before Christmas and Porky's strip club, on Darlinghurst Road, is the only shop to have made a festive effort. There are three trees on its awning, decked in tinsel and blue lights. It is one of those Sydney nights in which a mad energy is brewing. All day the air has been thick and the distances purple. It is still thirty degrees as I walk home at midnight. From a tree in the Fitzroy Gardens, above the El Alamein fountain, one of the koels, which migrate to the city each spring from Indonesia, keeps up its melancholy day-and-night cry with an upward inflection, as if working toward a climax that can never be achieved. Even the harbour smells like sex. Anything is possible. Fire. A riot. Orgasm. Apocalypse. It is only after one o'clock that the Southerly Buster comes at last, and it slams into the dark city. Steamy air is replaced by cold. A door bangs shut. The windows shake so viciously that, in spite of the heat trapped inside the flat, I have to almost close them. The branches on the gum outside thrash wildly. The next morning the floor is covered in thin, burned leaves. The sky is grey. It is the end of the jacaranda flowers.

On hot nights like this, when I was a student, the phone would ring after midnight. 'I'm thirsty.' My friend's voice on the other end was childlike and emphatic. We would leave our essays and drive in her old Datsun to Kellett Street – it was always possible to park in the Cross then – and drink jugs of cocktails beneath the slowly turning ceiling fans.

It has always seemed to me that Sydney is most itself in summer, with its days of intense humidity that break into storms and weeks of rain. Fennel grows to human height by railway tracks. The sea is moody. One day, on the drive to swim at Nielsen Park, the eastern suburbs are a vision of perfection, palm trees and neo-Tuscan mansions gleaming, the harbour a chalice of gold light. It is possible to feel a benign happiness at the sight of the huge private schools perched on the cliff's edge, the Bridge a misty dream beyond, the sea-planes droning as they take off from Rose Bay. Within the shark-net, the water is a tranquil jade, sun bouncing back up from the sand. A day later and the weather is dirty. Cats' paws pit the surface of the sea, and rolling waves slap at your face. The air looks swollen, bruisy. The traffic winding back down the hill, and through the flat bayside shopping strips, is intolerably slow. You could kill the Chinese family in their people-mover, hogging the right lane as they point out yachts beyond the sea-wall. You feel contempt for the lobster-red British tourists, shorts plastered against their legs, as they trudge with their eskies and deck chairs toward a free concert in the Domain. This intensity, this unevenness of mood, is almost hormonal. There is a feeling like puberty in the air: musky, eruptive; silly as a two-bob watch; given to fits of gloom.

In my early twenties I spent a whole summer in pitilessly bright Chippendale wearing cheap bottle-green silk trousers, a silk singlet and sturdy shoes. The cloth was like wearing nothing but a second layer of warm air. The shoes let me walk everywhere swiftly; they made me feel certain. The terraces I strode past were still unapologetically pre-heritage, wearing the colours their immigrant owners had given them: mandarin, Aegean blue, violet, purple. As it wound through Newtown, King Street fell into distinct zones: a student area of notoriously poisonous eateries that morphed into a run of Thai restaurants; a gay belt around Kuleto's Cocktail Bar and the Newtown; old Greek women shopping at the hot bread stores around the junction with Enmore Road; and from here, only the Sandringham Hotel showing signs of life among the tiny Fijian supermarkets and failing hobby shops, some with squalid student flats in their tops. A host of images crowd in now. Naked boys chasing cockroaches that had flown through the windows of upstairs terrace rooms so hot the only relief came from pressing your limbs against the bare walls. A friend taking his shirt off in the Court House Hotel to show me the tiny blue tattoos on his brown skin. Evenings sitting on front steps in Balmain or Forest Lodge, as the sun pressed down on the west like a crimson comet.

And now, as I sit at my desk, I feel a force I have been resisting sweep into this book like a change in the weather. It is my violent love for my city, a feeling as irrational as its geographic assertions – a love for its mix of tolerance and dirt, its sunshine with an undertow, its pride in its own darkness. And of course it is tied up, as everyone's version of their city must be, with nostalgia for my youth. Yet surely no other city's pleasures are so bound up with revulsion, or their beauty so dependent on the knowledge of corruption. It is no coincidence that the stone-masons in early Pyrmont classified the grades of Sydney's sandstone as 'hellhole,' 'purgatory' and 'paradise.'

*

If I had to choose a single story to sum up my city, it would be this. It takes place during a sultry dusk in December, several years ago. The light on New South Head Road, a brute gold filtered through fumes, was horizontal, but still strong enough to almost knock me down. Sydney is hostile to walkers, and you would be hard-pressed to find a more difficult place to cross, over eight lanes of cars that pass on either side of the eastern suburbs railway line, and in and out of the Cross City Tunnel. As I waited for the lights to go through their long cycle, I became aware that the traffic was heavier than usual: in fact, it was at a standstill. Through the glare I began to notice a long convoy, stretching up the hill as far as Edgecliff. The cars all had their headlights on. There were red Styrofoam menorahs on the top of some, and 'Happy Hanukkah' banners on others. I realised there must be a celebration on the other side of town. As the lights still refused to change, and the cars idled through the intersection, I became aware of two young men now standing beside me. Tall, bleach-blond, lugging an esky, they radiated a lean sense of menace that might not have been out of place at the Cronulla riots. As the traffic boiled, they peered in at the nearest driver. Hatted, bearded, he nervously peered back. Slowly, they read out the banner on his car. Then their faces broke into grins, and they began to chant and pump their fists: 'Ha-nu-kkah! Ha-nu-kkah!' As the traffic started to move again, the drivers honked their horns back. 'Ha-nu-*kkah!*'

Like most of the city's magnanimities, this was a moment that could have easily gone the other way. The story reminds me of another. In the eighties, in Camperdown, there was a famous piece of graffiti on the car park at the corner of Parramatta and Missenden roads. On the blue wall someone had spray-painted *God hates homos.* Beneath it, another hand had added, *but he loves tabouleh.*

It is this irreverence that I missed terribly in Melbourne, when we moved there at the turn of the nineties. It was good to come back to my hometown a decade later, where, as an editor once said to me, 'you can open up your chest and take a deep breath.' When I first agreed to write this book I made myself a promise that I would not play the cities off against each other, because their rivalry is a cliché, and because I wanted to reflect the truth: while Melbourne regards the northern city as Gomorrah, Sydney rarely thinks of Melbourne. Yet the fact is that I can imagine neither of these moments occurring south of the border, and they seem to invite me to understand better Sydney's quicksilver wit and ease. Our city is so big, so golden, each implies, that we do not need to overthink things. This is Sydney at its best, as a joyful melting pot. Yet a veiled aggression underpins the boys' enthusiastic cries of 'Ha-nu-kkah.' Join our light-heartedness, they suggest, or be too serious at your peril. That is why the second graffito is brilliant in harnessing the powers of the city's enforced brittleness for good. It is the hate-filled spray-painter who is instead revealed as abnormal; as too *intense.*

In Melbourne, that flat, planned city, you can construct a perfectly ordered existence for yourself. There are starched tablecloths in the cafés; transport is predictable; you can even park in town. More than likely, the same pubs you have been visiting for years are relatively untouched by renovation, the same crowd greyer and paunchier beneath their short-sleeved shirts and little hats. The weather may be miserable, but it is more often neutral. It doesn't matter anyway, as many of the city's entertainments – and it still has a vital centre – are reliably indoors. People stay, their friends stay, in the same places. Melburnians structure their lives around the real possibility of satisfaction. In fact, if any new restaurant or pub is mooted, it can cause distress.

It is Sydney's wild mix of the stunning and unplanned, of glitz and rot, by contrast, that gives it its very distinct cultural and intellectual life. In Sydney we are shaped spiritually by damp abrasion and the democracy of grit. The sublime and ridiculous are never far apart. Our pleasures, though at their best beyond compare, are rarely unalloyed with disappointment. There is a high chance at a sunny outdoor café that a bogong moth will dive bomb your perfect cappuccino; or, as happened to me quite recently, it will drown in the cheese on your focaccia, and you will be relieved, at least, as you stop yourself from taking a bite just in time, that the black antennae are not pubic hair. A simple downpour will bring the roads to a standstill, or you will find yourself jammed on the F3 with everyone else heading north for Christmas, even while the dry bush to either side of you thrums with joyful heat, and the bays below turn into tender mirrors. As a result, Sydney may be impatient, pushy, volatile, aggressive – but it is rarely *righteous*, because it is never surprised. Imperfection and making do are part of our aesthetic. Only Sydney would nickname one of its public artworks, with graphic precision, 'Poo on Sticks' (Ken Unsworth's *Stones Against the Sky*, outside the 'Elan' apartments in Darlinghurst); and only here would a body corporate deal with a heritage order that forbade it from removing the sculpture by repainting it from faecal brown to grey.

*

The Japanese have coined a word for the fifth taste beyond bitter, sour, salt and sweet: *umami* ('savouriness'). It is brothy, mushroomy, earthy: the smell of cheese, the deepest element of stock. This is the secret force in Sydney's freighted air. It is not just heavy with humidity, but with sulphury mangrove, kelp, the iodine of dead marine animals, humus, salt and mould. Over the top of this base, made more profound and lingeringly sad by it, are the sweeter smells of eucalyptus and frangipani, jasmine on baking wooden fences, gardenias, and the sun-hot needles of pines. When it has been raining hard it is sometimes possible to smell the layer of fresh water on top of the salt brew of the harbour – although the brackishness is always beneath it, giving a funky body, a pulse almost, to the air.

'There are spots in Sydney,' says one of the gay boys who visit us from Melbourne, 'that feel dirtier than almost anywhere else in the world.' And he is right. In Kings Cross the drunks and junkies lie in caked vomit in the recessed front of the empty bank; and when the plane trees seed in late summer, the fluff adheres to the spatter. The uncovered bins are high with rotting prawn heads and oyster shells. Ibis, their white coats a grubby brown, their stench arid, root about inside them. The public toilets beneath the police station reek of raw shit, and, if the wind is in the wrong direction, the smell blows, hot and funky, across the park and into the Gazebo Wine Garden. The seeds from the date palms form a thick dust on the footpaths, like Japanese soybean powder. Pigeons peck in the McDonald's; bats and possums leave feral scent markings on the trees in the park; cigarette butts float in the urine, both animal and human, that pools in the gaps in the footpath bricks around their roots. If it rains, everything washes down the stormwater drains and into the harbour, and it is a good idea not to swim for several days.

Much of the inner city is like this. Perhaps I am particularly aware of it because my aunt kept fifty cats at one time in her home in Drummoyne; as a child there was not an inch of that yard that I could poke a stick into without digging up clots of fur and waste. I have the same sense of dank layers metres deep when I pass many of the terraces and cottages around now-fashionable Surry Hills, Darlinghurst and Newtown. Here, I find myself thinking, as I pass a cramped house with its low gate in Macdonaldtown, is the home of a baby farmer who starved and disposed of the children desperate mothers entrusted to her care. Here, in Rushcutters Bay, I tell myself, with its mock Tudor shingles and separate back door, was the abortionist's house, and here behind it is the courtyard where they bundled the surgery's sad waste. Any history of the Rocks will recount the private wells in people's yards, in which drunks and children sometimes drowned. Look at photographs from the turn-of-the-twentieth-century backyard butcheries, chains of sausages hanging in the air and blood pooling in the gutters. It is all still caught up in the bricks and soil, in so many parts of the city, along with chaff from its granaries, smoke from its factories and the acrid lining from the brakes of trains.

Of all Australian cities, Sydney has most known poverty and overcrowding. Ruth Park's novel *The Harp in the South*, which won the *Sydney Morning Herald*'s inaugural novel competition in 1946, told the story of the struggling Darcy family in Surry Hills. Her Irish-Catholic heroes were the respectable poor, yet no one living in such close quarters, in dank homes with peeling cladding, Park pointed out, could avoid the bed bugs that swarmed out of the walls and furniture at night. Park knew what she was writing about. Struggling to survive on writers' earnings during the war-time housing shortage, she and her husband D'Arcy Niland rented a room above an old shop in Devonshire Street, near the corner of Riley, just up from where the Shakespeare Hotel now stands. Park was pregnant, and squeezed into a single bed with Niland; his brother slept in the barber's chair downstairs. The closeness and lack of sun would cause her lifelong kidney problems. Her new daughter failed to thrive until the family moved to the only fresh air they could afford, in remote and phoneless Collaroy.

Sydney knew much of its population lived in poverty, but it could not bring itself to thank a writer born in New Zealand for pointing out that it had slums. When it was serialised, Park's book was slammed by *Herald* readers as 'immoral' and 'filthy.' It was only later that *The Harp in the South* would go on to become one of the city's most-loved novels. Thanks to Park's writing, these terraces would be knocked down and replaced by the grim Housing Commission units that now stand on Devonshire Street, something Park has admitted to having mixed feelings about.

*

It is cool inside my friend's lounge room. The art nouveau waratahs on the ceiling have long since turned the yellow of clotted cream, and the paint is peeling from their spiky wreaths of leaves. Owned by an elderly landlady, the house is in the grounds of an old paper factory. A plane on its descent into Mascot makes the roof tremble for a moment. Like a light, the sun flicks off, then on again. The room smells of mildew, and incense, and disinfectant. A year into the new millennium, my friend is just holding on, in this decaying cottage with its low rent, to the textures of our past.

For it was houses like this that we lived in as students, with their hastily enclosed verandas, plastic bags balled into the gaps of the fibro, and windows too swollen by damp to close. Everything was jerry-built. There were thunderboxes outside, with wooden seats, and bricks that bore a faint hint of the night-soil that was once carried away along the lanes behind them. Indoor toilets had been hastily added in cupboards, beneath stairs, in the crooks of landings. Outdoor paint had been slapped on the skirting boards, but peeled back quickly to reveal thick layers of black mould. There was always a Hills hoist, or tree stump, or some other immovable object out the back that rendered the tiny space unusable; often an old bed frame or rotting bench.

I shared three houses platonically with this friend. There was a one-storey terrace in Stanmore, with Greek tiles over its central archway. The girl whose room I had taken still boarded her pet rats in the walk-in pantry and returned to bathe them in the bathroom sink. Another was a house-mind while the owner was in rehab, his hundreds of copies of *Pilgrim's Progress* lining the hall, smelling sweetly of mouldy bindings. The house's alcoholic atmosphere soon began to affect us. For the two months we lived here my friend, who scrubbed dishes part-time in the university's staff club, did not wash his clothes, soaked with bleach and scraps of food: even from outside the front door, the smell was overwhelming. My favourite was the last house, in Chippendale, which we shared with my partner; it had a purple feature wall and yard filled with huge fennel plants that had reseeded themselves from the wasteland that surrounded tiny Macdonaldtown station behind us. It was here I began to write; each day I would buy my lunch for two dollars from the Thai couple who had taken over the Greek sisters' corner shop.

These suburbs were still semi-industrial, with their railway workshops and silos, the houses yet to be hollowed out and renovated. Not far away a poet friend lived in a flat of spectacular grubbiness, on the top floor of an old federation mansion, squeezed between the deaf hospital and a detox centre. As he prepared dinner, he would brush, as a reflex, with his left hand at the tiny cockroaches that swarmed up the sides of the chopping block. In his bathroom there was an old gas water-heater that you had to light to take a shower, a toilet squeezed at a precarious angle into the corner, and a lugubrious axolotl that observed from its filthy tank on the washing machine as you performed your ablutions. Late one night, the poet said, he had looked out the window into the moonlit backyard of the deaf hospital, to see a naked game of touch football being played in perfect silence.

The thing is, we loved it. Perhaps my generation was strange, I think now, in making a fetish of filth. What is the seediest thing you have ever seen in Sydney? I ask friends my age, and they answer with glee. The Golden Grogan, says one: a competition held by the university's engineering students to defecate in the most creative spot on campus; one year the winner targeted the dryers in a college laundry. Several volunteer 'Trough Man,' who lay in the urinals at the Mardi Gras party each year: a sight seared on the minds of straight boys of my generation. Perhaps ours was a reverse snobbery, a means of rejecting whitebread Sydney childhoods. Or perhaps it was another way in which Sydney taught us to undercut our pleasures. It was a means of not mooning and thrilling over the deep shade of the gums in the cemetery of the old Newtown church; at the yellow flowers on the paperbarks; at the soft industrial dusks over the water at Glebe Point – all of which we had, quite miraculously, to ourselves.

*

It would be easy to assume that Sydney's easy-going climate is responsible for attracting its huge gay population. The Beauchamp Hotel on Oxford Street is named, after all, for that enthusiastic cruiser, the seventh Lord Beauchamp: an English bachelor interested in artistic matters, who governed New South Wales from 1899 to 1900. 'The men are splendid athletes,' Beauchamp reported, 'like Greek statues. Their skins are tanned by sun and wind, and I doubt whether anywhere in the world are finer specimens of manhood than in Sydney. The lifesavers at the bathing beaches are wonderful.'

The city was certainly a smorgasbord of beats. The Botanic Gardens area was always popular. And from the nineteenth century until after the Second World War the section of Hyde Park between the Archibald Fountain and College Street was a well-known destination; so much so, according to activist Lex Watson, that the footpath was narrowed in 1956 to 'eliminate' gay men. But like so many aspects of the city's life, Sydney's gay history has to be understood in relation to its dark opposite: repression. The beats existed for a reason. Extreme vigilance for any gay activity – the police archives are filled with photographs of cycad-shaded toilet blocks and shadowy tunnels that invite the imagination to dwell and lurk – carried on from the colony's paranoid fear of the potential convict vice. Sodomy and murder were both punishable by execution: 'For either of these crimes,' Governor Phillip said, 'I would wish to confine the criminal till an opportunity offered of delivering him to the natives of New Zealand, and let them eat him.' Alexander Brown was the first person to be hanged for sodomy, in 1828. As late as 1951, the NSW *Crimes Act* was amended to make 'buggery' a crime (carrying a sentence of fifteen years imprisonment), with or without consent, effectively diminishing any legal defence that consent had not been given. The state only decriminalised homosexuality in 1984.

In fact, the Gay and Lesbian Mardi Gras, the city's biggest party outside of New Year's Eve and, more recently, Chinese New Year, might not have come into existence except for a police crackdown, on 24 June 1978, on a march by gay rights protestors – ironically, to commemorate New York's Stonewall riots against police harassment in Greenwich Village. The day had begun with a march of 400 gays and lesbians through the CBD demanding a repeal of anti-gay laws. A public meeting followed. Later that night 2000 men and women chanting, 'Out of the bars, into the streets, join us,' made their way down Oxford Street towards the city. Though they had permission, by the time the march reached Whitlam Square, the police swooped, confiscating the PA system and lead truck. But on this occasion, the community fought back, streaming up College Street to Kings Cross and gathering more supporters. In Darlinghurst Road, garbage bin lids flew; bottles smashed. Police removed their numbered badges and laid into the crowd. 'Let them go!' the protestors chanted, following the paddy wagons. It was terrifying, witnesses reported, but also exhilarating. 'I was wild, ecstatic and scream- ing up and down the street. "Up the lezzos!"' one woman recalls. 'I did get arrested for saying that.' The newspapers published names and many involved lost jobs and friends. It will surprise few residents of NSW to learn that no charges were laid; a year later the police claimed to have lost all paperwork.

Moved to steamy March, Mardi Gras grew into a huge annual event, with marchers spending months on choreography, floats and costumes. And just as reliably each year Uniting Church minister and NSW parliamentarian Fred Nile has led his Festival of Light followers in prayer for rain to fall on the parade. (It is almost always a fine night.) Although he is seen by many as a risible figure these days – and has moved on to trying to halt Muslim immigration – it is worth remembering that Nile came close to getting the event banned in the late '80s, during the height of the AIDS crisis. For in a terrible irony, this disease would decimate the beautiful young men who had come to Sydney to be fabulous – bringing Mardi Gras in the '80s much closer to its religious significance as a brief bacchanal before the sorrows of Ash Wednesday. Yet these were also the great years of Mardi Gras, as it not only cocked a snook at those who wanted to define the group by their disease, but gloriously asserted life. In fact, its after-party would become so popular with young straights that the organising committee would find itself embroiled in fiery debates about whether ticket sales should be limited to gay-only membership lists.

Now Mardi Gras is so firmly on the tourist calendar that mem- bers of the police force march, and families bring children to pose with the drag queens in the marshalling area in Hyde Park. Still, its contrary wit distinguishes it from other Mardi Gras parades around the world. Marchers have carried a giant joint, Nicole Kidman's fake nose from *The Hours* and Vicky Virus, courtesy of the AIDS Council, a skull painted in fantastic fluoro colours in the spirit of the Mexican day of the dead. Politics is a popular subject, with ex-Prime Minister John Howard being memorably depicted on one float as a dog sniffing George W. Bush's bottom. But the most popular float in the history of the Mardi Gras was probably the work of the bearded and cross-dressed Sisters of Perpetual Indulgence who, in 1989, as the crowds whistled and roared, marched, carrying a six-foot high model of Fred Nile's head, complete with his characteristically vigorous dark hair and eyebrows, on a platter of papier-mâché fruit. It was the 3D equivalent of the anonymous graffitist's 'but he loves tabouleh.'

*

The greatest and most fundamental difference that distinguishes Sydney and its pleasures from other Australian cities is that this is the only one to have known itself as part of the eighteenth century. You can still trace the Georgians' influence on our habits of body and mind. But as historian Grace Karskens points out, that era arrived here fraught with internal conflict. The great majority of convicts were from working-class and rural populations, and brought with them a culture that was pre-industrial, and which collided with the values of a more educated officer class. With its slippery goat tracks and heavily timbered slopes, the Rocks swiftly became home to a convict population that mistrusted government, and had ways of dealing with the problems of daily life that predated Sydney's civil institutions. If a robbery or murder occurred, the residents would band together to try to solve the crime themselves. Home remedies were trusted over the new hospital at the bottom of the cliff, which they referred to as a 'slaughterhouse.' They built their houses to suit themselves, without surveyors. Following rural rather than military time schemes, they organised their working hours, often around the daylight, the seasons and the tides. Suicides were buried at crossroads with a stake through the heart, a detail that more than any other suggests a mindset that was still not so far removed from the medieval. The Rocks citizens were also suspicious of any interventions into their private sexual lives by organised religion. Until well into the nineteenth century, among England's rural and working-class populations, Karskens writes, non-traditional marriages were common and accepted, an arrangement that was particularly advantageous for women, who were able to hold on to their legal right to their children, property and name. It is hardly surprising that so many were keen to avoid formalised marriages in the new colony, as they quickly began to own businesses, like hotels and shops.

It is easy to see how the pragmatism and self-reliance of the Rocks residents lingers as a kind of psychic Tank Stream that runs below our city. There is a sense in which, somewhat like contemporary Romans, we enjoy the city's anarchic tendencies, the creativity of its corruptions, even as we decry greedy developers and our failing public transport.

The eighteenth century left another legacy, which was just as strong: an abiding wowserism. For many of the educated settlers, especially the Anglican clergy, this was the first time they had come across their fellow citizens' pre-industrial traditions like common marriage. The result was an almost obsessive wringing of hands at Sydney's 'immorality.' Reverend Richard Johnson, holding the first divine service under a tree in 1788, complained that the convicts stayed away while the soldiers beat their drums in church. In 1806 Reverend Samuel Marsden was moved to come up with the notorious 'Female Register,' which classified every woman in the colony as either 'married' or 'concubine': denying even sanctified Catholic or Jewish unions, along with the notion that a single woman could possibly be moral, he arrived at the staggering ratio of 395 to 1035. In a sense Fred Nile was following a long tradition of Protestant ministers when he declared, 'If Jesus wept over Jerusalem, he must be heartbroken over Sydney.'

The ghostly tug-of-war between the sober habits of the wowsers and the feral masses explains why our pleasures are so baroquely realised, so stridently and so avidly pursued. Sydney is the most over-regulated of Australian cities. Move here from interstate and you will suddenly find your car needs a blue slip, a pink slip, a green slip, and annual inspection. Our liquor laws are equally complicated. Coming here from Melbourne, a bar-owning friend was horrified by the difficulties he faced in trying to set up an open-air street venue for the 2000 Olympics. The red tape was endless. More worrying were the intimidating phone calls and veiled threats he received.

Paradoxically, our bureaucracy is the cause of our dedicated drinking culture. Any system of restrictions so complicated and so petty will encourage more and more inventive ways to get around it. Sydney's legendary drinking stories are legion. On VJ day, 15 August 1945, for example, at *Smith's Weekly* where the poet Kenneth Slessor worked, the staff convinced the publican of the closed Assembly Hotel next door to run a hose up from the back yard to their first-floor window. They drank the cellar dry. Temperance unions had been campaigning for prohibition since the Victorian era. They finally had some success when six o'clock closing was introduced to improve public morals during the First World War – except rather than sending men home sober and early to their families, as they had hoped, the new closing hours were the start of Sydney's culture of binge-drinking. During the notorious 'six o'clock swill,' men would crowd the bars to get as big a skinful as they could between the end of work and early closing. The very architecture of pubs changed as they were turned into liquid feed-lots: gone were their billiard saloons and small rooms, replaced by long bars with troughs at their base for men to piss in as they stood, and hoseable tiles on the inner and outer walls for vomit. Smaller and more convivial establishments were unable to compete. The effect of these strictures is still felt. Until only a few years ago, visitors to cafés and small bars had to go through the charade of ordering an item of food – or at least pretending to have the intention of eating – in order for the café to justify a licence. At the same time, compared to other states like Victoria, where anyone with a design degree and a couple of thousand dollars could open up a cool small bar, our licences were outrageously expensive. Only the most cashed-up, or mobbed-up, could afford them.

You could argue that wowserism conjured up the state's most colourful identity, Abe Saffron, or 'Mr Sin.' Kings Cross, the centre of Saffron's enterprises, had been the hub of organised crime since the razor gangs had moved in with sly grog shops around the First World War. By 1947, when Saffron opened the legendary Roosevelt, a Hollywood-style club, with cigarette girls and tuxedoed waiters, a sophisticated parallel economy was flourishing, in which the most influential people in Sydney (that sense of special privilege) could be relied on to put a word in the right ear, while police hived off healthy percentages from its after-hours liquor sales, illegal baccarat games and brothels. The top of this pyramid stretched up to the state premier, Robert Askin; at the bottom were the bouncers and standover men. As Saffron's son, Alan, writes in his biography of his father, the result was the 'most corrupt state in Australia.' Abe Saffron, like any good businessman, was 'able to capitalise like no other – after all, he was simply providing entertainment to the masses, in defiance of archaic restrictions.' Monopoly was the key. The more pubs Saffron acquired, the more alcohol he was able to buy legally – then he could redistribute it illegally to his late-night ventures, without relying on third parties. Inevitably, Saffron expanded into prostitution and sex clubs. He was under police surveillance for years, but in what is almost a cliché of organised crime, he would only ever be jailed, for seventeen months in 1987, for tax evasion.

Still, wherever there was crime, the public imagined Saffron. He was rumoured to have been involved in the Ghost Train fire at Luna Park in 1979, although his son denies this. For a very long time he was also thought to have been involved in the disappearance of Juanita Nielsen. Nielsen's unknown fate would become the archetypal story of Sydney's greedy dark side, traumatically tied to a moment that can be thought of as a 'return of the repressed,' when Sydney's history of radical private interest seemed to grow all the stronger for its infiltration of the complicated machinery designed to crush it.

Juanita Nielsen was an upper north shore girl, who, like so many other women before her, had come to Kings Cross for its bohemian attractions. The flat-fronted two-up, two-down terrace her father bought her is still standing at 202 Victoria Street, opposite the Soho Hotel and the steep sandstone Butler Stairs, where a plaque recalls her life. On that western side the wealthy families of doctors and merchants had long since moved out of the huge Victorian terraces perched on the sheer cliff over Woolloomooloo; these had been divided into low-rent flats inhabited by pensioners and working people, unmarried couples and members of the loosely anarchist Sydney Push. But in 1969 this side of the street had been reclassified as part of the Central Business District by the Askin government, and Frank Theeman, the Osti lingerie magnate-turned developer, had quietly been buying up houses. He planned to demolish them and turn them into high-rise apartment towers with overhead walkways, at a profit of millions; the local council was behind him.

In 1973 an alarmed National Trust moved to classify the street and its buildings as the 'Montmartre of Sydney,' and Theeman swiftly issued eviction notices to his residents, who numbered about four hundred. A radio documentary captures their voices, with a working-class inflection one rarely hears in the inner-city these days: there were always children running around then, one older woman says, and 'none of this violence business.' 'As a seaman I travelled a lot,' a man recalls, 'but I was always coming home to that beaut pad.' Those who stayed formed the Victoria Street Residents Action Group, while Juanita Nielsen began relentlessly agitating for the poorer residents in her community newspaper, *NOW*.

Things heated up very quickly. Some were offered small payments to leave, and cramped new rooms elsewhere; others found their belongings missing, or water pipes broken. Police from the Consorting Squad made random visits, looking for drugs. Then chief protestor Arthur King was forced into the boot of a car and held for several days on the south coast, freed on the condition that he quit his association with the group. As the street emptied, only a hard core of squatters remained, behind a system of barricades. But they had achieved a significant victory: the Builders Labourers Federation instituted a series of green bans, meaning no union member would work on the site. These lasted for two years, until 1975, when Jack Mundey was dismissed as the leader of the NSW branch by the national leader Norm Gallagher, who would later be convicted of taking developers' bribes.

The battle seemed to be lost, until Nielsen quickly went to the Water Board Union, and convinced them to enact their own green ban.

It is worth pausing here for a moment to note that although Sydney has lost much of its heritage, this did not happen without vehement community opposition; it is also worth remarking how many of the people involved in this action were women, from the women of Hunters Hill who brokered the first historic green bans with the BLF to save Kelly's Bush, to Ruth Park who was motivated to write her *Companion Guide to Sydney* by the sound of jackhammers rampant in her beloved old Sydney. Still, it is hard to get a sense of Nielsen, who remains an elusive presence; a stilted voice on the radio speaking of her years spent abroad before returning to the Cross, which she loved because of its thousands of people; photographs of her with fashionably pale lipstick, thick mascara and jetsetter's beehive. There seem to be no tender observations of her on the record. Instead, one has the sense of a lone operator, obscured by her own glamour, or perhaps her middle-class femaleness. One older woman door-stopped by the television cameras clearly disapproved of her interference. In another interview, recorded not long after her disappearance, the real-estate agent who sold her her house struggles painfully, as people did then with any name that seemed faintly exotic, with his pronunciation of her name – 'Yoo-nita.'

On 4 July 1975, Nielsen went to the Carousel nightclub (now the Empire Hotel) on the corner of Roslyn Street and Darlinghurst Road, supposedly to discuss an advertisement for the club in *NOW*. She was never seen again. The number of suspects says a lot about Sydney's rich criminal ecosystem at the time. Some thought of Fred Krahe, former NSW police detective and suspected murderer, who led the team Theeman employed to harass residents from their homes. The Carousel was owned by Saffron, so others felt he was somehow involved, especially as he was rumoured to have lent money to Theeman, a regular patron of another of Saffron's clubs, the Venus Room; then again, James Anderson, who managed the Carousel, owed Theeman thousands. In 2008 journalist Peter Rees claimed to have solved the case in his book *Killing Juanita*. According to Carousel receptionist Loretta Crawford, Nielsen had been shot in a basement storeroom of the club by Anderson, employee Edward Trigg and another man; this was corroborated by Marilyn (now Monet) King, Trigg's transvestite boyfriend at the time, who claimed Trigg had come home covered in blood, with a false receipt for an advertisement in his pocket. But since the book was published, others have come forward, claiming that

Juanita had compiled a dossier on organised crime, and this was the real reason for her death. Police are still suspected of a cover-up: they never investigated the Carousel premises after she disappeared.

Nielsen's body was never found. For decades, it was rumoured that it had been buried under the third runway at Sydney Airport, or ground up for pig food, or interred in the foundations of the new 'Lego Buildings' themselves. For they did go up – although, thanks to her years of agitation, at a third of their planned height of forty-five storeys. They are once more the homes of the wealthy.

*

The other evening, I was having drinks with a friend in Newtown. It was a warm night in the beer garden, and several cockroaches passed one another along the edge of the parterre. I'd forgotten them, she says; though, after fifteen years of living overseas, there is a delight in her squawk of horror. She has not been back since she used to rent the bottom floor of a boarding house in Balmain, in an old triple-fronted terrace; it was ten minutes from my place in Chippendale, on empty roads, in her old car. There was a bay tree and a beehive in the old back garden; a platform bed in the dining room spoke of wild times in the sixties; and three old men who shared a floor upstairs. One day, when she went to take one of them his betting slip, she found him dead by the TV. Today, she tells me, she went back to the old house and crept down the dunny lane to try to peer over the fence, but it was new and too high.

My friend has moved from the house in the paper factory, I tell her. The kitchen sink had backed up; a pigeon died in the roof and dropped maggots in the bathtub; the landlady had been slow to fix a puncture in the water pipes in the dunny, which directed a thin arterial spray onto anyone sitting on the seat. His new wife from Melbourne tried to tidy the place up, then persuaded him to get a mortgage on a tiny flat in Ashfield.

There must be something wrong with us, we say, to miss all this; when I got out at the station, I admit, and took a walk around the back streets, it made my heart tight with nostalgia to pass the filthy market with its leather jackets and smell of old shoes, the messy paperbarks and a flying fox, hanging dead from the power line, silver with flies. But it was nights like this one, we agree, when the air almost seemed to decompose around us, that the best things happened; when sweating bodies met, afternoon drinks turned into foodless dinners, or a shared cigarette on a back step became a night of driving across town between parties.

The thing about this city is that you always feel the dark pull of the earth, along with the urge for sea and sun. Perhaps this is the city's most pleasant haunting. For it is likely that those eighteenth-century farmers and mudlarks also brought with them some primitive version of humoral theory, which understood people as vessels for humours – blood, bile and phlegm – that were always seeking their perfect balance; which were attuned, in turn, to the elements. It cannot have been hard, in this new city where birds dropped out of the sky from the heat, to imagine themselves as part of the tide of planets; as earth, fire, air and water. No wonder the Victorians never quite left their mark on Sydney – there is a fiery madness about our pleasures, which only flare more wildly the more they are contained. We burned bright in those dank streets when we were twenty. As I passed the parties of young people, picnicking in the large green common around the cemetery, I admit, I felt a little jealous.

Edited extract from Sydney

It's Peter Dom

Richard Flanagan

In this world
we walk on the roof of hell
gazing at flowers
                        —ISSA

In March 1996, just before setting out on a solo trip to walk the rugged Western Arthurs in Tasmania's south-west, Peter Dombrovskis called. He wanted to talk about a forthcoming book of his photographs of Mount Wellington for which I was writing an introductory essay. The mountain defines Hobart and links it to the great wildlands of Tasmania. For generations Hobartians have walked, climbed, camped, tobogganed, swum and played over the mountain. Peter worried that the growing emphasis on notions of 'sacred wilderness' created a lie, or rather that it was the other pole of a lie. He lived on one of the mountain's higher flanks, and for him the mountain showed that the natural world wasn't something separate from human beings but the essence of us.

Peter talked of doing a book on gardens to further explore this idea. In a world in which humanity is ever more autistic to the natural world, he felt that anything that allowed people communion with nature mattered. Looking back on it now, I think he found all ways of being part of nature at once rich and mysterious. Rather than being dogmatic, Peter was curious.

He asked me about the boulders on the upper Huon River. He knew I was one of the few who had kayaked it and he wanted to know what they were like.

Why? I asked.

Because Olegas told me that they were beautiful, he said. One day I'd like to photograph them.

Olegas was Olegas Truchanas, a Lithuanian who arrived in Tasmania post-World War II and established a considerable reputation as both an explorer and landscape photographer. Truchanas had been the first to kayak the upper Huon, as well as the Gordon River. In one of several ironies, he worked as a draftsman for Tasmania's Hydro-Electric Commission, which, with its dams, was systematically destroying the wildlands that Truchanas was exploring, photographing and fighting to protect.

In the 1960s Truchanas began staging slide shows in the Hobart City Hall, showing the threatened wildlands with accompanying classical music. From the beginning these seemingly innocuous couplings of image and music were understood as the most political of events.

Then, in the great bushfire of 1967, his home and with it his slide collection was lost. Truchanas, now ageing, returned to the south-west to try to rebuild his archive of images of all that was on the verge of vanishing. In 1972, on a kayaking trip down the now threatened Gordon River, he lost his footing on a submerged log and disappeared into the dark, tannin-stained waters.

'He had been destroyed, with Biblical simplicity,' wrote Truchanas's friend Max Angus, 'by two of the elements, fire and water. Five years had passed between their brief and terrible visits. He had perished in the river he sought to save. Classical mythology affords no stronger example of the drama of the incorruptible man who passes into legend.'

It was a young man who three days later found Truchanas's drowned body. He was the fatherless son of a Latvian migrant, born in a refugee camp in Germany in 1945, for whom Olegas had become a father-figure, teaching him canoeing and photography. His name was Peter Dombrovskis.

A month later Dombrovskis returned to Lake Pedder, which Truchanas through his kayaking trip had been attempting to help save. From the same spot on the Coronets where Truchanas once had taken a photograph, he took an almost identical picture of the lake and its famed beach.

'I like to think,' Dombrovskis later said, 'I'm carrying on where Olegas left off, in my own way, finishing the work he started.'

But Lake Pedder was as doomed as Truchanas. Within three years it would vanish.

Yet Truchanas's influence soared in the 1970s and 1980s, spurred on by the publication of a book of his photographs, *The World of Olegas Truchanas*, in 1975. As the environmental movement went mainstream, Truchanas passed into myth as a martyr. Meanwhile, with the publication of Dombrovskis's early books *The Quiet Land* (1977) and *Wild Rivers* (1983) and his bestselling wilderness calendars, he became seen as Truchanas's heir. His photograph of the Franklin River at Rock Island Bend became the most celebrated landscape photograph in Australian history. Used by conservationists, it was said to have helped sway the federal election of 1983 in favour of Bob Hawke's Australian Labor Party, which promised to save the Franklin River.

It is perhaps not possible to convey what powerful effect the example of Olegas Truchanas and Peter Dombrovskis – the artist as adventurer; the merging of life and art; the radical and liberating possibilities of the natural world – had upon many Tasmanians growing up in the benighted, marginal and often self-hating Tasmania of the 1970s and 1980s. They created another Tasmania; an invitation to dream open to all.

*

Outside of Tasmania, the work of Truchanas and Dombrovskis has often appeared baffling. To some, their representations of landscape seem at best conventional, drawing from a romantic tradition that seems outdated, even reactionary. That their work has endured is strange; that it had radical political edge even more mysterious, and in some ways reprehensible. For the antipathy to art and artists in Australia that remains such a strong and destructive force in our national life sometimes appears to have been internalised and taken up by the Australian art world itself. It expresses itself variously: that great Australian lack of generosity to difference as well as a fear of any art that has political connotation, or, for that matter, spirit. It has also led to a culture of the corral: unless an artist is on the inside, part of a grant and gallery and critic system, they are not an artist.

Truchanas was a draftsman. Dombrovskis made a journeyman living, selling his images as postcards, calendars and books. They lived in Tasmania and made art about Tasmania, an island at once alien and marginal to Australia. It's hard to imagine artists more on the outside.

To the extent they had a politics, it was not the monocultural nationalism of the Labor Party that had so often been the bedrock creed for how Australian art was divined. Since Federation, Australian art was seen to have a mission to make a single national culture in the image of either its great coastal cities or its mainland dry outback. Whatever the aesthetic it wore as its motley, that was the goal.

Though a nation, Australia is not one country but many, and one of these is the country of Tasmania. Both men created an idea of Tasmania that could not be dismissed as regional or small, and that, like all powerful artistic ideas, contained a universe within it. For many on the island, these two artists were liberating – they showed us we lived not imprisoned in a small place dully conformist to a weary, century-old trope, but as part of a world of infinite possibility. But in so doing they also drew attention to the profound human choice that went with that world. To seek to know it better, to love it, or to agree to its destruction.

Talent is love, Tolstoy once said. The idea that great art is made out of love and can only be comprehended through love recurs through history in defiance of schools, traditions, aesthetics and ideologies. Love unleavened, of course, leads to kitsch. But with the yeast of circumstance, history and ambition added, enduring work sometimes arises.

Dombrovskis's work has been criticised as determinedly false, refusing to acknowledge the human element of the natural world by rarely showing humans or human artefacts. But the argument seems to make no more sense than applying it to abstract art. Dombrovskis spoke of how a photograph had to be filled with the character of the photographer or it was nothing. His images are, finally, an idea of humanity. But it is a particular and haunting idea of who we are and what we might be.

It is true that the conservation movement of the 1980s promoted a sense of 'wilderness' in which man had never been and should never intrude upon. Given human history in Tasmania is at least 40,000 years old and man has played a key role in shaping these wildlands for that long, such an idea was both demonstrably untrue and, as Dombrovskis understood, damaging to our souls. Though both men were environmentalists, and though that same movement used their images to promote environmental causes, as the years pass, as the politics recede, the images endure and seem to speak of something much larger and more evocative than the battles of that era. Much of Dombrovskis's later work finds erotic images of women in abstracted landscapes. The close-up still lifes of kelp-wrack, broken sea shells, myrtle leaf swirls, sand rib, snow-gum bark and river spume grow ever more mysterious, open and powerful.

I sometimes think both Truchanas's and Dombrovskis's attitude to the natural world of Tasmania can only be understood as a response to the immense human horror of World War II in Eastern Europe. At the edge of the world, where the contours of progress were more visible than at its centre, two photographers, refugees of the last great global conflict of nation and ideology against nation and ideology, perhaps came closer than many of their more celebrated peers in speaking of the conflict to come – of man against the natural world, and the terrible cost not just to our environment and economy, but to our humanity if we did not try to prevent it, if we did not try to understand ourselves and our world differently.

The storyteller, writes Walter Benjamin, is the man who would let the flame of his story consume the wick of his life. Peter was precise about language, and he may have dismissed such an idea. Certainly he would have seen no relevance to himself. But sometimes there is about an artist's life a profound and terrible poetry.

The Monday following my phone call with Peter I was driving to Salamanca through black clouds and heavy-dropped rain that sweeps and slaps rather than falls, while Hobart's higher suburbs were being coated in snow. The radio news said a solo walker had failed to return from a walking trip to the Western Arthurs. I rang a friend who worked in police search and rescue.

It's Peter Dom, he said.

*

They searched in blizzards for three days. Far below, floodwaters rose and covered the beautiful boulders of the upper Huon River. They found him kneeling, looking out to the south-west wildlands. He had been dead for some days, killed by a massive heart attack. As the weather was about to change, Peter had fallen to his knees, bowing before the world he had invited us to love and discover ourselves anew in.

Art & Australia

The West: New Dreams from Noongar

Andrew O'Hagan

In the summer of 1976, a thing happened in our house that seriously challenged my notion of international relations. The
English came to stay. Ours wasn't the kind of house where people came to stay: it was a council house twenty-five miles from
Glasgow full to the brim with noisy boys, unhappy dogs, phantom parents and football gloves. But my father had met this man
on a building site in Coventry and rashly – or, one might say,
merrily – asked him and his entire family to come and stay in
what he now and then called Bonnie Scotland. The discussions
and tears before the visit went on for weeks: my mother immediately christened them 'The English' and threatened to go on
strike. I remember her saying she hadn't a clue what to feed The
English and where would The English sleep? Did they go to bed
at a normal time, The English? And when they got up in the
morning did The English have cornflakes or porridge or did
they expect a banquet from Harrods?

I'd like to be able to tell you that when The English turned up
– all five of them, tumbling out of a hippy caravanette – everything went well and peace and understanding broke out in the
land of Robert Burns. But it didn't. The English colonised the
house exactly as my mother had predicted. The kids jumped on
the beds and laughed at the three-bar fire. The English daddy
never stopped talking in his big English accent and the mother
went straight upstairs for a bath and started smoking in the

bathroom. I knew the English were different because the children were doing handstands in the hall up against my mother's woodchip and the English mammy and daddy were always having naps. My three brothers and I sat silent on a green sofa. My father examined the *Daily Record*. My mother was in the kitchen with smelling salts and one of the English children sang a rude song that included the word 'bastard.'

'Are they Protestants?' I asked my mother.

'Aye, they are,' said my mother. 'And worse!'

Long after the English had gone south, my family discussed, for years actually, the true horror of the summer invasion – but in my antithetical, note-taking way, I found myself wondering about them. Who were these exotic beasts, the English? They were individualists – or at any rate, they weren't a family in the same way we were. Maybe I was secretly quite pleased that The English had muddied my mother's Anaglypta. Maybe I just reckoned they were freer than us. But my first experience of the English left me with the beginnings of a theory, to be expounded here, that whereas the Scots and the Irish were a people, a community, full of songs and speeches about ourselves, the English were something else altogether: a veritable riot of individualism with no real sense of common purpose and no collective volition as a tribe.

I was still thinking about the English the following summer, when the Queen's Silver Jubilee brought bunting and arguments to our street. Allegiance wasn't much of an option round our way, though the Orangemen of the town wouldn't have agreed, and soon another antithesis floated over the airwaves in the shape of an English group called the Sex Pistols, whom my brothers loved to death for singing a song that included the words, 'God save the Queen / She ain't no human being.' We were happy to go through the motions with the ice-cream and jelly on Jubilee Day, but everybody I knew thought the Queen was an English joke and a sign of our neighbour's conformity. The sound of the Sex Pistols sounded more like it – they sounded like a riot, like a political yawp, an altogether different kind of Englishness. Or was the song a mistake, an aberration? In any event, the record was soon banned and we went back to imagining the English as incapable of standing up for themselves or their songs.

I gather you had your own English invasion over here, so I come to you in sympathy. In Scotland, we were never out gathering jilgies or harvesting yams, and we had starlings flying overhead, not the green and red of the Western Rosella. But on Scotland's west coast, as here on your own vast western edge, we felt we were out on our own. We felt that we were in some sense, as you are, at the bottom of the world. But as I'll tell you now: we were really at the top of the world, and the journey between the two is a modern journey, the journey of self-realisation.

The problem with the English was not that they were bigger than us, but that they were *south* and their imperialism was always of the lazy kind. Everything we trusted was to the West. Ireland and America and John Wayne – not that John Wayne wasn't imperial, but at least he wore a nice hat and drew a gun real fast. Many good human efforts tended towards the West, towards the clean breast of new discovery. We wanted away from colonial assumptions and old-style Southern familiarity. It just seemed that life was to be found in the West, and the big task was to work out how to embrace your own Westernness. The task was to see, at last, that discovery was the better part of your nature.

In my childhood, the journey to Australia was a search for a better life, for a climate of change and possibility. Truth is, we Scots, in tune with our legacy of Jekyll and Hyde, were both colonisers and colonised and it wasn't, perhaps, our own Perth that would show us how to live with this, but yours. George Fletcher Moore, the Irish lawyer who sought his fortune in the Swan River colony in 1830, recorded the words of Yagan, the Aboriginal seer who saw what was happening and named it. 'You came to our country, and disturbed us in our occupations: as we walk in our own country, we are fired upon by the white man. Why should the white man treat us so?'

I have to tell you, my mother, in her own sweet-tempered way, would have understood the feeling, long after The English had gone off with their cigarettes and their baths in the middle of the day. But the notion of the West was complicated for all of us: we knew what it was to feel marginalised, but we, unlike the native people of Western Australia, knew what it was to take the other role and stamp on people's ground. Some of my ancestors came in convict ships and ended up panning for gold in the

Kalgoorlie gold fields of the 1890s. We were Westerners who sought our advantage, and for many of us the instinct to go west survives the ages.

*

I'm sure as soon as I could walk I wanted to go west. I wanted to be there at the going down of the sun, and in the morning, to see what the world was all about. A writer is born, sometimes, with a heart already filled with early promises and lost horizons, and I loved the idea embedded in the seasons and in the turn of every new day that life could begin again. It would take years for me truly to realise that Westernness was deep in our DNA. We lived in a kind of suburban dream of improvement, but the new housing estates of Scotland's west coast led to country fields and hedges aslant the sea, where the water seemed like a lesson in timelessness. I remember as a boy going there to read T.S. Eliot – we didn't get out much, or, when we did, it was to raise our voices in utterances beneath the lyrics of T.S. Eliot. But I remember his words by the Firth of Clyde; these lines from *The Four Quartets* felt like an invocation to the growing imagination. They felt real. And they felt like the key to a way of being.

> *What we call the beginning is often the end*
> *And to make and end is to make a beginning.*
> *The end is where we start from. And every phrase*
> *And sentence that is right (where every word is at home,*
> *Taking its place to support the others,*
> *The word neither diffident nor ostentatious,*
> *An easy commerce of the old and the new,*
> *The common word exact without vulgarity,*
> *The formal word precise but not pedantic,*
> *The complete consort dancing together)*
> *Every phrase and every sentence is an end and a beginning,*
> *Every poem an epitaph.*

That already sounded very homely to my Scottish ear. 'In my end is my beginning' were the last words of Mary Queen of Scots, and I felt, as I looked out, that history was speaking through the mercy of poetry to a new age. Here we were in the West, but what was out there? What was beyond?

I found one answer in 'The Dead,' the famous story by James Joyce that closes the Irishman's beautiful collection *Dubliners*. In that story, the West – the west of Ireland – comes to represent a repository of native essentials, a zone of pure belonging. Gretta, the woman in that story, is struck dumb on the stairs when she hears an old song, 'The Lass of Aughrim.' Her husband, Gabriel Conroy, sees it happening, and he discovers soon enough that she is still haunted by the death of an old lover, a young man called Michael Furey who died for her sake. The story becomes a great and beautiful beacon of truth about how we exist, and the West is at once the past, the ghostly present and the future in that story, which to me is James Joyce's masterpiece. Listen to the Western voices echoing through the story, at its very end:

> A few light taps upon the pane made him turn to the window. It had begun to snow again. He watched sleepily the flakes, silver and dark, falling obliquely against the lamplight. The time had come for him to set out on his journey westward. Yes, the newspapers were right: snow was general all over Ireland. It was falling on every part of the dark central plain, on the treeless hills, falling softly upon the Bog of Allen and, farther westward, softly falling into the dark mutinous Shannon waves. It was falling, too, upon every part of the lonely church-yard on the hill where Michael Furey lay buried. It lay thickly drifted on the crooked crosses and headstones, on the spears of the little gate, on the barren thorns. His soul swooned slowly as he heard the snow falling faintly through the universe and faintly falling, like the descent of their last end, upon all the living and the dead.

Did you hear that? 'The time had come for him to set out on his journey westward.' As a boy, I imagined that was a journey we all might wish to make. Standing on the coast, I thought of the Ireland my people had come from – I have an Irish name, O'Hagan – and, beyond Ireland, further west, there was America, a place that was coming to absorb my generation and whose culture seemed set to absorb the world. They were each out there, the past and the future, the great hunger and the maddening feast, and it seemed possible that Westernness and its discontents would become a subject of lasting interest for the likes of me. And so it proved. For in that beautiful story of Joyce's, there was also politics and the throb of a changing world: when Miss Ivors wants to insult Gabriel, she calls him a 'West Briton.' Ireland wasn't enough for some natives, she seems to imply, not for those who must see themselves attached to the glory of a bigger nation. This process of 'Westernisation' has been a problem for many of our cultures – not least Australia's – and Gabriel rightly sees it as an affront to his sense of progress.

On my own spot of land, my own tiny western amphitheatre of Ayrshire, the sea performed its duty, serving up evidence of Western power in the shapes of submarines. I began taking note of the American submarines that swept Scotland's coast. They sailed from Faslane, the American base among the glens, and carried the Cold War nuclear threat past our very windows. From that moment on, I believe my own sense of the West became a co-mingling of the romantic and the annihilistic: on the one hand, as I said, it was a zone of dreams, of the pioneering hopes that could lead good people into western lands. But on the other, as conjured by those black shapes on my childhood horizon, the West was also a threat to the safety of nations.

We have lived with the West in both senses now and have come, at last, in 2011, to a moment when the double-dealing of what we call 'Western' governments – selling arms to nations who oppress their people – is seen clearly for the immoral horror that it is. Those black submarines of my childhood are caught now, perhaps, in the floating nets of global freedom-fighting – the social networks of activism – and the world will never be the same again. It was not American and allied invasions of foreign lands – or centuries of 'Westernisation' – that brought people in Tunisia, Egypt and Libya to see the way out of oppressive darkness, but a generation of the intelligent young, who, in company with their mobile phones, set out to question the old order of military and economic networks. Those corrupt governments were often boosted by the West to the advantage of tyrants everywhere and to the enslavement of ordinary people. The West, as we knew it, can never be the same. And on certain days it is necessary to admit the possibility that this has given the West a bad name. Those rolling covered wagons that once carried the pioneers westward – whose tracks, at one time, were said to be visible from the air – they had carried dreamers to a land of milk and honey. That was the frontier spirit, and we all followed it in one way or another. Many of you here come from people who followed it directly. But I would argue that the pioneering spirit – the deep work of the individual imagination, and of our communities – has always known something that even government geographers forget: human imagination and idealism is a moveable feast; the journey west also leads to the East; and our search for betterness for our children, for our nations, is not a journey from A to B, but from A to a better A, and in my childhood that A stood for Australia.

Here's a theory: The West can only realise its true glories when it finds its way fairly through the East. That is human nature but it is also modern history. The West, as a privileged zone, has had its day, and the future might take its example from places like Perth, where the West stands proud at the frontier of an eastern promise. There is no nation but the imagination: and in that place, Perth, Australia may stand as a kind of lesson. The journey down and away might lead you to a point where Westernness changes its meaning. With a bit of luck and more hard work, Perth, Australia might stand for some of life's great alternatives: a place not of moral finagling but of civic dignity; a place not of religious piety and racial intolerance and economic bullying but of a new kind of West, the kind that says, like the best of literature, 'Nothing is simply one thing. We are all plural. We are nothing more, each of us, than our power to imagine each other's reality.' Perth is not a backwater but a frontier, and it must shout that fact from the rooftops of modern Australian life. A national government that kow-tows to old-style American interests is not a national government doing well: it is, rather, a government not looking for the meaning of its own more modern kind of Westernness. Turn off your delinquent American TV channels and go out and look at your own culture, for it tells more beautiful stories.

We live or die – our culture fades or survives – by our ability to imagine life afresh and see our territories anew. If France today behaved, internationally, like France in the nineteenth century, it would be a byword for tyranny. If England today defined its interests as it did in the 1760s, America would still be struggling under a notion of allegiance to a foreign power of the sort that it now expects to receive from other nations. America, and a new notion of the West, was founded on the principles of freedom and self-governance enshrined not only in the Constitution but in the literature that gave its language to the Constitution. Literature is like that: it helps us to live our lives and helps nations to know themselves.

Nationhood is not a badge, or a threat: it is a benediction. And we must be free to define it how we like. We may apologise for the past, but we should not do so only to counter righteous anger. We should do so in order to admit that anger into our moral understanding of how to do better today, not only for ourselves but for the people we are apologising to. Travelling on the outskirts of Perth in 1922, D.H. Lawrence wrote a letter home, in which he spoke of 'the primeval ghost in the Bush.' That ghost, that sense of the past warily haunting the present, may finally be coming to rest.

Perth is a living example of the postcolonial spirit making contact with its own past, ghostly present and future, as we said earlier of James Joyce's Ireland. Perth is closer to Jakarta than it is to Sydney – it used to be called the most isolated city on earth – which may explain a number of things. It may explain why the city should seize its moment to become a kind of international byword for independence of mind: to me, as a writer, the condition of bliss that writers must learn from their greatest cities is to be industrious and socially valiant, keeping, all the while, to your own style. That is Perth. And its example of Westernness, a new way of being West, can indeed be heard in Jakarta if not so much in Sydney. In my childhood there was a rabbit-proof fence around the world, from Berlin to China to Iran to Alabama and – bizarrely, to some – it was not only struggle but the ferment of ideas that brought it down. Perth must take its place, and the job never ends, of pioneering a new Western habit of taking down fences.

Acts of the imagination are themselves the best offence to tyranny. Talk to the dissidents of Tahrir Square in Cairo, as I have, and what you discover is modern individuals busily cancelling the assumptions of their political trackers. They are saying no to old concepts of dictatorship but also to old concepts of Western paternalism, the dictatorship of 'benign intervention,' 'security' and 'economic advisers.' The events of this year mean that, wherever we come from, from whatever former site of oppression and fear, we will not go back to Moore River, and Perth knows in its cultural bones, I hope, what it means to build a society that knows when the rights of a stolen generation will have their day. We sometimes think we are far from the great world. That was one of the clichés of my own youth. But the black submarines showed me we were closer than we knew. It was the job of literature to connect us to worlds both greater and smaller.

*

A man I knew once organised a tour of America for Dylan Thomas and remembers him the last time he saw him, drunk of course, and standing on the steps of a plane out of Nashville. 'I'm going further and further west,' he said. 'Further away from Wales. Further away from home.' But I would argue for another notion of the West – that we go there to find the home of homes, and while we leave it, we come back, and we know it again as if for the first time. Among many of the wrong-headed notions that kept me growing as a boy, perhaps one was right: the notion that only poetry can bring us to the heart of human power. I certainly thought so as I read the poems of Robert Burns, another Ayrshire writer who taught us so much about how to feel. At least at the end, even if our imaginative plans fall short, we can sit with a whisky and be warmed by the fire of our former hopes.

I've been talking to you here about how writers can act as a lightning gauge for change across time. And I'd like to pause with you over Robert Burns, because he is, for me, an exemplar of how language and landscape and politics can merge, and go hand-in-hand with a need for transformation in individuals but also in whole societies. What Les Murray did for Australia he also did for the world; what the novelist Tim Winton does for Perth he also does for all of us, and Robert Burns is one of those writers who constantly renews our capacity for living. I first heard the words 'Robert Burns' when I was a skiving wee blether at a primary school in Kilwinning: the headmistress, Mrs Ferguson, was looking for a young male victim, aged seven, to accompany her on the piano as she rattled out a version of 'My Luv She's But a Lassie Yet.' 'But let her stand a year or twa,' I sang – red-faced, mortified, banned forever from the legion of footballing heroes and non-sissies – 'and she'll no be half so saucy yet.' But I didn't care. I loved the words and the eternity of bare human feeling that lived inside the words. I knew that Burns would never spare my blushes: he didn't that day, and he didn't any day, including all the days of his own life.

Burns was a magician of fellowship. He was a magician of compassion, such as we feel when we use his words to oppose needless wars and inequality. He was a man of his time, but for all time, showing us how to enlarge ourselves in company with others. Years after the humiliation at Mrs Ferguson's piano, only the year before last, I was standing in front of the cameras to present the first of three BBC films. It was a cold day – the BBC always want everything to look sunny, and if you watch our films you'd think we had filmed them in Barbados, but it was cold that day and I was preparing to speak to the camera about Burns and Jean Armour outside the Ship Inn down at the harbour in Irvine. Half the crew were English, so they weren't what we call au fait with the old Burnsian enthusiasm. The girl from the BBC put a blob of something under my eyes to conceal last night's hangover, and I stood looking down the lens, trying to remember Mrs Ferguson's point that a man who couldn't speak in sentences was probably a criminal.

'*Action!*' shouted the director. And just at that point, a sonsy-faced, well-oiled, sleekit auld man fell out of the door of The Ship.

'Rabbie Burns, is it?' he shouted. 'I'll gi' ye Rabbie Burns. Ye don't know the first thing aboot the man, ya bunch a university tossers!'

So. That just about summed up the situation. The truth is there are as many Robert Burnses as there are people to admire him, and I'm happy to embrace them all. But when we're speaking about the Immortal Memory of Burns, what we're often talking about if the effort to keep his work and his memory alive for new generations of kids, especially those, like me, who grew up in households that weren't made for poetry or immortality, unless you're talking about the kind of immortality that can be achieved on a football field.

To me, Burns's great legacy is in the way he linked men up no matter what their class or creed. He is one of history's great unifiers, one of its great democrats. He's the libertarian's libertarian. And, as you know, he was seldom the recipient of equality for himself. Scotland has always wished its great writers to be men of the people – even if those writers were not that way inclined – but few in any language had such a natural instinct as did Burns for inclusion. The popularity of Burns may be a testament to our lust for plain speaking. The national poet hated unfairness and the abuse of power; that is his signature, giving intellectual and emotional life to notions of common sense and the common good.

Can a single poet summon the essence of a nation? Does Goethe do it for Germany? Pushkin for Russia? Whitman for the United States? Seamus Heaney for Ireland? I once took Heaney up to Alloway, home of the Robert Burns Birthplace Museum. We were standing outside the Tam o'Shanter Experience, an 'audiovisual journey through the poet's life and times,' when the great Nobel Prize-winner shook his head and exclaimed at what a life had grown up around Burns's talent. Seamus likes a bit of carry-on and I said to him that Ireland would show us the Seamus Heaney Experience before too long. 'And what's going to be in that,' he said, 'bar a confessional box and a couple of auld butter churns?'

We must never forget what literature can do. We love Burns not for his consistencies or even for his convictions, but for the sound of his mind and the song of his humanness. It wasn't a legislator or a party animal who wrote a Marseillaise to the human spirit, but a farmer's son from Ayrshire with an uncanny connection with people's cares and people's wishes for a better life. 'It's coming yet for a' that,' he wrote, 'that Man to Man, the whole world o'er, / Shall brothers be for a' that.'

The schools I went to were only ten miles away from his birthplace, and I remember reading him in my bedroom with the rain against the window. With my first typewriter I sat and typed the whole of 'Tam o'Shanter,' trying to understand the turns and periods in the poem, the source of the narrative's urgency and comedy and truth.

Literature is not a compendium of special effects or a log of political attitudes, but a repository of human vision, and Robert Burns compels readers – all of us – to understand our own capacity for fellowship. It was the American poet Wallace Stevens who said that the reading of poetry helps you to live your life, and in Burns's hands the reader comes away humanised, better equipped to tolerate our own failings and appreciate the world's glories.

Robert Burns was not merely Scotland's gift to the world, but humanity's gift to Scotland. Up in the wards, when my daughter was born, and the London traffic seemed to hush the crowds in honour of this brand-new person, I thought of Robert Burns's first love poem as I looked into her face.

> *O once I lov'd a bonnie lass,*
> *An' aye I love her still,*
> *An' whilst that virtue warms my breast*
> *I'll love my handsome Nell.*

Great poets follow us, long after we followed them, and they linger like spies in the shadows of the mysterious. Now and then we turn in an empty street and see them light a match: perhaps, we say, you were my best friend all along. You shadowed me. That is not to suggest that poetry is always a source of comfort, but merely to say it is always a source of presence.

Burns was one of those Western voices that have haunted my sense of what is possible for a writer. But you hear it again and again, in those writers, for example, who sung their anthems for doomed youth at the Western Front. And another West appears before us, to break our hearts with a vision of discovery, at the close of Scott Fitzgerald's masterpiece *The Great Gatsby*. I have spoken tonight of beginnings and endings – of a West that opens up possibility, and another West that closes it down – but it is Fitzgerald's great last paragraphs in Gatsby that summon how literature itself might embrace the hopes we invest in the West. The narrator Nick Carraway, like Gatsby himself, came to New York from the West, and the search for new dreams, the horror at old politics, will lead him back West again, in search of goodness. Here's Nick Carraway sprawled out on the sand:

> Most of the big shore places were closed now and there were hardly any lights except the shadowy, moving glow of a ferryboat across the Sound. And as the moon rose higher the inessential houses began to melt away until gradually I became aware of the old island here that flowered once for Dutch sailors' eyes – a fresh, green breast of the new world. Its vanished trees, the trees that had made way for Gatsby's house, had once pandered in whispers to the last and greatest of all human dreams; for a transitory enchanted moment man must have held his breath in the presence of this continent, compelled into an aesthetic contemplation he neither understood nor desired, face to face for the last time in history with something commensurate to his capacity for wonder.
>
> And as I sat there brooding on the old, unknown world, I thought of Gatsby's wonder when he first picked out the green light at the end of Daisy's dock. He had come a long way to this blue lawn, and his dream must have seemed so close that he could hardly fail to grasp it. He did not know that it was already behind him, somewhere back in that vast obscurity beyond the city, where the dark fields of the republic rolled on under the night.
>
> Gatsby believed in the green light, the orgiastic future that year by year recedes before us. It eluded us then, but that's no matter – to-morrow we will run faster, stretch out our arms farther … And one fine morning –
>
> So we beat on, boats against the current, borne back ceaselessly into the past.

And here you are, too: at the most westerly point of all. Why shouldn't the West be among your greatest subjects? Here in Perth, perhaps, we see the Western voice distilled and changed: speaking to the new Orient as much as to the old kingdoms across the sea. New republics indeed are rolling on under the night, and it might take a place like this, a place innately happy to live out on its own, at the furthest edge of the Western consciousness, to teach us a lesson in how to move the tectonic plates of human understanding into a new formation. History is back, but it will not be history as we used to know it. If there are revolutions, as we have seen, they will be revolutions married to technology and culture; they will be uprisings of the flashing cursor and the instant message; coalitions will spring up across borders and states; we are living through the era when change will appear not from the barrel of a gun, but from the common wishes channelled from a million box bedrooms. The West is not longer in charge of the world, or not for long. The outbacks have found their voice and their moment: there is nowhere too remote to make its mark on our understanding. We are each a principality and each an agent of change. That is what we discovered and literature plays its part. The West is not out there or out here anymore: it is inside, in our heads, a place in all of us where ideals might become realities. In *Land's Edge*, Tim Winton wrote, 'West coasts tend to be wild coasts, final coasts to be settled, lonelier places for being last.'

But we may not be last anymore: we may be first. I have spent some time this week at the National Museum of Western Australia. Writers live by symbols and sleeping truths, and that wonderful place is a repository of such things. But at the end of the largest room, next to the displays of Kings Park and the aluminium roofing of the suburbs, next to a colonial house and a display of gold diggers' pans, next to models of megafauna and echidnas, next to digging sticks used by Noongar women, there are five TV screens transmitting live webcam pictures from cities around the world. We see Ulan Bator, we see Paris. There's Los Angeles and Glasgow and Venice. We see London, Istanbul and Siena. It felt to me, as I watched them again this morning, that they represented a brand new point in your history. All these world cities, viewed at last from the ancient land of Mooro, this district of Yellagonga, as if to show in one great moment that Westernness had finally come home to itself. Here we are, wherever we are, at the still point of the turning world – today, and now, all frontiers seeming to dissolve in a golden hope of plurality in Western Australia. Under the citicams of the world there is a quotation from Veronica Brady's 'This I Believe.'

Nor do we humans exist separate and apart. We are part of

this great polyphony of being as it is played out on our small and vulnerable planet suspended in infinite space.

In closing this festival, let us call it a consummation. The end of the old West is in sight, and, in that ending, we may find a new beginning. This is Noongar land, and this is Perth, and this is the world itself as it reaches for a new definition that protects us all. All roads in literature lead to the domestic interior – that is what we heard again and again this week during the festival. The small business of life standing for the universe. And it is true of the most global innovations: we take steps to create a better world if only to invest in the future smiles of our children, and let the grace and rhythm of literature cast a spell on them, forever to free them from prejudice and chaos. I came to Perth, I tell you, as if coming to visit an old part of myself, a part that wants Western ideals constantly to outfox our Western depravities. There is a new notion of the West's potential for light: let us, for now, call it a Noongar of the mind, a Perth of the heart, and let it carry the best human ideals across all boundaries into a world where is no need for a place called the West, the East, the North and the South.

And so we return to T.S. Eliot, to 'Little Gidding,' and the notion of the returnability of life – the endless West once before us and now, day by day, hour by hour, behind us.

> *We shall not cease from exploration*
> *And the end of all our exploring*
> *Will be to arrive where we started*
> *And know the place for the first time.*
> *Through the unknown, unremembered gate*
> *When the last of earth left to discover*
> *Is that which was the beginning;*
> *At the source of the longest river*
> *The voice of the hidden waterfall*
> *And the children in the apple-tree*
> *Not known, because not looked for*
> *But heard, half-heard, in the stillness*
> *Between two waves of the sea.*

Address to the Perth Writers' Festival

Publication Details

Gail Bell's 'In the Rat Room: Reflections on the Breeding House' appeared in the *Monthly*, July 2011.

Inga Clendinnen's 'In the Pines: A Girl Skulks Along Memory's Edge' appeared in *Australia: Story of a Cricket Country*, edited by Christian Ryan, Hardie Grant Books, Melbourne, November 2011.

Peter Conrad's 'Can We Be Heroes? Chris Lilley and the Politics of Comedy' appeared in the *Monthly*, May 2011.

Helen Elliott's 'Death and Distraction' appeared in *Griffith Review 31: Ways of Seeing*, February 2011.

Delia Falconer's 'Sweating' is an edited extract from her book *Sydney*, New South, Sydney, 2010.

Richard Flanagan's 'It's Peter Dom' appeared in *And What Do You Do, Mr Gable?*, Vintage, Sydney, 2011. It was previously published as 'The Outsiders: Olegas Truchanas and Peter Dombrovskis' in *Art & Australia*, volume 48, number 1, Spring 2010.

Lian Hearn's 'The Work of Catfish' appeared in the *Monthly*, May 2011.

Shakira Hussein's 'Nine-eleven-itis' appeared in *Griffith Review 33: Such Is Life*, August 2011.

M.J. Hyland's 'The Trial of Mary Bale' appeared in the *Financial Times*, 25 March 2011.

Clive James's 'How Broadway Conquered the World' appeared in the *Atlantic*, November 2010.

Paul Kelly's 'In the Wee Small Hours' appeared in *How to Make Gravy*, Penguin, Melbourne, 2011. First published in 2010. Reproduced by permission.

Anna Krien's 'Out of Bounds: Sex and the AFL' appeared in the *Monthly*, April 2011.

Anthony Lane's 'Hack Work: A Tabloid Culture Runs Amok' appeared in the *New Yorker*, 1 August 2011.

Amanda Lohrey's 'High Priest: David Walsh and Tasmania's Museum of Old and New Art' appeared in the *Monthly*, December 2010–January 2011.

Morris Lurie's 'On Not Writing' appeared in *Meanjin*, volume 70, number 1, Autumn 2011.

David Malouf's 'Happiness in the Flesh' formed part of *Quarterly Essay 41, The Happy Life: In Search of Contentment in the Modern World*, Black Inc., Melbourne, 2011.

Robert Manne's 'The Cypherpunk Revolutionary: Julian Assange' appeared in *Making Trouble: Essays Against the New Australian Complacency*, Black Inc., Melbourne, 2011. A shorter version was published in the *Monthly*, March 2011.

Gillian Mears's 'Fairy Death' appeared in *That's it, for now...*, *HEAT 24 new series*, edited by Ivor Indyk, Giramondo, Sydney, 2011.

Andrew O'Hagan's 'The West: New Dreams from Noongar' was delivered as the closing address to the Perth Writers' Festival, March 2011.

Peter Robb's 'Real Food' appeared as 'Stardust Memories: In Search of Real Italian Food' in the *Monthly*, July 2011.

Nicolas Rothwell's 'Living Hard, Dying Young in the Kimberley' appeared in the *Australian*, 30 April 2011.

Andrew Sant's 'On Self-Knowledge: A Ring and Its Keeper' appeared in *Griffith Review 33: Such Is Life*, August 2011.

Craig Sherborne's 'A Handful of Thoughts Before the Dust' appeared in the *Australian*, 21 May 2011.

Maria Tumarkin's 'The Whisperers in the Jungle' appeared in *Meanjin*, volume 70, number 3, Spring 2011.

Notes on Contributors

The Editor

Ramona Koval has presented *The Book Show* on ABC Radio National since 2006 and before that *Books and Writing* from 1995. She has published several books, including a novel, *Samovar*, and has written for many newspapers and international journals. Her most recent book is *Speaking Volumes: Conversations with Remarkable Writers*.

Contributors

Gail Bell has worked as a pharmacist, educator and writer. Her books include *The Poison Principle* and *Shot: A Personal Response to Guns and Trauma*.

Inga Clendinnen's books include *Reading the Holocaust* and *Dancing with Strangers*, which both won New South Wales Premier's awards. Her most recent book is *The Cost of Courage in Aztec Society*.

Peter Conrad is a writer, academic and regular contributor to the *Observer*. His books include *Verdi and/or Wagner*, *The Art of the City* and *Modern Times, Modern Places*.

Helen Elliott is a Melbourne-based writer and journalist.

Delia Falconer is the author of two novels, *The Service of Clouds* and *The Lost Thoughts of Soldiers*, both published by Picador. Her first work of non-fiction, *Sydney*, from which this essay is extracted, was shortlisted for the Prime Minister's Literary Awards, the Kibble Award, the *Age* Book of the Year Award, the New South Wales Premier's History Awards and the Colin Roderick Award.

Richard Flanagan's books include *The Sound of One Hand Clapping* and *Gould's Book of Fish*. His latest novel, *Wanting*, won both the Queensland and Western Australian premiers' awards for fiction. A collection of non-fiction pieces, *And What Do You Do, Mr Gable?*, was released this year.

Lian Hearn studied modern languages at Oxford University and worked as a film critic and arts editor in London before settling in Australia. A lifelong interest in Japan led to study of the Japanese language, many trips to Japan, and culminated in the *Tales of the Otori* series.

Shakira Hussein is undertaking a postdoctoral fellowship on Muslim women, gendered violence and racialised political discourse at the Asia Institute, University of Melbourne.

M.J. Hyland used to be a lawyer. Her latest novel is *This Is How*.

Clive James is the author of more than thirty books. As well as verse and novels, he has published collections of essays, literary criticism, television criticism and travel writing, plus four volumes of autobiography including, most recently, *North Face of Soho*. In 2003 he was awarded the Philip Hodgins memorial medal for literature. His latest book is *A Point of View*, a collection of his BBC Radio 4 broadcasts.

Paul Kelly is recognised as one of the most significant singer-songwriters in the country. He was inducted into the Australian Recording Industry Association Hall of Fame in 1997 and in 2011 he received the Ted Albert Award for Outstanding Services to Australian Music. His memoir *How to Make Gravy* was published by Penguin in 2010.

Anna Krien is a writer of journalism, essays, fiction and poetry. Her book on the Tasmanian forestry wars, *Into the Woods*, won the 2011 Victorian Premier's Literary Awards People's Choice Award and a 2011 Queensland Premier's Literary Award. Her work has appeared in the *Monthly*, the *Age, frankie* and the *Big Issue.*

Anthony Lane has been a film critic for the *New Yorker* since 1993 and his writings up to 2002 for the magazine are collected in *Nobody's Perfect.* In 2001, he received the US National Magazine Award for Reviews and Criticism. He lives in Cambridge, England.

Amanda Lohrey's most recent book is *Reading Madame Bovary*, a collection of short stories that won two 2011 Queensland Premier's Literary Awards. She is the author of several novels, including *Camille's Bread*, and two *Quarterly Essays.*

Morris Lurie is the author of some three dozen books, for adults and children. They include *Flying Home*, selected by the national Book Council as one of the ten best books of its decade, *The Twenty-Seventh Annual African Hippopotamus Race*, winner of the inaugural YABBA Award as voted by the schoolchildren of Victoria, and his Banjo-winning autobiography, *Whole Life.* He received the Patrick White Award in 2006.

David Malouf is the author of poems, fiction, libretti and essays. In 1996, his novel *Remembering Babylon* was awarded the first International IMPAC Dublin Literary Award. In 2000 he was selected as the sixteenth Neustadt Laureate. His most recent novel is *Ransom* and his most recent book *The Happy Life.*

Robert Manne is professor of politics at La Trobe University and a regular essayist and commentator for the *Monthly.* His books include, as editor, *Goodbye to All That?* and *W.E.H. Stanner: The Dreaming and Other Essays.* His most recent book is *Making Trouble: Essays Against the New Australian Complacency.* In 2011 he authored *Quarterly Essay 43, Bad News.*

Gillian Mears's books include *The Mint Lawn* (winner of a

Commonwealth Writers' Prize) and *Fineflour*. Her latest novel is *Foal's Bread*.

Andrew O'Hagan's first book, *The Missing*, was published in 1995. *Our Fathers*, his debut novel, was shortlisted for the 1999 Booker Prize. His second novel, *Personality*, was published in 2003 and won the James Tait Black Memorial Prize for Fiction. His latest novel is *The Life and Opinions of Maf the Dog, and of His Friend Marilyn Monroe*.

Peter Robb is the author of *Midnight in Sicily*, which won the Victorian Premier's Literary Award for non-fiction and was named a *New York Times* Notable Book. His other books include *A Death in Brazil* (the *Age* Non-Fiction Book of the Year in 2004) and *Street Fight in Naples*.

Nicolas Rothwell is the author of *Wings of the Kite-Hawk*, *The Red Highway*, *Journeys to the Interior* and *Another Country*. He is the northern correspondent for the *Australian*.

Andrew Sant co-founded the literary magazine *Island* in Tasmania and served as its editor for ten years. Since 2000 he has been a writer-in-residence at institutions in England and China, and is currently Writing Fellow at Goldsmiths College, University of London.

Craig Sherborne has published three books of verse, including *Bullion* and *Necessary Evil*, two memoirs, *Hoi Polloi* and *Muck*, and writes regularly for the *Monthly*. His first novel, *The Amateur Science of Love*, was published in 2011.

Maria Tumarkin was born in 1974 in the former Soviet Union to a Russian Jewish family, which in 1989 emigrated to Australia. She has written three books, *Traumascapes*, *Courage* and *Otherland*. She lives in Melbourne with her two children.